CHURCH AND CULTURE

Church and Culture

German Catholic Theology, 1860–1914

THOMAS FRANKLIN O'MEARA, O.P.

UNIVERSITY OF NOTRE DAME PRESS

NOTRE DAME   LONDON

Library of Congress Cataloging-in-Publication Data

O'Meara, Thomas F., 1935–
    Church and culture : German Catholic theology, 1860–1914 / Thomas F.
    O'Meara.
      p. cm.
    Includes bibliographical references and index.
    ISBN 0-268-00783-7
    1. Catholic Church—Germany—Doctrines—History—19th century.
    2. Catholic Church—Germany—Doctrines—History—20th century.
    3. Theology, Doctrinal—Germany—History—19th century.
    4. Theology, Doctrinal—Germany—History—20th century. I. Title.
    BX1747.059 1991
230'.243'09034—dc20   90-50971
                                                  CIP

for
John O'Meara

Contents

Introduction

WHEN WE LOOK at a painting whose canvas is full of intricate colors and abstract forms but lacks nature's landscapes or human figures, when we consider how the drives and desires of a single human personality can fashion economics and politics, or when we ponder electronic networks linking markets of paper money with corporate offices, we are catching a glimpse of the abstractions and technologies of the modern era. We live in a world where science, freedom, consciousness and process are central. There the talents of the human self create technology and art, economics and politics, and there the forces of collective personalities like nations and religions bring sweeping or inescapable, beneficent or dangerous changes.

Toward the end of the eighteenth century Immanuel Kant and J. G. Fichte convinced Europe that much of what human beings know is fashioned from the activity of their own consciousness. Their precocious disciple Schelling in 1800 intuited that the self, whether ours or God's, also has a history; indeed, is history. In this history, Hegel distinguished politics, religion, and art—the totality of world and God becoming. Schopenhauer sought the dynamics of the absolute and the totality in will, Marx in economics, Nietzsche in life, Freud in the unconscious. The modern world began with a revolution in the individual and collective selves at the end of the eighteenth century; through variations and metamorphoses this elaboration of our world-producing self continued on to the end of the twentieth century. Today architecture and advertising, psychoanalysis and minimalist music are extensions of a culture which creates itself anew out of constellations of symbolic forms. This is the modernity which inevitably begins not with cosmos and eternity but with self and history.

* * *

Roman Catholicism had not found it easy to deal with modernity. Would not the human freedom advocated by philosophy from Cartesianism to existentialism claim independence from God? Could not

1

subjectivity become blind to objective revelation? A meaningless or point-illist history could end in atheism where the Christ would be absorbed into psyche or myth. From Gregory XVI to Pius XII, from the *Syllabus Errorum* (1863) to *Humani Generis* (1950) there had been no lack of condemnations of modernity. It was long thought that every encounter between Roman Catholicism and modernity from Kant to Freud inevitably had ended (and must end) in magisterium's theological rejections of not only pantheism but also democracy.

In fact, the dialogue between modernity and Catholicism was more complicated. An earlier book, *Romantic Idealism and Roman Catholicism: Schelling and the Theologians*,[1] sketched how German Catholic thinkers from 1795 to 1845 took seriously the philosophies of Kant, Fichte, Jacobi, Hegel, and particularly Schelling. As a result of this intersection of idealism and Romanticism in Germany around 1800, a contemporary, culturally engaged Catholic speculative theology flourished through the first half of the nineteenth century. The following pages continue that history into the latter part of the century.

Church and Culture looks at the cultural epoch from 1860 to 1914. The 1850s formed a prologue to this segment of time and the years immediately prior to World War I were its conclusion. Did the schools of Munich and Tübingen, the traditions of Joseph Görres and Franz von Baader, the systems or F. A. Staudenmaier and J. A. Möhler survive through the second half of the past century? After the upheavals of 1848, the cultural and ecclesiastical climates changed. Idealist and historical theologies found themselves out of step in a more conservative ecclesiastical age, and a vigorous neoscholasticism more and more dominated. Catholics were themselves pushed back from the political arena of the age; fissures opened between them and the Reich of Protestants and liberals. Moreover, into this German climate came Rome's relentless insistence on restoring medieval thought to dampen contemporary theology.

Some Catholic theologians, bishops, and lay leaders, however, viewed Catholic life as incompatible with social isolation. There were philosophers and theologians who sought to express faith and revelation in terms of subject and process. Some of these were censored; many books were placed on the *Index librorum prohibitorum*; the anti-modern papal decrees of 1907/1908 had a serious impact. Nonetheless, there were figures in Catholic intellectual life who were neither "neoscholastic" nor "modernist." They continued the tradition of romantic idealism.

Prejudicial views of this period have long dominated wherein devout neoscholastics were pitted against heretical or selfish modernists. Modernity was equated with relativism and positivism, and cultural conversation was always considered dangerous because church and faith were ruled by a monist bureaucracy. The lives and writings of significant German Catholic theologians from 1860 to 1914 are little or inaccurately known outside of Germany and Austria. Often their heresy has been presumed even as their creativity was left uninvestigated. There are few books in any language which survey Catholic theology from 1864 to 1914 and few articles.[2] This era was long forgotten, and church histories and seminary textbooks for Germany, France, and America have presumed that it should be described only in terms of papal discipline and the triumphs of neoscholasticism.[3]

But the nineteenth century was not one unit. Rather, its years fall into several distinct periods marked by a central division toward the end of the 1840s.[4] Theology from 1860 to 1914 had its own conversation with science and culture; its philosophies are drawn from natural science, from idealism revivified and from metaphysics understood as epistemology. Although most of Catholic theology and philosophy of this period was neoscholastic—and thus deaf to modern thought—there were, nonetheless, Catholic theologians who appreciated modern philosophy. Accepting a historical and critical stance, they struggled to develop social ethics or philosophy of religion in terms of the thinkers and thought-forms of the 1880s or 1890s. This culturally open theology as it was developed in Germany from 1860 to 1914 is our focus.[5]

The following chapters do not attempt to provide a complete history of Catholic theologians, schools, and specializations during the second half of the nineteenth century. That vast task awaits much detailed research, for the period is little known. The following pages aim merely to sketch first the shifts and directions of Catholic theology and then its important figures.

The theologians selected for presentation here worked largely within systematic and fundamental theology, areas where philosophy is most influential. Not all the themes of Christian theology are treated. It would be valuable to trace how J. A. Möhler's return to the church fathers continued through the century, for instance; or how the history of moral theology showed itself to be simultaneously neoscholastic, idealist, and positivist; or how Christology became an addendum to other theological interests, while ecclesiology and apologetics captured the spotlight, but that is not possible at present. The following book, then, is not a chronological survey of many subjects and figures but a narrative of theological struggles and directions, and a presentation of major exemplary theologians. Thereby we glimpse a period and see its contours.

A struggle to integrate modernity critically and vitally with tradition and science marked philosophy and theology in the nineteenth century. Catholic intellectual life was inevitably challenged by the need to hold two worlds together: revelation and idealist philosophy. *"Glauben und Verstehen"* (believing and understanding) was the century's dialectic, and the correlation of revelation with modernity remained in a particular way the Catholic problem. There could be no deeper issue: revelation stood for the totality and explicitness of a special divine presence on earth, while free subject-in-process sparked modernity's cultural epoch.

Describing these theologies, however, is not easily accomplished. The relationship of Catholicism to a German culture which appeared alternately creative and suspicious is complex. Catholics were divided over the very sources and nature of theology, and new schools arose precisely to oppose older methods. If grandiose theological systems were more or less absent during this period, nevertheless issues of great import were considered: the merits of Catholic as opposed to state universities, the meaning of newly created term "ordinary magisterium," the extension of Roman authority into areas as diverse as apologetics, a universal catechism, labor unions, and social reform movements. Lay assemblies, social activists, politicians, journalists, and artists as well as meetings of German bishops took up theological and cultural issues. Beneath the life of German Catholicism four basic tensions were active: (a) that between science and theology; (b) between Prussian Reich and Pian Rome; (c) between transcendental philosophy and apologetics; (d) between society, the press, and the church. Each was but an aspect of the relationship between revelation and modernity.

*   *   *

The following study of Roman Catholic theology in Germany from the 1860s to the onset of World War I is fashioned along the lines of a triptych. Its central panel contains the theological portraits of leading dogmatic and fundamental theologians from this period.

Part One offers the historical background for the theologians whose lives and writings make up the core of this book. A first chapter describes characteristics of culture and philosophy which permeate and vivify the latter nineteenth century. They gave a cultural identity to this period and show how different it was from the earlier period of romanticism and idealism. They influenced the approaches of Roman Catholic life and thought after 1860. Catholic life mirrored the metamorphoses in politics and science within the German states absorbed into Bismarck's Reich. The *Kulturkampf* brought Catholics into a greater solidarity with their inner church life, but it also set up patterns of social discrimination which lasted for decades. The *politique* of the Vatican questioned the militancy of science, Prussian hegemony, and late idealist philosophies of religion, but its mode of leadership frequently misunderstood the vitality of the German church. A second chapter sketches the two directions in Catholic theology and philosophy in the second half of the nineteenth century. The "old" German theology, open to modern thought, was replaced by the "new" neoscholasticism skeptical of all that is not baroque and medieval, Aristotelian and Thomist. Traces remained from the earlier time of idealist systems and romantic restoration, influences from Schelling, Baader, and Möhler, but the period was dominated by the rapid and broad hegemony of neoscholasticism, The two directions in Roman Catholic theology—a minority of culturally engaged thought and a majority of ecclesiastical restoration of the past—dominated church life up until World War I. The Vatican became increasingly hostile toward modernity in all its forms. It condemned German books and theologians as it sought to find an alternative to a culturally engaged Catholic thought in a revival of medieval philosophy and theology and an assertion of church authority.

Part Two looks at five theologians who were arguably the most important Catholic thinkers in the latter nineteenth century. Their theologies show how Roman Catholic theology—in a historical and idealist approach rather than in a neoscholastic one—understood and realized its mission during the years from 1860 to 1914. In the careers and writings of M. J. Scheeben, Alois Schmid, Paul Schanz, Herman Schell, and Carl Braig we learn how theologians avoided ecclesiastical neoscholasticism and addressed modernity, and how they saw the nature of Christian revelation, the task of theology, and the contributions to it from philosophy. These theologians taught and wrote in dogmatics and fundamental theology. None was a neoscholastic (although Scheeben's sympathies lay more with that direction than with post-Kantian philosophy). Each represented a major school of theology—Munich, Tübingen, Würzburg, and Freiburg— with Scheeben illustrating the move of theological education, that is, seminary education, away from the universities to the diocesan seminaries. All were influenced by the earlier time of romantic idealism and by the figures of the era of Kant, Schelling, and Hegel, but the new issues in epistemology and psychology, in science and politics were taken seriously. Scheeben died young in 1888, but the others flourished in the years around 1900.

Part Three recounts the end of this era. The autumnal climax to the nineteenth century, the *fin de siècle*, is a cultural epoch ending with the First World War. As a result of the Vatican's censures talent and expansion in German theology became increasingly infrequent during this period. In the years after 1890, however, Catholics found a new vitality in cultural, social, and pastoral areas. It was writers and political leaders who were arguing for the importance of living within one's own age, a time whose modernity produced engines and laboratories rather than transcendental philosophies and neoclassical architecture. Catholic publications rejected the isolation imposed by the Kulturkampf and the campaign by the Vatican against any rumored aberration in Christianity's contacts with the modern world. A first chapter narrates how, as a new century was arriving, movements for cultural engagement, education and social needs were brought together under the slogan "*Reformkatholizismus*." A number of Catholics wrote programs for the church's existence in the coming century. They espoused freedom for science, philosophy and theology, advocated ecclesiastical reform and urged a moderation of Roman control by more emphasis on lay activity. A second chapter narrates the climax of the Vatican's campaign against modernity, which added measure to measure in order to control and stifle theology. German Catholic intellectual life, blocked from movements of reform and disciplined for creating modern theologies, passed beyond neoscholasticism and epistemological apologetics to focus on the arts and literature, and particularly on a variety of social and political issues. Nevertheless, watched and controlled by both Rome and Berlin, Catholics entered the First World War deprived of a traditional international perspective, and they met the arrival of the twentieth century uncertain about the forms which church and theology would take in the future.

* * *

To the Catholics who were developing in 1900 programs for the church in the twentieth century, Catholicism in Germany seemed embattled and oppressed. To Paul Schanz and Herman Schell the future held out little hope for a culturally engaged theology. But to us, beyond two world wars, beyond existentialism and secularity, lies the event of Vatican II. To some, Vatican II has appeared as something quite new and unprecedented, but in many ways its renewal is a realization and a critique of Catholic Christianity living in the modern world. Postconciliar theologies take up anew the issues of the past century. The themes and approaches of this influential council lie partly in the nineteenth century, in what was left unsaid at Vatican I, in the conflicts sketched below. The system of Schell is not so dissimilar from the theologies of Karl Rahner or Pierre Teilhard de Chardin. Henri De Lubac's rearrangement of nature and grace recalls J. E. Kuhn's disagreements with young neo-Thomists. The world-altering ecclesiology of Möhler at Tübingen reached Yves Congar, and through him the forms of the Catholic church changed throughout the world.

* * *

To walk through the galleries of the Neue Pinakothek in Munich (one of several museums devoted to nineteenth-century art in the Bavarian capital) is to see a variety of aesthetic viewpoints, each presenting era and person. Color and form, light and line disclose in diverse ways nature, history, and self. Large canvasses portray history and myth; smaller paintings depict daily life in the nineteenth century. All the while the dynamics of modernity are pushing beyond realism toward expressionism, impressionism, and symbolism. Nineteenth-century art illumines the various periods of the past century, a succession of different cultural epochs. A Friedrich and a Schleich paint nature from different viewpoints; history is unfolded by von Uhde and Piloty; distinguished men and women are portrayed by Kaulbach and Lenbach. The paintings' styles bear the mysticism of *Geist* but also the positivism dominant in past myths and the present bourgeoisie. Canvasses unite universal values and banal strivings. In this Pinakothek one might pause before five paintings, finding them markers in a changing century, five actors of the past century in diverse styles: Goethe, Schelling, Ludwig I, Döllinger, Graf Keyserling. One can see in each face not only an influential personage but a cultural moment in the past century.

As portraits of a century's personages capture not only the face but the epoch, the following chapters would offer narratives of ecclesial movements and pictures of fundamental theologians, sketching thereby a kind of chart and geography of Catholic theology and church life in the latter decades of the nineteenth century.

PART ONE

The Contours of a Century

1

The Second Half
of a Century (1840–1914)

THE YEARS 1880 TO 1910 are not as distant from us as we might suppose. A parent or grandparent can remember the first years of this century, and the First World War with its many changes is not yet ancient history. In every age philosophy interprets and explains Christianity; this philosophy is an expression of the *Zeitgeist*. If at times church and faith do not easily discover or accept the useful models for their self-interpretation, still, an incarnational faith will not pronounce a major culture or healthy era evil and unsuitable to express Christianity. Our narrative explores a difficult time for Catholic theology but it records that in those decades, too, faith— with reserve and critique—could express itself through modernity. This exploration is not church history but the history of theology. How did scholars, writers, theologians, professors, lay movements and university schools unfold Catholic intellectual life from 1860 to 1914? Our special interest within theology is fundamental theology, that intersection of philosophy and religion, which in the last analysis involves the cultural expression of faith.

I. The Different Ages of One Century

A century is an arbitrary segment of human chronology. A hundred years do not necessarily correspond to a cultural epoch, and a new century, whether it is 1200 or 1900, does not inevitably introduce the next epoch. In many ways the nineteenth century is not one time; its first half is as different from the second as romanticism is from industrialization, as Hegel is from Nietzsche. Ernst Bergmann wrote in the 1920s:

> The nineteenth century has no form; it can have none. . . . The number of cultural areas which expanded, individually and in their ensemble, is enormous. One cannot easily unify their motives and tendencies, the richness of methods within the work of the human

11

spirit: in art there is classicism, romanticism, naturalism; in world-views, spiritualism, materialism, mechanism and vitalism; in philosophy, epistemology and ethics.[1]

In the broadest sense the nineteenth century begins with the writings of Kant after 1781 and ends with World War I. The most serious division in the past century falls between two periods separated by the years of the 1840s. Moreover, the years 1900 to 1914 continue the final decades of the nineteenth century.

Let us look briefly at the overall pattern of the past century. The liberations of the Enlightenment seemed destined to last a long time, but by the end of the eighteenth century, romanticism—born of the new natural sciences and Fichte's analysis of the free self—had rapidly introduced quite a new culture, idealist and then romantic. With Schelling's move from art to religion after 1806, and from knowing self to human will and complex godhead after 1810, romanticism entered its later stages. By the 1830s Hegel was dead and Schelling had failed to publish the awaited world-directing system. In the conservative 1840s such transcendental systems seemed academic games, unable to resolve political needs.

The period from 1830 to 1870 was a time of considerable change in Germany.[2] Alterations in science and philosophy, in church and society appearing from the 1840s to the 1860s prepared for the period from 1870 to 1914. Both the union of the states of Germany under the hegemony of Prussia and a worldwide Catholicism under the leadership of Pius IX furthered a conservative atmosphere. They clashed as Bismarck's policies warred against the independence of the Roman Catholic church. From 1880 to 1907 German Catholics, wounded and marginalized by the *Kulturkampf*, had to work at achieving an identity which was both Catholic and German, ecclesial and contemporary. This struggle entered a further, not particularly healthy phase after 1895 as Rome worked in the mode of condemnation while Catholics struggled against their marginalization from German professions and politics.

German Catholicism at Mid-Century: From
Romantic Restoration to Imperial Minority

Still partly rooted in the sacramental vision of the baroque and unhappy with the rationalism of the Enlightenment, German Catholic life and culture had found a renaissance in romanticism after 1800.[3] The systems of cosmos and religion composed by Schelling and Baader, the advocacy of liberal monarchy and conservative church in the writings of Joseph Görres, the programs of liturgical and church reform, the faculty of Tübingen and the new Benedictine monastery of St. Bonifaz—all these furthered a new time of vital Catholic romantic restoration. Nevertheless, while this was an important and significant time (having its counterparts in France, Belgium, Italy, England, and Ireland), it did not deal fully with the modern world. As 1848 neared, there were deeper modernities in politics and technology and in a liberalism which was now secular rather than romantic. The revolutions of 1848 expressed the need for metaphysics to become more than theory, to show how the liberated individual and the free society could actually produce a government. After 1840 Catholic life more and more did not control but was controlled by cultural shifts.

The 1840s and 1850s were decades of transition, moving beyond the coherent system of romantic idealism to the aggressive politics and positivist science of Bismarck's Reich. Gregory XVI, a member of the Camaldolese Order and known for his only book (an exaggerated apologetic for the "triumph of the Holy See"), became pope in 1831. His 1835 letter *Dum Acerbissimas* condemned writings of the Catholic scholar Georg Hermes, who had died four years earlier (It was said that Metternich was behind the measure, fearful that "rationalism" could lead to "revolution.") Through Hermes the University of Bonn had become a center for introducing an entire generation to modern conceptualities, although Hermes was, with his philosophical theology focused upon Kant, an exception to the Schools of Munich and Tübingen which had been stimulated in the 1820s by Schelling and romantic idealism. Hermes' rationalist expressions of Christianity attracted the educated middle class and offered an alternative to the traditional baroque forms of piety. Because Prussia controlled the Rhineland, a Vatican condemnation of Hermes, professor in a state university, was inflammatory and could be seen as a prelude to the later conflicts between Prussia and Catholicism. Prussia (and its annexed neighbors) was a largely North German, Protestant state, while the western provinces of the Rhine and Westphalia (which Prussia acquired in 1815) had a less agrarian and more urban Catholic population; their intellectual class, precisely through its Catholicism, was open to liberal ideas from France, Belgium, and Bavaria. The establishment of the University of Bonn in 1818 with Catholic and Protestant faculties had been a move by Berlin to influence Catholic clergy and intellectuals. Consequently the condemnation of Hermes was seen as a move by Rome to control theology and church life.

Subsequent years witnessed disputes between church and state over marriage, the enforcement of anti-Hermesian measures (bishops removed seminarians from Bonn) and the widely publicized imprisonment of the idiosyncratic archbishop of Cologne, Droste zu Vischering, for resisting governmental intrusions into the realms of education and marriage. Rome pursued an aggressive policy toward Germany, appealing to public opinion in the late 1830s and finding there strong support (Joseph Görres' political and theological tract compared Droste to Athanasius). The 1840s began with the coronation of Friedrich Wilhelm IV (1840–1861), a Prussian monarch in a romantic key and an admirer of medieval forms in Catholicism. He was sympathetic to resolving controversies over episcopal authority in social and ecclesial life. As a sign of royal goodwill the completion of the Cologne Cathedral (musically depicted in Schumann's Rhenish symphony of 1850) was taken up again. But romantic gestures did not obscure the new tremors in German Catholicism: conflicts over modern theology and traditional piety, a Vatican on the offensive, a breakdown in various principalities of the union between throne and altar, an alienation of liberals from religion and of Protestants and Catholics from each other. New Catholic movements were more conservative in theology and politics, drawn into the search for modern social, political, and scientific developments. K. Schatz writes:

> At the end of the 1840s it was clear that the face of German Catholicism had basically changed. . . . Secularization had destroyed the earlier unity between church, state, and society in the *"Germania sacra."* The result for the Catholic church was at first isolation in church and kingdom, subjection under the state, and minority existence. Only slowly, proceeding from small "circles," did a process of renewal begin, a change in ecclesial consciousness.[4]

A second transitional decade, the 1850s, also centered around a condemnation: the writings of the Viennese Hegelian, Anton Günther, which were proscribed in 1857. The *politique* of Gregory XVI continued with Pius IX, pope from 1846 to 1878. Now it was not simply the antiquarian policies of a Camaldolese pope at work but a broad ultramontane movement, pan-European and increasingly quick to reject everything "liberal" and "modern." Some German bishops and cardinals opposed Günther's condemnation, which came to represent symbolically the rejection of every Catholic theology that was in dialogue with modern philosophy. As 1860 approached, the Curia achieved more control over marriage and education, while anticlerical forces inside Germany increased their influence over politics and the press. Liberals were encouraged by the unification of Italy, the end of the papal states, and finally by the victory of Protestant Prussia over Austria at Königgratz, a manifest proof that hegemony had been given not to Catholic Austria but to Protestant Prussia.

So in midcentury German Catholics had entered a middle land over which two great forces struggled, Rome and Berlin. Conservative and liberal ideologies led to strange paradoxes such as the state's curtailment of religious freedom and the Vatican's support of it. With so many far-reaching social changes, with so many serious and unresolved issues in both life and faith, the conflict could only increase as the century unfolded.

The Shift from Philosophy to Science

Histories of philosophy devoted to the latter half of the nineteenth century are few. Herbert Schnädelbach sees the second epoch of the past century beginning not with 1848 but with 1831 (this recalls the censure of Hermes). That year Goethe entered the last months of his life, Hegel died, Schopenhauer left academia, and Schelling still hesitated over his final system. These events ended an age which had embraced German classicism, idealism, and romanticism. There was a certain cultural uniformity from 1770 to 1830, but by the 1830s the age of science and of historical culture had ushered in the beginning of the crisis of European humanist civilization, the true extent of which was to be revealed by the world wars.[5] A break with the style of romanticism in art and system led to new cultural directions. As Schelling left Munich in 1841 to succeed Hegel in Berlin, he informed the royal family that the future world would be dominated by historical research and politics.[6] A number of cultural alterations distanced the years after 1830 from the earlier nineteenth century. There was, first, a movement away from absolute idealism to science, thus precipitating a profound identity crisis for philosophy. *Wissenschaft* had meant for Schelling and Hegel the metaphysical and systematic elaboration of the grounds and networks of all areas of culture: now it sought the framework for the empirical sciences with their experiments and technologies pursued for the benefit (or, in the case of war, harm) of society. Second, the future lay not with philosophies of history but with historical research. Third, analyses of the structures of life and consciousness became fundamental in the interpretation of reality.[7] Modernity appeared to have an increasingly post-Christian character. The most striking symptom was the dissolution of the idea of God. Hegelian philosophy became atheistic, materialistic, and revolutionary interpretations of the left, while theology became epistemology or anthropology.

The German intellectual spirit, far from being exhausted by the firmament of geniuses from Schiller to Wagner or by philosophers from Schopenhauer to Marx, continued to exert influence. "The years between 1831 and 1933 were the century in which German-speaking science, which is essentially university science, won undisputed world-wide acceptance," writes Schnadelbach.[8] This age may also be described as the century of *Bildung*, of culture in the German sense of that word, of the cultivated bourgeoisie.

History became a realm of research, a detailed science of eras, individual figures and forces. The German drive for system could not be extinguished, but von Ranke and others saw their field as the narrative of humanity (not of the transcendental self), of how individuals and nations became conscious of themselves.

> The pace of conceptual change was astonishing. Whereas for Kant what was cultivated only in the historical sense had remained on the periphery of genuine culture, in the nineteenth century (after a radical change in the meaning of the word "historical") it was precisely the person who was historically cultivated who was regarded as the cultured person.[9]

The task was to bring history as close as possible to the individual and the state.

The industrial revolution led to a revision of the very idea of science and a new reverence for empirical research. Science altered people's self-understanding and their social configurations from monarchy to nation, from farm to city. The universities placed in their libraries the multivolume works composed in the spirit of Schlegel and Schelling on a unified field of natural science—and then they built laboratories. Science soon became the unquestionable source of legitimacy. The new science tested and attacked faith and church and eventually questioned even the state.[10]

Thus without always being aware of it, the society was led deeper and deeper into the realm of the self, but the self viewed positivisticly. It is no accident that as the nineteenth century became more scientific, the subject whom this science was to serve with the gift of life became more and more abstract, ending in the spiritual art of Kandinsky, the unconscious of Freud, or the collective will of fascism.

The Course of Philosophy

Charting the course of philosophy in the latter nineteenth century, we see two currents of philosophy flowing from the figures of Hegel and Schelling in Berlin in 1831 and 1841: the first one is a weaker continuance of idealism in Fichte's son, I. H. Fichte, and in C. H. Weisse and H. Lotze; the second is one of radical critique in Engels, Feuerbach, and Marx. The period up to 1865 was the age of the epigones re-presenting Fichte, Schelling, or Hegel. The new directions from 1865 to 1910 are divided into neo-Kantians and theoreticians of method (Windelband, Cohen), psychologists and biologists (Wundt and Dilthey), philosophers of life (Nietzsche), and monist and theist metaphysicians (Brentano and von Hartmann). Toward the end of the century we see a further move from the metaphysical to the hermeneutical philosophy of life in Spengler, Klages, and Simmel, and in disciples of Bergson and Dilthey. The older idealism continued in the Marburg and Freiburg schools of neo-Kantianism, and in the lines from Brentano, Meinong, and psychologism to Husserl and phenomenology.[11]

Philosophy split into two directions, "positivism" and "materialism," both philosophies derived from science. Catholic intellectuals arguing for the truth of historical revelation saw these two as their enemies. Positivism meant an empirical science with its research free from the metaphysics of the past, thus free from the superstitions of religion and the prejudices of faith and theology. The victorious march of the sciences verified in technological application ushered in an age where reality was disclosed in the factory and the laboratory. Positivism even proposed to replace Catholicism with a substitute church (linked to the state and supported by the religious theories of Feuerbach, Nietzsche, and Haeckel). With the affirmation of religion as a part of the developmental struggle of the human psyche, a new religion of the liberal state or of mass assemblies of workers could be created. While positivism is a method, materialism is a conclusion about the content of reality: only material beings and material events exist. Positivism engendered materialism as its laboratories located the empirical in the material, and both positivism and materialism avoided not only religion but the philosophies of the past century from Kant to I. H. Fichte. By the 1850s popular books were applying materialism to the soul, explaining it as a composite of physiological brain functions. Thus psychology was born (and epistemology furthered) through a materialism where logic could be derived from neurology.[12]

In a reaction to the dominance of technological science, Dilthey and Nietzsche explored the subjectivity not only of knowing but of living in society, past and present. "Life" does not refer primarily to the biological domain but to personal struggle and the full personality. In their thought life process and subjectivity were joined to individuality and interpretation. Here the issue is not life in natural philosophy but the concrete life of the individual, based upon self-experience, struggle, limits, history, destiny, anxiety, and guilt. So its precursors are Pascal, Schopenhauer, and, above all, Kierkegaard. To begin with human existence is to transcend both an idealistic absorption of the individual into absolute spirit and the positivist or materialistic narrowing of existence to material being and activity, and so it struggles on a double front: against the idealism of the past and the materialism of the present. Multiple modes of experience formed a balance to rationality and experimentation. The motif of life could include much that the late nineteenth century loved: biological evolution, forms of the irrational, individuality, freedom, and the search for identity. Epistemology and human experience were two paths leading to psychology—first in a materialism of the brain and then, with Freud, Adler, and Jung, in the psychology of the unconscious. "Life" was the slogan of the youth-movement, of *Jugendstil*, of late romanticism, of educational reform—life as biology and life as renewal.

The late idealists viewed religion as a single, developmental phenomenon: an unfolding of the transcendental drive or the psychological depth of the human personality. Christianity as a form of religion, whatever its merits, did not escape historical and psychological critiques.[13] God was analyzed in terms of a divine personality, but what resulted was not a theodicy as much as an analysis of the divine subject through a sterile transcendentalism. Although these philosophies (and liberal theologies) searched for a new system, they failed, because the idealist foundations, the nature of system, and Christian forms had all been called into question. The crisis of late idealism was that the more it pondered the philosophy it had inherited, the more it withdrew into a metaphysics of self and God. But society turned to science and politics. The younger Fichte never left the foundations of Kant and of his father as he fought against the pantheism of Hegelianism; he sidestepped history and society even while composing an ethics. Thus, in him philosophy withdrew into an austere theism, abandoning religion and revelation and ending in a spiritualism amid transcendental and psychological forces.

From 1890 to 1914 a brief renaissance of interest in Fichte, Schelling, and Hegel appeared, along with the birth of various neo-Kantian movements. Kant lived on in Hermann Cohen, Paul Natorp, Ernst Cassirer, and Heinrich Rickert; Fichte in Fritz Medicus and Richard Falckenberg; Schelling in Otto Braun and Hubert Beckers; Hegel in Adolf Lasson, Wilhelm Dilthey, and Kuno Fischer. But ultimately philosophies of life from Nietzsche and Dilthey to Eduard von Hartmann led not in the direction of new systems but toward psychology. The year 1900 would find a preoccupation with the human mind whether in experimental psychologies or in Kantian forms.

The Freiburg theologian Bernhard Welte perceived in the age a drive toward individuality and away from unity. Science isolated individual entities with their natural powers or a particular fact or figure in its history. The scientific mind was concerned with facts and numbers, even as the individual struggled for a life in a world of new political forces and social problems. Beyond scientific progress for the Reich and the late romanticism of the *fin de siècle* lay many new ways of being conscious of reality. Theology piled up researched data and programs for religious method and epistemology, but it could not summon up a perspective of the whole. What the age could not achieve was unification and synthesis.[14]

II. Catholicism in the Latter Nineteenth Century

As the century progressed, Catholics were pushed away from the mainstream of philosophy and theology, pushed so far that by the 1880s they may have forgotten that they ever composed theological systems in the 1820s inspired by Schelling and Hegel. Why? First, after the 1840s their contemporary cultural efforts were rarely supported by church leadership. Second, potential intellectual leaders became sidetracked by the neoscholastic revival. Catholicism did not produce a Kierkegaard or a Dilthey. The excesses of the Hegelian left and of liberal Protestant philosophers and theologians amounted to the substitution of philosophy for revelation and offered poor models.

Catholics, whose lives had been deeply altered by Napoleon's secularization and rearrangement of society, at the end of the 1860s had to define again their relationship to Germany, to the new state led by Prussia. In the Reich—in contrast to Baden, Bavaria, and Austria—they would be a minority. The Center Party had been founded in 1870 to serve as a confessional political advocate for Catholics, although it supported a pluralism of views. It followed the progressive tradition of Catholic social views initiated by Adolf Kolping in the 1840s and continued by Bishop Wilhelm von Ketteler from 1850 to 1877. Workers' cooperatives and Christian trade unions were organized to combat the evils of unbridled capitalism and to assist the poor. This new political situation altered the role of the hierarchy even as it furthered the voice and activity of the laity. Karl Egon Lönne writes, "If political Catholicism unfolded in close connection with the ecclesiastical hierarchy, in individual areas and in the long view importance was shifted to the laity, offering an independence not only from aristocratic states but from the church's hierarchy. This implied a strengthening of the individual's responsibility for political activity even when [its goals were] drawn from the resources of Catholic faith."[15] But these vocal Catholic associations, a socially conscious hierarchy, and the Center Party aroused fears in Berlin.

Embattled Catholics

At first the relationship of Catholics to the new Germany was debated tranquilly. Was a shift toward conflict forecast by Pius IX's 1864 *Syllabus Errorum*, which aggressively attacked new intellectual attitudes?

Every liberalism (which the pope viewed as the pedagogue for indifferentism and church decline) was dangerous, according to this document, and it roundly condemned the view that the pope should accommodate "progress," "liberalism," and "modern civilization." J. J. I. von Döllinger, church historian at Munich, saw in the *Syllabus* a threat to the modern state based on law, although he appreciated the role of the recently strengthened Catholic church in criticizing a politics which was too powerfully Hegelian.

While the political revolutions of 1848 did not bring republican governments, they did advance the cause of democracy. They furthered the civil rights of Catholic populations in areas where state and liberal parties discriminated against them. Bishops' meetings in 1848 (Würzburg) and 1851 (Freiburg) insisted upon the rights of bishops to educate and appoint clergy, to erect schools, to supervise church life and property, and Bishop Ketteler of Mainz drew up a strong draft of rights in 1853. Thus, as 1860 approached, the church was already struggling with liberal and Protestant parliamentarians over institutional independence. In some states concordats were drafted and violently debated; in others satisfactory compromises were written up. Andreas Kraus concluded: "What was feared was an obedient decisiveness in the Catholic clergy which might threaten the bonds of the state church, and this fear was escalated to pure hysteria by the results of Vatican I."[16] An alienation of Catholic intellectuals from the public life, not just of Prussia but of Baden and Bavaria, was furthered by actions of the press and parliament together with a conservative shift in Catholic theology and church led by a Vatican unsympathetic to modernity. "The development of the Catholic Church in terms of various aspects of European life at the end of the 1860s offered a framework in which tensions between German Catholicism and the leading German political and social powers involved with the foundation of the Reich could become explosive."[17]

A dual alteration had occurred. German Catholics no longer found allies in liberals with progressive ideas. Some Catholics, aware that separation of church and state would please neither Berlin nor Rome and that the earlier revolutionary and progressive years of the 1830s and 1840s were not congenial to Rome, sought a defender in the state. But this patron, while sustaining some rights and offering protection from injurious ecclesiastical programs, could abolish other rights and could control German Catholics, if not the Catholic church, from inside the imperial ministries. In the later 1860s the size and the power of Catholic assemblies increased as bishops and people worked to develop their identity outside the Protestant government. A delegation of five hundred brought Pius IX twenty-three volumes containing 250,000 signatures congratulating him on the fiftieth anniversary of his ordination. Heinz Hürten observed, "The implication was clear that the pope could help this people if the government abandoned them, and Pius and his successors effectively furthered this implication through the encouragement of larger and larger groups of pilgrims."[18]

Nowhere was papal infallibility debated so intensely, both before and after its definition at Vatican I, as in Germany. Not just Protestants and liberals but Catholics—historians, pastors, neoscholastic professors, bishops—voiced their views in articles and books of varying seriousness. Forty-five German and Austrian bishops met and then addressed the pope concerning the doctrine's inopportuneness. Those who did not cease to oppose the definition left before the vote at the council. The German bishops foresaw difficulties with the states. Johannes Lutz, the Bavarian prime minister, notified the bishops that the decrees of the council could not be put in force (or even published) without the government's *placet*, a challenge which the bishops, of course, ignored.[19]

The Center Party gave a voice to Catholic views in so independent a way that it was described by Bismarck as an artillery group breaching a wall. The liberal press after 1870 depicted the Vatican and the Italian church as seeking a paternalistic control without any appreciation of intellectual gifts or cultural differences. Church-state disputes in Baden, driving a wedge between the Catholic and Protestant populations, were a prelude to the Kulturkampf. On the other hand, those content with the church's new conservative direction were frightened by the end of the papal states and identified faith with obedience to every Vatican whim. The German bishops could not fight Rome; they followed its policies even while many of them over the next forty years doggedly supported movements and theologians engaged in meeting the issues of the age.

Kulturkampf

Prussia, except for Schlesien, did not have large Catholic populations within it, but the incorporation of the Rhineland in 1815 changed that situation, and a way of dealing with Catholic areas had to be developed. If the power of the papacy was the subject of increasingly public conflict, another volatile issue was the role of Catholic bishops within this new and self-sufficient empire.[20] Paradoxically it was in the country where the Catholic church had the greatest intellectual independence that the most severe persecution by the new modern state occurred: Germany.

Bismarck and his liberal minister Adalbert Falk decided to force the Catholic church out of the public life of the new Reich through various laws. An attack on the Catholic church could forge a political will to restore everywhere a traditional Prussian church style while at the same time trumpeting the maxims of liberalism toward religion. This could both defeat the ultramontane party in Münster and Mainz and assimilate the eastern provinces with their Polish populations. Regardless, the church must be separated not only from the state but from the school.

In July 1871 the Catholic section of the Kultusministerium was dissolved; Catholic church life was to be administered by Protestant offices. The bishops of the areas under Prussia gathered in Fulda to plan their defense, but Bismarck admitted no dialogue in the following years. Clusters of laws were enacted in 1871 and 1872: schools were taken over by the state; the Jesuits were dealt with through expulsion; and by 1875 most religious orders, even those caring for the sick, were dissolved or exiled. Their institutions were seized and the remaining members, male or female, were interred. Seminarians were to be educated in universities unless the bishop had permission for a seminary, and the state would control the curriculum. The government was happy to receive the support of the liberal press who interpreted the subjection of a "Roman sect" to "German *Geist*" as progress.

While the liberal party wanted to do away with the church altogether, the state's measures were highly illiberal, running roughshod over human rights and constitutional law. In 1875 the Reich's constitution was changed to end the right of bishops to administer the life of the church; those who refused to step down were penalized by heavy fines and imprisonment. State financial support flowed to the Old Catholics with the hope that they would be an attractive replacement. Non-German authorities (e.g., pope, Curia, superiors of religious orders) were to be excluded from exercising authority, and the state asserted a veto over all ecclesiastical offices from rural pastor to archbishop. The Prussian bishops, followed by all but a few clergy and laity ("state-Catholics"), adopted a plan of passive resistance to all the measures involving the clergy and church institutions. An attempt to replace an episcopal church with a congregational form completed the alienation of Catholics from the government. Soon most dioceses were vacant, but through designated clergy the bishops in exile could direct their churches. As over a quarter of the Catholic parishes became empty (in 1881 in Trier over a quarter of the clergy were in exile), liberals began to doubt the wisdom of what had become an unpopular and losing war. The battle then stalled; Bismarck could foresee no victory but refused to compromise with Pius IX lest such a step appear to be a new Canossa.

Within a few days of his election in February 1878, Leo XIII wrote to Kaiser Wilhelm I to initiate a rapprochement.[21] The goal of the Holy

See was to avoid conflicts and recriminations with politicians and parties and to restore the freedom of the diocesan and international church to function in religious areas. The various meetings from 1879 to 1887 included compromises on both sides and were frequently directed by the pope.

The Kulturkampf ended with a truce between Berlin and Rome which pleased neither but saved face and restored church operations. Financial normality for the Catholic dioceses came in 1891; bishops' elections (involving not only Rome but chapters of canons) were permitted; the Redemptorists returned in 1894. In 1902 a Catholic theological faculty was established at Strassbourg, and in 1904 the law expelling and imprisoning the Jesuits—a symbol and slogan of the entire Kulturkampf— was withdrawn. The ending of the conflict strengthened the authority of the papacy and the image of Leo XIII enormously. Clearly, in Rome secular sovereignty had been metamorphosed into a more powerful religious authority. Wilhelm II during his three decades in office occasionally mentioned the Protestant nature of his house and empire, but he found understanding words for Catholics and Catholic institutions. Rudolf Lill writes:

> So the Kulturkampf must be evaluated, along with the persecution of the socialists, as the most severe mistake of Bismarck in international politics. He realized it must be remedied by a clever resolution of the conflict. The laws of persecution and marginalization questioned the credibility of the state and the role of law for Germans. The needed evolution of civil structures and the integration of Catholics into the national state were foolishly delayed. Relationships with the church as well as between Germany and Poland were injured.[22]

Did the other states follow Prussia in this persecution? How could there be a battle against Catholicism in baroque Bavaria? In the years before unification Bismarck found Catholics in South Germany repeatedly frustrating his plans, and the Central Party brought disturbing elements right into Berlin. The elections of 1868 in Bavaria and Württemberg were devastating defeats for the North German political aims. But caught between the power Bismarck had proven against France and Austria and the idylls of a disturbed Ludwig II, Bavaria entered the unifying Reich. In Kraus's view "Economics determined, then, the destiny of the German states. The [threat of] economic isolation alone, if one passes over all the other factors at work, forced Bavaria to yield."[23]

Liberal politicians were largely in control of the Bavarian parliament; they found Vatican I and papal infallibility a provocation. The presence in Munich of Ignaz Döllinger, the leader of liberal Catholic theologians and the representative of historical and theological disagreement with infallibility, gave support to the liberal era beginning under Prime Minister Lutz in 1871, as the formation of the Old Catholic church supported every critique of Rome. The Landtag debated whether Bavaria should not pass a law protecting all who rejected the Vatican dogma.[24] Lutz favored the Reich's leadership in the area of church questions after October 1871, and this encouraged the Kulturkampf, so far limited to individual German states, to expand further in Germany. For Bavaria this meant a stronger dependence of Bavarian politics upon outside influences.[25] Bavaria accepted some of the decrees of Berlin: in July 1872 the Jesuits and other religious congregations were expelled. Battles began over the finances of the dioceses and religious education. But antichurch measures existed largely at the administrative level: the population would not have supported the expulsions and closures imposed on Prussian areas. The government remained hostile to Rome, withdrawing its positive agreement with the bishops of 1852 and returning to the Napoleonic-Enlightenment edict of 1818, and this political mood lasted until the end of Lutz's regime in 1890. Kraus concludes:

> The Kulturkampf in Bavaria did not reach anything like the violence of Prussia, because in Bavaria the church and the Catholic party worked together in developing defenses. Yet the state upheld its claims of dominance basically up to 1918. The field of battle was always the same: the edict on religion, the finances of the state drawn from religious sources, the education of clergy, the naming of bishops.[26]

The Kulturkampf isolated German Catholics, and they reacted, as groups forced into a ghetto usually do, by depending on their own powers and viewing the outside, all that was new, as hostile.[27] These conflicts where the political extended into the cultural were amplified by a liberal press, and they form an important backdrop for understanding Catholic theology in the final decades of the nineteenth century. While creative theologians were in danger of being rejected by Rome for any thinking which was not blandly neoscholastic, they were accused by the state as being un-German. Even in the government of Bavaria, the ideas and *politique* of the Vatican appeared as intrusions. But we must now leave the broad horizons of philosophy and politics for theology, for the history of Catholic fundamental theology in this period of triumphant modernity, a time when storms were frequently gathering around faith and church.

2

The Two Directions of German Catholic Theology (1864–1914)

IN THE SECOND HALF of the nineteenth century a militant and successful neoscholasticism brought energy and formal clarity to Catholic theology; it also brought limitations, controversy, and intolerance. So for the century after 1860 Catholicism contained within itself an antagonistic dualism between Aristotelian and idealist philosophies; the triumph of neoscholasticism included a hostility to every contemporary form of thought and an increasing forgetfulness of modern philosophy, past and present.

If generally the spirits of self and history now inhabited the empty rooms of disappointment, nevertheless, a dialogue between Roman Catholicism and modernity was continued by a few theologians employing post-Kantian thought. To prepare for a look at individual theologians in non-scholastic modes we should first sketch the history of theology in the late nineteenth century. Neoscholasticism and transcendental idealism, the "Roman" and the "German" paths, were both present after 1848; they reached a state of tension and crisis by the 1860s and ended in a worldwide neoscholastic revival which was normative in the 1880s and dominant by 1900 (and remained so until 1950). From 1848 to 1868 neoscholasticism made inroads in schools and among scholars. Roman fears that the university and the Reich were fashioning a culture unsympathetic to the Catholic faith brought forth conservative measures by popes, bishops, and nuncios. The condemnations of Vienna's Anton Günther (1857) and Munich's Jakob Frohschammer (1857, 1862) displayed the censorious side of the Vatican's stance toward any theology whose language and conceptuality were contemporary. Close supervision of publications proceeded from two curial congregations, the Holy Office and the Index (distinct from the Holy Office until the restructuring of Pius X). The Munich nunciature served as a kind of clearinghouse for suspect writings in southern Germany.[1] If neoscholasticism provided the matter for the conservative Catholic religious thought of Rome from the 1850s to the 1950s, Vatican censures were the form.

I. Theologians in Conflict

J. J. I. von Döllinger, who lived through most of the nineteenth century, from 1799 to 1890, represented not just historical research but Catholic university life itself. Along with most Catholics studying and teaching at universities, he advocated a double front: the Catholic church had nothing to fear from honest research into its origins and history, while the minority status of Catholics in the universities could only be countered by high standards of scholarly effort. Deeply worried by the victories of philosophies and movements which he believed would cripple Catholic intellectual life, he delivered two lectures in 1861 at the Odeon theater in Munich describing a new stage in the relationship of German theology to Rome. He calmly argued that the collapse of the Papal States (which he was convinced would soon occur) did not mean the end of the papacy, and he then turned to the hostility of European governments toward Rome, due, he said, to the archaic and authoritarian style of papacy and Curia. Döllinger's Odeon lectures gave a provocative picture of the relations between papacy and modern society.

The opposition of ultramontane neoscholasticism to any other form of theology led him, along with theologian Johann Baptist Alzog and Benedictine Abbot Bonifacius Haneberg, to invite German-speaking scholars (Austria and Switzerland were included) to assemble in Munich in September 1863.[2] A copy of the invitation was sent to Cardinal Giacomo Antonelli, secretary of state in Rome, by the Munich nuncio, Matteo Gonella. The nuncio sent Rome his reactions: "The Holy Father should take some opportunity to remind the bishops of Germany to be more vigilant over the tendencies of many professors . . . who elevate themselves to the status of judges and custodians of true Catholic doctrine and its ways of propagation . . . (in) pseudo-councils where attempts are made to adapt the doctrine and discipline of the church to the so-called spirit of the times."[3] This independence from the bishops displeased Pius IX, who contrasted the "purity of faith" with nonepiscopal "discussions."

Young conservatives and old liberals, exegetes and historians, philosophers and dogmaticians assembled in the Benedictine Abbey of St. Bonifaz, built by Ludwig I after 1835 to begin the restoration of monasticism; eighty-four scholars attended the opening mass celebrated by Munich's Archbishop Gregor von Scherr.[4] Tübingen would not come to Munich (had they insisted upon a more limited participation by the neoscholastics, or upon a lesser role for Döllinger?); the Jesuits and the Mainz neo-Thomists were also absent.

Döllinger's keynote address was a description of the tensions between theological schools and a declaration of rights for theology. His opening survey depicted the decline of theology in France, Italy, Spain, and England and the shift of theological leadership to Germany. "In a signal way Germany has carefully and basically cared for the two eyes of theology, philosophy and history." Theology makes process through science not through ecclesiastical censures. "Freedom is to science what air is to breathing."[5] The scientific consciousness of the church changes from age to age, influencing the content and form of theology; theology does not arrive once and for all with church or Bible. "In Germany today there are two theological directions; this is not an evil but rather in many ways a gain, presupposing only that we are scientifically true to what each is, and each grants freedom to the other."[6] Although he advocated a pluralism and a synthesis between the two theologies, he had critical words for neoscholasticism. It had not overcome its persistent one-sidedness, was not born of the German spirit, and tended to an ahistorical formalism. Moreover, in an image which offended neoscholastics Döllinger said that historical-critical theology defended Catholicism with canons, while neoscholasticism used bows and arrows. The hoped-for synthesis of theological parties did not occur. This meeting of neoscholastic and postidealist directions in fact brought the curtain down on the restoration dialectic between Catholic theology and romantic idealism begun in the last years of the eighteenth century.

The assembly telegraphed a letter to Pius IX professing obedience and asking for his blessing, while indicating that church authority was not denigrated by theological science. At the end of the congress a telegram came from Rome with the papal blessing, a communication quickly published.

Subsequently Rome had less benign reactions. Reports of the nuncio and others on the atmosphere of the congress and the text of Döllinger's address led to papal displeasure. A papal letter, *Tuas Libenter*, reached Archbishop Gregor von Scherr in Munich in early 1864, destined for the other German-speaking bishops. A certain negative Augustinianism can be detected in its superficial and negative evaluations of the German church and theology. There is little understanding of the contemporary world, whose science is filled with error and its whole culture is profane or Protestant. Theology is to judge other areas of thought, a theology born not from thinking about faith for an age but from "holy and immortal doctrines" drawn from the views of bishops and the Holy See.[7]

The dramatic meeting of the theologians at the Munich assembly is an overture to our survey of systematic theology in the late nineteenth century. Döllinger's blustery but failed assembly, much like the introductory scenes to the operas of Wagner's *Ring*, sums up the previous events and forecasts dimly what is to come. It marks the end of the age of Baader and Möhler (it was reported that young neoscholastics could hardly understand Martin Deutinger's address;[8] its conflicts are the conflicts of the future.

The new nuncio, Pier Francisco Meglia, described the theologians of Munich, Tübingen, Würzburg, and Bonn as seeing themselves as German scientists ready to dispute the exercise of church authority. Some theologians, like Alois Schmid, Karl Werner, and F. X. Dieringer, would try to mediate in the coming years, but Döllinger and his young followers at Munich sought out new battles, and their opponents were combative lay neoscholastics like F. J. Clemens and Constantin Schäzler, who in their thirties were already arrogantly attacking the orthodoxy of Tübingen's J. E. Kuhn. Rudolph Lill writes:

> The opponents of German theology were convinced they were serving the church and the purity of its teaching . . . in a struggle with the ideas of the age. On the side of the Curia is the fact that the worldview of liberalism which dominated most scientific disciplines was frequently filled with a powerful and prejudicial enmity toward the church; thus Rome, not knowing the distant German universities adequately, could come to the conclusion that "modern science" and faith were mutually exclusive.[9]

With seminaries, institutes, and chanceries avid for the new scholasticism, Catholic resistance to neoscholasticism and ultramontanism in Germany quickly came to be centered within the universities.[10]

Döllinger spoke at Munich of "two directions."[11] This chapter will sketch both directions as they unfold in a succession of historical periods.

Bernhard Welte has located theology in the second half of the nineteenth century within a changing cultural milieu. "The age changes fundamentally; changes its thought, structures and capabilities. With this alteration in thinking, the mode, structure and style of theology changes decisively."[12] The projects and systems of Fichte and Schelling disappeared, "burnt up like a fire whose source has been extinguished." The original ideas which the past had spewed up—and which had insufficient time to unfold their brilliance—could reach, after the middle of the century, an increasingly smaller audience. Catholic intellectual life was not just a dispute over philosophies but an event of cultural change. Philosophy now explored the activities of the mind or the research of sciences, and so the collective intellect of the age adopted a hostile, polemical tone toward the broader worlds of religion and metaphysics.

The return to scholasticism was based on an ecclesiastical conservatism more than on aesthetic nostalgia. Were not idealist systems something of the past, and had they not ended in pantheism and atheism?

After 1850 part of the German clergy and bishops looked not to universities and periodicals but to seminaries and Catholic clubs for leaders in Catholic life. Good and active priests were desired rather than research scholars publishing a dialectic of abstract theories. A simple if austere chain of proofs and definitions given by neoscholasticism's mix of Aristotle and Aquinas could provide a unifying theology for the church's mission in increasingly secular societies, and scholasticism justified itself not just by medieval brilliance but by global condemnations of other approaches.[13]

II. The "Old Theology": The Perdurance of Catholic Romantic Idealism

Did anything remain of the influences of Schelling and Hegel (inspiring Drey, Möhler, Hirscher, Görres) after 1870? That cultural time of philosophical systems so radiant in the 1830s had faded, and we find few self-professed disciples of Schelling or Friedrich Schlegel. A very small number, however, continue romantic idealism within German Catholicism, although they are minor in comparison with an ever extending neoscholasticism.

At Munich, if Martin Deutinger (1815–1864) was Schelling's last substantive Catholic theological disciple,[14] the most committed proponent of that tradition as it continued in a different world was Hubert Beckers (1806–1889). It was Beckers who had introduced Deutinger to the *Essay on Freedom* at the seminary in Dillingen. Beckers had heard Schelling in Munich unfold the grand tripartite system of transcendental philosophy, mythology, and revelation. Beckers's inaugural address at the University of Munich in 1847 looked at philosophy and at Schelling in light of changing times, as did his address to the Royal Academy on the occasion of the Swabian philosopher's death in 1854.

Beckers argued that philosophy must be in touch with the empirical, recognize the multiplication of schools, and renounce the search for an exclusive, permanent system.

> It is a fact that philosophy today as a science has fallen into discredit among most people, even among reflective and well-disposed spirits.... Our age requires a clear, pure concrete knowing—a knowing of things as they really are, not simply as they are thought; thus, of the entire reality. It was Schelling's great merit to have underscored this task of philosophy, namely the elucidation of reality, with sharpness and decisiveness. Earlier it was nature and

later experience and history which, drawn into the circle of speculative research, effected a new, vital metamorphosis in the area of
philosophy.[15]

In 1875 Beckers's studies of Schelling's metaphysics, natural philosophy and theory of immortality were fashioned into a synthesis, *Schellings
Geistesentwicklung*[16] where the author explained how identity and process stimulated a metaphysics of the absolute evolving and how the final
synthesis of myth and revelation was not pantheism. In the late 1880s the
Munich philosopher liked to call himself "the last Schellingian,"[17] like
his master a seeker for theoretical totality.

Jakob Frohschammer arrived at Munich just as Schelling left for
Berlin but his philosophical studies were done with Görres, Thiersch, and
Schubert. His natural philosophy and psychology have many similarities
to the idealist *Naturphilosophie* and by the 1870s his work on science
seemed somewhat dated. Frohschammer proceeded from an identity of the
real and ideal, searched for the process of unity in diversity, and preferred
the category of life to matter; he was conscious of the boundaries brought
by time and finitude.[18]

Johann Nepomuk Huber (1830–1879) was a professor of philosophy at Munich whose books on Cartesian and Platonic theodicies, creation and Darwinism, pessimism and the proletariate had a modestly
idealist approach. He opposed the rise of scholasticism, which he called
"Jesuitism"[19] and carried on a controversy with Albert Stöckl over the
very value of medieval thought.[20] Huber both criticized the exegesis of
D. F. Strauss and theories of evolution and protested the placing of his
own *Philosophie der Kirchenväter* on the Index in 1860. After 1869 Huber
worked with Döllinger on the journal *Janus*, authored attacks on Vatican
I and infallibility, and ultimately became a leader of the Old Catholic
movement.[21]

Wilhelm Martin Rosenkrantz (1821–1874) sought to develop the
teaching of Schelling in a Catholic mode while avoiding pantheism and
rationalism. Active in the legal system of Bavaria, Rosenkrantz wrote in
both philosophy and theology. His *Die Wissenschaft des Wissens* explored
through Platonic and Kantian categories the structures of knowing and
willing in a format where being follows upon idea, intuition, and knowing.
His *Prinzipienlehre* of 1875 is a curious combination of philosophical
principles followed by topics in theology with references to Aquinas and
Augustine as well as to contemporary dogmaticians like Heinrich Klee.[22]

Friedrich Pilgram (1819–1890) grew up a Protestant in the Rhineland and became a Catholic through an attraction to romanticism and
Hegelian process. Hegel's writings, he believed, could make sense out

of the human condition in an industrial world. The categories of reality were not fixed but capable of critique and dissolution by thought, and idealism could give access to the real. In the summer of 1845 Pilgram heard Schelling lecture on mythology and revelation in Berlin. "Pilgram found in Schelling's positive philosophy the great discovery he had already made on his own: reality precedes all thinking. One suspects that the Christian conclusions of Schelling's system in cosmic cross and purified church furthered Pilgram's path; after reading Augustine, Newman, and Ranke he became a Catholic in 1846, moved to Bonn and joined a circle around the dogmatic theologian Klee."[23] Uninterested in the customary priestly access to a scholarly career, he became politically active in 1848 and worked in the first Catholic lay movements. His *Irrwege des modernen Denkens in der Auffassungsweise katholischer Wahrheiten* (1852), conceived in the spirit of Möhler, sketched similarities between Protestants and Catholics, while the inventive *Soziale Fragen betrachtet aus dem Prinzip kirchlicher Gemeinschaft* described the new situation of the modern state from the perspective of political science.

Pilgram's *Physiologie der Kirche*, which searched for the "philosophoumena" of the church—temporal forms where faith becomes concrete in community—appeared in 1860. In this original ecclesiology the church is the assembly of human and graced relationships. The "natural side" of the church, its inner link with all that is human and real, exists in a dialectic between sin and redemption, unity and diversity. Pilgram developed the idea of the church as fundamental sacrament, effecting what it is.

> To receive all that is necessary for sanctification and immortality the human being first enters into community, relationship, contact, and society. By doing this a channel is open to sanctification. Since the church does not just influence this relationship but is the community, it restores the primal relationship of human beings to each other. . . and to God. Thus it follows that the church working for itself in a sanctifying way is in itself sacrament.[24]

Pilgram wished to reach Protestants and nonbelievers, intellectuals and scientists in his own age, and he was among the first to protest against "ultramontanism." After 1855 neoscholastics accused him of a subjectivism drawn from Schelling, a transcendental faith like Jacobi's, and a sociology in sympathy with de Lamennais.[25] Sadly, the private scholar found no audience for his pioneering works in social ethics and ecclesiology. His theological projects had reached a point beyond his times. After 1870 Pilgram withdrew into private study, particularly of Hegel and Aquinas, but nothing was published. Today he is seen as a pioneer of the ecclesiology of Vatican II.[26]

Thus Schelling's ideas (and those of Baader and Görres) continued at Munich from Vatican I into the 1880s, Döllinger and Alois Schmid were teaching history and dogmatics, while in philosophy Beckers and Frohschammer covered the central courses from logic and metaphysics to history of philosophy and philosophy of nature. Döllinger's followers, such as Huber, Johann Friedrich, and Adolf Pichler, composed "the young Munich School," which was viewed after the Munich assembly as independent and arrogant.[27]

When we turn to Tübingen, we recall that its leader in midcentury, Johannes Evangelist Kuhn, had absorbed his early orientation—subjectivity, the interplay of finite and infinite, history and process—from Jacobi and Schelling (as had his teacher J. S. Drey). The Tübingen theologians remained knowledgeable of and sympathetic to the great figures of past philosophy. The influence of Schelling moved from Tübingen to Freiburg with Franz Anton Staudenmaier. Among the more prominent Catholic theologians, one finds influences of idealism in Herman Schell, through his education in Freiburg with Brentano; in Carl Braig, whom Heidegger said opened up to him the tradition of Hegel and Schelling and their influence in Catholic theology; and in Paul Schanz, Kuhn's successor, whose interests were apologetics and the natural sciences. Alois Schmid arrived at the University of Munich only three years after Schelling had left for Berlin. He heard lectures by Görres on the cosmic development of the history of the world and on parapsychological and mystical phenomena, as well as Baader's lectures on Catholic theology. A bridge between this era of the system-builders and the new interests of Thomism and apologetics, Schmid saw himself as part of the Munich tradition. His survey of Catholic currents referred to intellectuals pursuing "neo-Schellingian systems."[28] But in 1879 Alois Schmid reminisced about Munich, the Bavarian Florence of Ludwig I in the 1830s:

> That was the time of youthful, creative romanticism which came out of the desolation of the Enlightenment (the leveler of every trace of poetry and history). It began with a captivating philosophy of nature, and after the difficult years of revolution moved to the historical powers of positive Christianity and Catholicism.... It was a beautiful time of courageous struggle and work; it is gone like a dream of youth. It was—and is no more![29]

In the rebirth of interest in the idealists from 1890 to World War I neo-Hegelians and neo-Schellingians emerged, but only neo-Kantians lived on significantly into the twentieth century. Schelling became the interest of Eduard von Hartmann, Rudolf Haym, and Kuno Fischer. Paul

Tillich was to write two dissertations on Schelling. A number of books treat Schelling and the Old Testament, Christology, revelation and mysticism, his connections to Schleiermacher and Schopenhauer. Rare Catholic contributions to this renaissance include a late article by Alois Schmid, some chapters on myth and aesthetics by a young Munich *Privatdozent* for literary history, and the histories of modern theology by Adolf Dryoff.[30]

III. The "New Theology": Neoscholasticism

It is difficult to narrate the early course of the neoscholastic revival in the nineteenth century and its virtual conquest of Catholic philosophy and theology. Unfortunately, nothing approaching a history of neoscholasticism in the nineteenth century exists and even books and articles on its figures and schools are rare.[31] Actually, the Western Catholic church had gone through not one but several periods when theology was expressed in medieval, i.e., scholastic, form and content. Presentations of Aquinas and Scotus occurred in the Renaissance, in the Counter-Reformation, in the baroque period and in the nineteenth century. Each had its own characteristics and even in one period one can see differences of emphasis. Moreover, the neoscholasticism of the 1880s is not that of the 1920s or the 1950s. The most recent renewal of Aristotelian and medieval metaphysics began in the 1840s and lasted until the 1960s. In the nineteenth century neoscholasticism was a reaction to Hermes and Günther, to French traditionalism and ontologism, and its parents were the early Italian neo-Thomists and the Jesuit Joseph Kleutgen.[32] Neoscholasticism after 1870 dominated Catholic philosophy and theology, even art and political theory, and was the standard against which every Catholic intellectual movement from Vatican I through the First World War to Vatican II had to be measured.

Scholasticisms and Thomisms

Some nineteenth-century scholars defined scholasticism as the thought of a period, i.e., the twelfth to the fourteenth centuries, while others saw it as a method. Great scholastics like Albert, Aquinas, and Scotus satisfied both views. While Tübingen and Munich theologians spoke of "a new theology of past sources," a "scholasticism redivivus" (J. B. Hirscher), or a "modern-scholastic doctrine" (J. E. Kuhn), in Germany and Rome the terms "neoscholasticism" and "neo-Thomism" appeared only in the late 1870s.[33] The pioneering historian of medieval thought, Martin Grabmann, defined neoscholasticism in this way: "The direction which has emerged since the mid-nineteenth century and usually found

in Catholic theology and philosophy; it takes up again the connection
with that ecclesiastical scholasticism interrupted by the Enlightenment,
searching to make fruitful for contemporary problems the thought-world
of medieval scholasticism, particularly of Thomas Aquinas."[34]

The nineteenth century did not instantly rediscover the breadth and
depth of Aquinas. There was a struggle to understand his principles, a
process to explore the breadth of his corpus, and a need to separate
his thought from baroque commentators. Only toward 1900 did historians glimpse the pluralism within the medieval period—e.g., with the
Jesuit Franz Ehrle focusing on Augustianism and the Dominican Heinrich
Denifle on Meister Eckhart. Sometimes self-consciously non-scholastic
thinkers like Kuhn or Schanz understood the fabric of Aquinas's theology
better than those writing textbooks on it. But how rapidly and thoroughly
German Catholic life was drawn to accept a neoscholastic monopoly
in theology and philosophy! There were certainly real weaknesses in
German philosophies of religion which prepared for this shift: the disappointment of the systems of Hegel or Baader; the absorption of Christ
into transcendental metaphysics; the universities being more concerned
with historical theories than with interpreting the faith of Christianity;
the reduction of revelation to religion, and religion to consciousness,
myth, and symbol. There were causes in the culture itself: the idealist syntheses had not provided cultural and political harmony but only
failed revolutions and rapid social change; as inevitably happens, liberal epochs are followed by conservative periods where precision and
certainty are sought. Science and government, Protestantism and philosophy seemed no longer irenic but now appeared hostile to Catholicism. Vigorous faculties at Mainz and Münster convinced more and more
bishops and professors to restore a single way of thinking based upon
Thomas Aquinas. By 1870 neoscholasticism was viewed as the intellectual and theological form of all that was ultramontane; it was linked
to the Jesuits as its special proponents and to Rome as a parent-school
and command center. Neoscholasticism held itself apart not only from
subjectivity and process but from a truth independent of church authority and from the history of theology and salvation history as sources of
Christian faith.[35] Thus political and ecclesial ideologies tended to replace
the intrinsic criteria of truth prized by the great medieval thinkers with
extrinsic arguments like the authority of the church, logical proofs, and
the isolation of certain principles. (All this finds its climax in the selection in 1914 by the Vatican Congregation of Studies of twenty-four
theses which would perfectly present the thought, i.e., the philosophy, of
Aquinas.)[36]

The renewal of scholasticism occurred in both theology and philosophy. Neoscholastic theologies were not just applying philosophical words and forms to central Christian beliefs but they altered the proper theological content, because Scripture and the history of dogma were neglected. As the nineteenth century progressed the great figures like Suarez, Molina, Bañez and John of St. Thomas became better known and the distinctions between major schools of the sixteenth and seventeenth centuries were appreciated.

Neo-Thomism is not identical with neoscholasticism, for there were restorations of the theology of Bonaventure and Scotus that were part of neoscholasticism; Jesuit intellectual life drew from Molina and Suarez, although these would not wish to be viewed as separate from the thought of Aquinas. Interpretations of Aquinas had differed, as the major neo-Thomist commentators like Capreolus, Cajetan, John of St. Thomas show. The discussion of the merits of various Thomisms before and after Molinism would be vigorously pursued for decades.[37] The Jesuits, despite their own interpreters like Suarez and the criticism of the Dominicans, saw themselves particularly bound to Aquinas. The combination of Dominicans and Jesuits enhanced the role of Aquinas and contributed to an inaccurate identification of his thought alone with medieval scholasticism. The Franciscans were not strong enough to establish their thinkers as the equals of Albert and Aquinas; this is unfortunate, for the Augustinian-Franciscan tradition might have found some affinity with the idealist-Neoplatonic one.

Seminaries which had followed an ecclesiastical program separate from universities enthusiastically joined the scholastic direction: Eichstätt with Stöckl and Cologne with Scheeben. By 1900 even the older universities had their neoscholastic representatives. "If we abstract from the Tübingen school, the theology of neoscholasticism is in fact identical with the systematic theology of the last century. Real theological progress is found only in apologetics and in segments like Mariology and ecclesiology."[38] This paradigm survived two world wars and ended only with Vatican II.

How can this large neoscholastic movement be charted? Can this network of texts and textbooks, of clerics and professors extending over half a century be enclosed in a framework? One could look at religious orders (e.g., the Jesuits), at the shifts in theological areas (from sacraments to apologetics), or at kinds of publications (from studies of Aquinas to textbooks). To attain some grasp of the movement's origins and progress we will look at academic centers, then at religious orders, and conclude with a delineation of this movement's historical periods.

Professors, Universities, and Centers

Universities like Munich, Tübingen, and Freiburg remained faithful to the older idealist directions, while Würzburg also contained neoscholastics. Münster and Mainz (where Catholic faculties were intertwined with seminaries) represented the dramatic advocacy of a scholastic remedy for modernity. There a new generation of traditionalist bishops, clergy, and laity set up or altered faculties and periodicals for the exposition of Aristotle and medieval theology.

Mainz

Mainz was an early center of neoscholastic restoration, a theological tradition going back to Bruno Liebermann (1759–1844) and to the Strassburg Jesuits. Some of its professors, such as J. B. Heinrich (1816–1891) and Klee (1800–1840), had been educated during the early years of the Catholic Tübingen school. Clergy were educated in Mainz in an atmosphere of liberal ideas from Belgium and France and a pastoral theology that emphasized remaining close to the people they served; a rather simple dogmatics prepared for but did not fashion the later neoscholasticism. In 1818 a philosophical and theological faculty was begun anew, although it was moved to nearby Giessen, a school established in 1830 as a university-like substitute for the Mainz seminary and whose faculty included Kuhn and Staudenmaier.[39]

In 1851, however, Bishop Ketteler, whose liberal stances in social issues did not hinder him from becoming increasingly fearful about speculative theology, withdrew his students from Giessen and reopened the seminary at Mainz. This *Priesterseminar* at times had the right to grant advanced degrees but was incorporated fully into the University of Mainz only much later.[40] A faculty committed to Roman directions ("the second Mainz school") was assembled after 1845 and included Heinrich, P. L. Haffner (1829–1899) and Christoph Moufang (1817–1890). It restored somewhat the educational format of the best Jesuit seminary education before the secularization and established a type of school concerned with educating the clergy rather than with university research and speculation. Initial inspiration for Mainz theologians came from Rome, from the multivolume works of Joseph Kleutgen. Haffner founded a chair in honor of Görres in the philosophy section, and in 1866 he became bishop of Mainz, a move illustrating the interplay, favorable to neoscholasticism, of prelates and professors.[41] Periodicals were founded to serve the return to scholasticism—*Der Katholik* and *Zeitschrift für katholische Wissenschaft und kirchliche Lehre*—and the school published sources for the neoscholastic revival.

Johann Baptist Heinrich has been called the head of the Mainz circle. Neither revolutionary nor rigid, he had studied with the great liberals at Tübingen and Freiburg but became critical of the Tübingen approach and of programs for reform such as J. B. Hirscher's. Nevertheless, his central role in founding the Görresgesellschaft indicates that he did not wish German Catholicism to retire fully from the cultural stage. He was in favor of Bishop Ketteler's measures to strengthen Catholic identity in German society, even as he argued in favor of Vatican I taking measures against historical-critical scholars. Editor of the *Mainzer Journal* and of *Der Katholik* from 1850 to 1891, he wrote perceptive articles on issues like Vatican I and composed an apologetics and a dogmatics which began to appear in published form in 1881.[42]

Moufang was the moral theologian at Mainz. He was professor from 1851 to 1890, serving at times as regent of the diocesan seminary. Editor of *Der Katholik* after 1870, he served as vicar of Mainz after Ketteler's death and during the Kulturkampf. Active in politics in Hesse, he organized the first *Katholikentag*, a quasi-national assembly (lasting to this day) where periodically a broad representation of German Catholics could hear and discuss important issues. His lack of historical and metaphysical depth forecast the pattern of neoscholasticism which would dominate the coming decades.[43]

Münster

If Mainz served as a pioneer of neoscholasticism, Münster assumed a leadership role after 1870. An *Akademie* with a theological faculty was founded in 1843 and became a university in 1875. A bridge-figure similar to Mainz's Heinrich was Anton Berlage (1805–1888). This student of Drey and Möhler at Tübingen went on to Munich to hear Baader, Schelling, and Görres[44] and in his early years looked positively on Hermes and Günther. He taught for forty years beginning in 1835, and his *Apologetik der Kirche* indicated for many the methodological directions of theology in the future: the tone of apologetics with the content of scholasticism. His approach to theology was speculative, while his gifts in language and conceptuality reflected a dual philosophical education. His goal was to move Catholics of a Hermesian sympathy away from that idealism where dogmatics were rationalist and moral theology was sentimental. *Christ-Katholische Dogmatik* in seven volumes[45] was among the most widely used reference books in ecclesiastical circles in the years after 1865. Münster furthered Thomism and Aristotelianism in textbooks, as the publications of F. Friedhoff (1821–1878) and F. X. Dieringer (1817–1876) show.

Franz Jakob Clemens (1815–1862) was a militant figure of the early generation of neoscholastics who led scholasticism to a first level of maturity. A student of the Jesuits in Rome, he attended lectures at Bonn and Berlin. Among the first Germans composing neoscholastic works in Latin (against which some scholastics in Rome such as B. Jungmann protested), he argued in *De scholasticorum sententia philosophiam esse theologiae ancillam* (1856) for scholastic philosophy as an exclusive if subservient minister to theology. His next major work was a critique of Günther.[46] The young layman (a delegate to the Frankfurt Parliament) became professor of philosophy in Bonn and moved to Münster in 1856 before assuming a position in Rome, where he died suddenly in 1862. But he had already formed such disciples as M. J. Scheeben. It was Clemens who began the controversy over nature and grace with J. E. Kuhn. His career alerts us to the role which laity (sometimes converts) played in this crusade for conservative Catholic structures. Moreover, as the years passed, the advocates of the new Catholic theological directions less and less had any experience of the university or of the German *Wissenschaft* they opposed.

Ernst Commer was born in Berlin in 1847 and died in Graz in 1928. After receiving a doctorate in law in 1869 he studied philosophy and theology at Tübingen, Würzburg and Breslau. He was ordained a priest in 1872 and received a theological doctorate at the Dominicans' Angelicum in Rome in 1880. He taught philosophy in Liverpool in 1877, at Münster from 1884 to 1888, and finally at Vienna from 1900 to 1911. Joseph Hasenfuss refers to him as "the co-founder of German Thomistic neoscholasticism,"[47] and he represents new links with Rome, that is, with the Dominicans and the Angelicum. At Münster he helped to found the *Jahrbuch für Philosophie und spekulative Theologie* in 1886 (titled after 1914 *Divus Thomas*). The journal became a sourcebook for the positions of the right in German neoscholasticism. It was not only the most significant organ for neoscholasticism (with a strong Thomist orientation) in the German-speaking world, but through reviews and articles it offered a survey of how the neoscholastics viewed church and culture in those years. Its scope was not rigid, particularly at the beginning. Studies of Greek axioms were followed by essays on Aquinas and socialism, or surveys of Trinitarian theology. Attention was paid to apologetics and to papal positions, but one finds here also new issues like the human "*potentia obedientialis*" for grace.

In the years after 1883 Commer published a four-volume philosophical system. We find there an important shift in the order of scholasticism, one contrary to Aquinas's method: from general metaphysics to natural philosophy with logic at the end. While the object of metaphysics is the nature of things as having being, Commer linked being immediately with our ideas and so general metaphysics proceeds (in a modern direction) from being and then from ideas moving to categories and causes. The content is a pastiche of Aquinas's various works.[48] His later works are more challenging: an apologetics for philosophy and a study on the "perennial philosophy."[49] His ecclesiology sees hierarchical constitution and clerical exclusivity in the clergy to be of divine institution; the baptized live from a sacramental union with Christ. Moreover, any move for a separation of church and state is to be rejected.[50] Commer had looked favorably on the liberal theologian Herman Schell in the 1880s and invited his friend to contribute to the *Jahrbuch*, but neoscholastic narrowness eventually made the famous theologian his foe. After Schell's books were placed on the Index, Commer pursued a campaign to discredit the Würzburg theologian in every way, and his diatribes make evident that he sees scholasticism as the only acceptable mode of intellectual discourse.[51]

A figure not located at Mainz but whose links to German neo-scholasticism come through Commer is Michael Glossner (1837–1909), a frequent contributor to the *Jahrbuch für Philosophie und spekulative Theologie*. Called by his foes the *"Oberscholastiker,"* he was always ready to reject Catholic theologians like Paul Schanz, Carl Braig, and Schell with their different perspectives. Ordained a priest in 1860, he was professor and rector of the seminary in Saratow, Russia, after 1864. In 1877 he assumed a position at the seminary in Regensburg and in 1891 moved to an ecclesiastical position in Munich. His first book, written from the solitude of Russia, was a critique of Kuhn's theology of grace. Two volumes of a dogmatics appeared in 1874, followed by attacks on "modern idealism" and "modern culture." Of particular interest is a confrontation of Albert the Great's Aristotelianism with the various branches of post-Cartesian philosophy.[52] *Der spekulative Gottesbegriff* surveyed the idea of God in several dozen major and minor figures from Kant through J. Sengler and M. Deutinger to H. Lotze, Ulrici, W. Wundt, and J. Michelet arranging them into groups of "unitarian theists" or "radical atheists." Glossner's method was a mixture of quotations and principles. He had *a priori* decided that a thinker with the slightest positive view of modern philosophy was to be condemned: for example, the thought of the pious Martin Deutinger, Glossner concluded, led to an absolutizing of human consciousness.[53] His books against Schell and Kuhn were followed by a long article depicting negatively the role of the Tübingen school over the entire nineteenth century.[54]

Joseph Mausbach (1861–1931), professor of moral theology, examined the issues of the time according to Catholic principles in works which were translated and widely used in seminaries around the world.

He opposed narrow-minded and polemical Thomisms (among which he included that of Viktor Cathrein). Opposing the growing prominence of casuistry, he employed Scripture and Augustine. His writings stood apart also in their address of contemporary issues such as the role of women in society and the promise of the Weimar government. He developed after 1911 a new kind of apologetics linking ethics, society, and faith and enlisted colleagues to writes its three volumes: *Religion, Christentum und Kirche.*[55] The topics are introduced in terms of contemporary issues and methodologies; neoscholasticism is absent in both terminology and metaphysical approach. Mausbach's opening essays begin with the nature of religion, the development of the philosophy of *Geist*, and contemporary derivations of religion from mental structures. These books present an exceptional theological experience for the years after *Pascendi.* Lest we think that this world of past theology lies far removed from us, we might recall that Karl Barth described amicably his frequent contacts with his Thomist colleagues at Münster, particularly with Diekamp and Mausbach.[56]

Seminaries

The ultramontane movement in Germany furthered the development of diocesan seminaries which were geographically and institutionally separate from the theological faculties of the state universities.[57] In place of the unsuccessful plan for Catholic universities, separate seminaries became centers of conservative theology to which they owed their very existence. M. J. Scheeben spent his career at Cologne, and at Dillingen there was Theodore Specht (1847–1918), who wrote a Thomistic *Lehrbuch der Dogmatik* and *Lehrbuch der Apologetik.*[58]

Founded in 1843 by the future Cardinal von Reisach as a Tridentine seminary distinct from a university, Eichstätt was a pioneer of neo-Thomism. Albert Stöckl (1823–1895) taught there from 1850 to 1862 and succeeded Clemens at Münster from 1862–1872. As teacher and rector he worked tirelessly for neo-Thomism in curriculum revision and publications. Stöckl assembled what some would designate as the first neoscholastic textbook for seminary philosophy and an early history of philosophy past and present. These works contained some texts and figures hitherto unresearched, but they were largely summaries lacking insight and synthesis and were as critical of medieval mystics as of modern philosophers.[59] Intent upon equating his view of scholasticism with Christian revelation and with the mind of Rome, he developed the Eichstätt seminary into a school for future priests from different regions of Germany whose seminaries had been closed by the Kulturkampf; thus its influence was considerable. There professors Matthias Schneid (1810–1893) and Franz Morgott (1829–1900) advocated Aquinas as the pinnacle of medieval thought and as an alternative to modernity. Morgott, Grabmann's teacher and Scheeben's supporter, corresponded with European scholars of a like mind. His neoscholasticism had a textbook format but included an extraordinary grasp of Thomism. A study of instrumental causality in the sacraments in Aquinas and his disciples influenced the way many, for almost a century, conceived of orders and sacramental efficacy.[60]

Fulda, seat of ancient German Christianity and of modern episcopal meetings, offered opportunities to Konstantin Gutberlet (1837–1928), who taught at that seminary from 1862 until the turn of the century (he directed the seminary when it moved to Würzburg during the Kulturkampf). His *Lehrbuch der Apologetik* attacked monism and materialism. He re-edited the dogmatics of Heinrich and founded with J. Pohle (1852–1922) in 1888 the *Philosophisches Jahrbuch* of the Görresgesellschaft.[61] Pohle finished his studies in Rome at the Germanicum in 1878 and after a time in England taught in Fulda from 1883 to 1889. Accepting Leo XIII's call for professors for Catholic University of America (founded in 1889), he was soon embroiled in conflict with J. Keane, rector of Catholic University (who in 1900 was exiled to Dubuque, Iowa, for modern pastoral views). Pohle returned to Germany to be professor at Münster in 1894 and in 1897 at Breslau; he left uncompleted a *Lehrbuch der Dogmatik*.[62]

Religious Orders

The history of the varieties of scholasticisms in the Catholic world is, in some sense, the history of the religious orders from the Middle Ages to Vatican II. In schools and traditions, in collections and textbooks they presented medieval, Renaissance, and baroque theologies interpreted through figures belonging to a particular order—for example, for the Jesuits, Molina or Billot; the Dominicans, Bañez or Garrigou-Lagrange. At the same time that the philosophical and theological restoration of neoscholasticism was taking place after 1850, the religious orders were themselves being reborn in the aftermath of the French Revolution and German secularization. It is important to see how the progress of neoscholasticism was linked to the orders and congregations. A school of neoscholasticism was both the theological tradition of an order's past and the intellectual direction of its rebirth.

The educational practice of the Jesuits before and after their suppression by the papacy in the late eighteenth century was tied to scholasticism, and the rebirth of this method was linked very much to the Society's influence. Through a number of scholars and publications the Jesuits in

Germany were of great importance in the neoscholastic revival. This was true before the Kulturkampf, during the Jesuits' difficult exile, and after their return. Joseph Kleutgen was a seminal figure in the revival and his importance was enhanced by the weakness before 1860 of the other orders of scholastic tradition, e.g., the Dominicans and the Franciscans, outside of Italy and Spain. Jesuit centers of research were established at Innsbruck in 1857, in 1872 at Valkenburg (their studium in exile), and at Maria Laach in 1862 and upon their return to Germany after the Kulturkampf. Valkenburg in Holland remained a philosophical and theological center until 1917 (it was still in existence as a scholasticate with a fine library and faculty up to 1942). The publications *Scholastik, Stimmen aus Maria Laach* on religion and culture (which became *Stimmen der Zeit*),[63] a journal on homiletic and pastoral theology titled *Chrysologus*, and an early periodical on missiology were all edited in Valkenburg. These periodicals and various series of textbooks gained an international audience, particularly in seminaries. A thirteen-volume course in neo-Thomistic philosophy, *Philosophia Lacensis*, and a collection of conciliar texts were produced after the Jesuits returned from exile to their intellectual center at Maria Laach (after 1893 the abbey was returned to the Benedictines and became an important liturgical and artistic center of Catholicism between the wars). Maria Laach's Jesuits represented a spectrum of scholastic approaches in philosophy, dogmatic theology, and moral theology. Social and individual ethics joined apologetics as the major fields of interest; the dogmatic areas of Christianity were pursued with less frequency and less imagination, but ethical conversation with the times, in line with the views of the Holy See, prepared for the new social encyclicals. Tilmann Pesch (1836–1899) carried neoscholasticism into periodicals and addresses, arguing that Catholicism offered as an alternative to the current return to Kant a return to "the philosophy of the Middle Ages—without doubt the greatest, unified phenomenon in the history of philosophy, the foundation for the future, the seed for development."[64]

Another gifted and influential Jesuit was Christian Pesch (1853–1925). His *Praelectiones dogmaticae*, in nine volumes published between 1894 and 1899, aimed not simply at repeating diluted scholastic texts but integrating a critical viewpoint and other theological sources within a scholastic framework. It quickly became one of the most widely used theological manuals. Pesch's own views, however, leaned toward a static conservatism as in his criticism of Schell and his position on the salvation of the nonbaptized. Viktor Cathrein (1845–1931) was a prolific moral theologian. The opinions of this Jesuit, noted for his strict adherence to Aquinas but also for applications of Catholic social theory to new situations, e.g., *Arbeitsvertrag und Streikrecht*[65] tended to please neither non-scholastic thinkers nor the more traditional Thomists. His *Moralphilosophie* (1890–91) was reworked into an apologetic framework in *Die Katholische Weltanschauung in ihren Grundlinien mit besonderer Berücksichtigung der Moral* (1897). Among neoscholastics in both centuries, Cathrein stood for what some saw as an inappropriate or impossible task: the total employment of Aquinas joined to the conscientious addressing of contemporary problems.[66]

In 1913 the Society founded an institute for scholastic philosophy at Innsbruck, one of whose leading speculative minds was T. Granderath (1839–1902). He engaged in a long controversy with Scheeben over grace, indwelling, and merit.[67] An adviser at Vatican I, he represented a narrow Roman scholasticism, an approach always present but not necessarily dominant in the Jesuit centers. And yet his *Constitutiones Dogmaticae* examined contemporary figures like Ritschl.[68]

Thomas Aquinas had been a Dominican, and his order did not need the neoscholastic revival of the nineteenth century to encourage the teaching of his thought. Dominican intellectual life was always centered upon the texts of Aquinas and few outside sources were permitted to complement them. The Dominicans had their own "school" begun with Capreolus, and after 1800 their interpretation of Aquinas was to no small extent based on the commentaries of Cajetan and John of St. Thomas. They wanted, however, to let Aquinas speak out of his own writings, to balance philosophy with theology, and to give weight to the philosophical distinction between essence and existence and to the theological axiom of grace drawing nature to its destiny.

The Dominicans, like many religious orders, reached a low point in their history outside of Italy and Spain in the 1830s. The order hardly existed at the time of the neoscholastic revival and the German Dominicans were few in numbers. Some years later centers of Thomistic research were developed at the Angelicum in Rome and at Fribourg in Switzerland. Fribourg drew on an international faculty: Pierre Mandonnet pioneered research into medieval figures such as St. Dominic, while Spaniards such as Norbert del Prado and F. Marin-Sola pursued within narrow neo-Thomist guidelines original speculation on divine existence or the evolution of dogma.[69] In Austria, H. Denifle pioneered the historical study of the Middle Ages.

Albert Weiss (1844–1924) was representative of a strict German Dominican neo-Thomism as it unfolded beyond technical studies. A native of the Bavarian Alps, he studied in Freising and Munich and was ordained a priest in 1867; subsequently he taught in the Freising seminary, only entering the Dominicans in 1876 when he was thirty-two. Active in

Graz and Vienna in examining Christian social issues, he taught sociology after 1892 in Fribourg and apologetics there from 1895 to 1910. A first book on pedagogics in the early church was followed in the 1880s by a five-volume apologetics which was translated into many languages and was still reprinted in 1923.[70] He wrote autobiographical memoirs, essays on spirituality, and a work on the psychology of Luther. *Liberalismus und Christentum* and *Der Geist des Christentums*[71] were among the most uncompromising rejections of intellectual and theological directions outside the preferred union of neoscholasticism and popular apologetics. *Die Entstehung des Christentums* read back into the first two centuries of Christianity the same issues that existed in 1900: the nature of progress, the distinction of Christianity (and Judaism) from all other religions, the possibility of revelation in paganism (which Weiss views as an admirable naturalism). The Dominican distinguished himself by writing against all reform movements at the turn of the century, not only those of "Reform Catholicism" but those with an integralist foundation. "With his broad knowledge he opposed on the social, apologetic and religious levels every form of liberalism."[72]

Thomas Esser (1850–1926) was born in Aachen and studied with both Schell and Commer. Ordained in 1873 but professed in the Dominicans in 1878, he taught canon law at Maynooth, Ireland, and then at Fribourg from 1891 to 1894. An expert on Tertullian, he wrote books on philosophy as he worked on Commer's *Jahrbuch*, e.g., *Die Lehre des Thomas von Aquino über die Möglichkeit einer anfangslosen Schöpfung*[73], and he edited with Mausbach an apologetics, *Religion, Christentum, Kirche*. He served on the Congregation of the Index during the important years of 1900 to 1917 and had the distinction of being the last secretary of that congregation.[74]

IV. Stages of German Neoscholasticism

Neoscholasticism had its own history and, although it aimed at a single conceptuality and metaphysics, in the scholastic revival of the nineteenth century it even had a certain diversity. In 1928 the German Jesuit Erich Przywara perceptively observed four moments in neoscholasticism's flourishing from 1870 to World War I. The first, which he titled *critical*, was repeated by the strict Dominican school at, for instance, the Angelicum or Fribourg. Not looking favorably on the Platonism of Augustinianism or on the critiques of Kant, it criticized all other philosophical and theological approaches by comparing them to its own clearly delineated tradition: Aquinas understood in light of the Dominican commentators through the centuries. It eschewed historical context in favor of metaphysical structure. Its drawbacks were one-sidedness and absoluteness. The second direction, a *historical* one, was begun by Franz Ehrle's and Heinrich Denifle's research into the diversity of medieval scholastic theology and mystical schools. The third direction Przywara called a *productive* neoscholastic philosophy serving theology and dogma by defending a philosophy of objectivity in logic and theodicy or by incorporating new discoveries from psychology and natural science into a neoscholastic framework. A fourth stage came out of positive conversations over the relationship of objectivity to creative subjectivity with such philosophers as Bergson, Husserl, and Scheler. This stage was different from the first three because it saw scholastic thought capable of conversation with modern thought and eschewing claims to solitary dominance. "We see that both an independently active neoscholasticism and an apologetical Christian metaphysics oppose in different ways the positivism which denies metaphysics, and yet they have points of contact with the philosophy of the age and with its inductive metaphysics, critical realism and epistemology."[75]

As difficult as it is to find the temporal pattern for so many names, multivolume texts, schools, and traditions, one can discern in the march of neoscholasticism in Germany from 1860 to 1914 three stages.

The first period (1850 to 1875) moved from discovery to stability. Figures like Schmid, Scheeben, and Heinrich, who were educated in the earlier German historical and idealist modes, studied the medieval thinkers but did not fully replace contemporary thought with neoscholasticism. At the same time there were also young enthusiasts who, knowing very little of German idealism, assumed an ideological stance on behalf of the hegemony of Aristotelianism. They turned a provincial, exuberant neoscholasticism (which did not yet grasp the inner richness of Aquinas or the diversity of medieval thought) into the dominant philosophical stance for German Catholics.

The second period, from 1875 to 1890, presumed that Thomism and scholasticism were well-known (more and more books on all areas of Aquinas had appeared) and were destined by church authority to be the sole intellectual format of Catholicism. Most facets of modern *Wissenschaft* and *Gesellschaft* in Germany were disapproved of not just critically but polemically. Isolationism and autocracy led to an exclusivist vision (as many neoscholastics rejected every thinker but Aquinas), while rigid and unimaginative authors like Glossner and Commer dictated theological acceptability.

With the third stage, beginning after 1890, four approaches are present: (1) the development of manuals and multivolume textbooks;

(2) works explaining the meaning of Aquinas, particularly on philosophical issues; (3) applications of Aquinas and Aristotle to social and ethical issues; (4) histories of medieval thought. Just when metaphysical rigidity might have become sclerotic, two groups of thinkers broke out and pursued, first, "scholasticism applied" and, second, the history of medieval thought.

What is most important is the rise of the historians of medieval thought after Ehrle and Denifle, reaching a climax with Martin Grabmann. "With the exception of Scheeben, all German neoscholastics of that period are outranked in significance by the scholars of medieval scholasticism (Ehrle, Denifle, Clemens, Baeumker and Grabmann)."[76] What makes them distinctive is that through history a knowledge of medieval philosophy and theology is gained which is both richer and pluralistic.

A pioneering historian of medieval thought was Ehrle (1845–1934). First serving as editor of *Stimmen aus Maria Laach*, he labored after 1885 on a history of scholasticism: *Biblioteca theologiae et philosophiae scholasticae selecta* in seven volumes. With Denifle he began the prestigious *Archiv für Literatur und Kirchengeschichte des Mittelalters* and became director of the Vatican library under Leo XIII. Ehrle's interest lay with the great figures of scholasticism and the research of writings which were largely available only in unpublished manuscripts. His discovering of an Augustinianism in reaction to Thomas Aquinas's Aristotelianism indicated a plurality of themes, approaches and schools in the scholastic era.[77] The Austrian Dominican Denifle (1844–1905) furthered historical research into medieval theologians by discovering new works in manuscript in England, Spain, France, and Portugal. He called attention to a medieval theological world which was not speculative—the Dominican mystics Suso, Eckhart, and Tauler (he discovered the Latin works of Eckhart). An expert in medieval church life and universities as well as in Luther and the Hundred Years War, he became Vatican archivist, established the Leonine edition of Aquinas, and to some extent rehabilitated the historical study of Martin Luther by noting his medieval roots.[78]

Ehrle's research into an Augustinianism reacting to Aquinas, and Denifle's discovery of the variety of mysticism were expanded by Pierre Mandonnet's delineation of the Latin Aristotelianism of Siger de Brabant and by Baeumker's discovery of the relationships between Muslim thought and scholasticism. There was also the perdurance of Platonism and a "metaphysics of light" in a second school coming from Albert the Great. Martin Grabmann emphasized research into the liberal arts and philosophy. Profiting from past research and synthesizing philosophical, theological, cultural, and mystical facets of the Middle Ages, Grabmann was able to publish a summary of the accomplishments of the history of scholasticism in 1913, but he did not transfer his insights on medieval culture and theology to his own age; he feared modern philosophy and a contemporary Catholic theology.[79]

V. Two Theologies in Conflict

This chapter began with the divisive meeting of 1863 in Munich. Now that we have traced the two directions of Catholic theology let us return to the 1860s for an introduction to prominent theologians of the age from 1860 to 1914. A controversy over nature and grace illustrates the growing conflict between scholastic and historical-idealist theologies. The debate is multifaceted, touching on science and faith, state and church, scholastics and Aquinas. Herman Schell and Alois Schmid grasped its centrality as did Pius IX and Pius X.

Johannes Evangelist Kuhn was born in 1806 and died in 1887, his life spanning much of the nineteenth century. An early student of Schelling and Jacobi and then of Hegel, he represented their presence in Catholic theology well into the latter part of the nineteenth century. Singled out by Drey and Möhler to be the speculative leader of the Catholic Tübingen school, he was professor in Tübingen for forty-three years, from 1839 to 1882.[80]

Kuhn's intellectual career was marked by an engagement with the public forces of his time in government and in philosophy. During the turbulent years of German politics in the middle of the century he was elected to the Württemberg parliament, and in the issues of church and state Kuhn argued for the rights of both. Paradoxically, in light of his later rude mistreatment in Rome, the monarchy in 1847 found him too independent and Catholic to be bishop of Rottenburg, for which he had been nominated by Rome and Vienna.

As we have just seen, the introduction of neoscholasticism was not simply a restoration: its warmest proponents were often self-educated in medieval thought and did not always grasp well the order or principles of the great thinkers. For theologians in Munich and Tübingen the arrival of Aquinas's thought could appear as a Trojan horse holding sectarian and legalist control.[81] Kuhn was already being criticized in the 1850s by the conservative school of Mainz for being too open to modernity and too influenced by Protestant theology. From 1856 to 1863 he was involved in a controversy with Clemens over the relationship between philosophy and theology.[82]

In Aachen, the city of Charlemagne, at the fourteenth General Assembly of the Catholic Unions of Germany in 1862 a plan was put forth by laity and bishops to establish a Catholic university in Germany.[83] Pope Pius IX sent a letter supporting the decision. Through Heinrich Andlaw, lay professor at Freiburg in Breisgau, the committee directing the discussion of the project sought out the views of the distinguished theoretician of the Tübingen school. Kuhn admitted the limits placed upon Catholic intellectual life in universities where Protestant or secular groups dominated, but nevertheless progress had been made there in recent years. He repeated the public call for a parity in the numbers of Catholic and Protestant professors, but he questioned whether there was "Catholic" medicine or chemistry. A separate Catholic university would insure that scientific research and teaching, precisely in its relationship to the Catholic faith, would be viewed as prejudiced or second-rate. Catholic theological faculties in the German universities would be marginalized through lack of support.[84]

A young Freiburg professor J. Lorenz Constantin von Schäzler attacked the Tübingen theologian's views.[85] Born a Protestant in Augsburg in 1827, after some time studying law he entered the military and in 1850 he became a Catholic in Brussels. He spent five years in the Jesuits, being ordained to the priesthood in 1856 and leaving the Society but not the priesthood in 1857. After studies in Rome and Louvain, two further years of theology at Munich gave him a doctorate on the topic of sacramental efficacy and he found a position teaching the history of dogma in Freiburg. He was present at the scholars' congress in Munich. Advisor at Vatican I, from 1873 he lived in Rome, serving as consultor to the Holy Office and writing books on papal infallibility and a Latin *Divus Thomas contra liberalismum* in honor of the jubilee year of Aquinas in 1874. He died in Switzerland in 1880.[86]

An article in 1862 by Schäzler accused Kuhn of infidelity to Augustine and Aquinas and of heterodoxy in dogma. It declared that Kuhn's deficient views on the mission and nature of a Catholic university flowed from his weak understanding of the supernatural. Kuhn's system was "a fully enclosed worldview where only one concept had no place: the supernatural. . . . There is no topic he speaks less about than the supernatural— but a professor of Catholic theology must speak about it."[87] From Munich, Ignaz von Döllinger advised his Tübingen colleague not to respond, but Kuhn did answer concerning the issue of the university.[88] While an exaltation of the hegemony of Catholic dogma might at first appear attractive, sciences lacking the latitude to operate within their proper principles would lead to cultural darkness. Albert the Great and Thomas Aquinas fought for an independence of each and did not advocate a sectarian subordination of science to theology.

The combatants in the discussion over nature and grace were the dominant figure in the flourishing second generation of the Tübingen school (and its most speculative theological mind) and a young but recognized representative of neo-Thomism. Ultimately the issue was not just nature and grace but their active relationship. Was grace to be understood as being or as activity? Was human nature a reality with independence or only a vehicle for divine actions? This polarity (which became an opposition) did not have its source so much in Aquinas's thought (where grace as a principle of supernatural life preceded acts) but in baroque and Enlightenment theologies of grace. Both theologians agreed that grace is unconditionally necessary for human beings and that it is something above nature. Schäzler saw the natural potentiality of the human person as less capable in its own sphere and the supernatural order as more distinct, more separate from the natural. This Kuhn found demeaning to creation and humanity. For Schäzler the principles of human knowing and willing must be "expanded" through a divine force, but for Kuhn the human faculties are active and need only an impulse and elevation by grace. Neither Schäzler nor Kuhn (and here they continue the general lines of Aquinas's thought as it has influenced Catholicism for centuries) emphasized fallen nature and widespread sin as the reason for grace. "The question between us is this: does grace act as a supernatural complement for my natural powers, an elevation of the capacity of my spirit, or does it make possible merely a particular use of my natural capabilities?"[89]

Mysteriously, after the publication of his incomplete *Gnadenlehre* in 1868 and a final article on original justice in 1869, Kuhn published almost nothing for the remaining years of his life. Was this due to his discouragement over an increasingly dominant neoscholasticism or over certain decrees of Vatican I against which he had advised but then quietly accepted? Schäzler interpreted some passages in conciliar decrees as directed against Kuhn.[90] By 1870 J. B. Heinrich's suggestion of heterodoxy found an echo among some—particularly the bishop of St. Gallen—who wrote to Rome suggesting Kuhn's writings be placed on the Index. It was rumored in Roman circles that he was a dangerous person, and curial officials approved a selection of theses from Kuhn's writings which might be condemned. German bishops and theologians, however, arguing against any such procedure, prevailed. Nevertheless, F. X. Kraus, professor in Tübingen, related in 1881 that "the venerable old Kuhn is still working on his treatise on grace,"[91] and the Tübingen *Vorlesungsverzeichnis* shows him still lecturing on grace in 1880.

* * *

The controversy between Kuhn and Schäzler attracted attention into the 1900s; it was simply an epochal example of the underlying struggle between history and metaphysics, revelation and culture.

Late nineteenth-century repetitions of medieval thought and baroque scholasticism determined Catholic religious education from catechism to seminary textbook. This restoration was more particularly of philosophy than theology, of Aristotle than of Thomas Aquinas, of logic than of christology. A nonvoluntaristic and free theology of grace found in Aquinas was re-formed into a theology of propositional faith, ontology, and church authority. A lack of sophistication in method, a questionable arrangement of disciplines, an absence of history, a moralistic interdiction of other theologies even when based upon Scripture and tradition characterized this theology. The great controversy between Kuhn and the neoscholastics in the 1860s reappears in different forms over the future decades as the neo-Thomist parties eschewed contemporary life and intellectual exploration.

This survey of the two directions in theology is preliminary to our task of offering some portraits from Catholic theological life at the end of the nineteenth century. Our interest lies more in the directions which neoscholasticism opposed. And in reaching the 1900s we are ahead of our story, for theologies drawn from the "older" currents of idealism and history did still exist in this period. The school of Tübingen, with Paul Schanz, continued, and the most creative theologian of the time, Herman Schell, despite his international influence, was condemned by Rome. The following profiles give us theologians, periods, and schools to illustrate how Catholics in the second half of the past century struggled to offer an alternative to a past scholasticism, a theology which would ponder and critique modernity rather than flee culture.

PART TWO

Theologians in a Divided Age

3

Matthias Joseph Scheeben:
A Transcendent Synthesis

OUR FIRST THEOLOGIAN was something of an anomaly. During the decades of transition, the 1860s, he belonged to no school. He pursued grand formats but published few books. Nevertheless, we include M. J. Scheeben in our history for two reasons: first, he represented poignantly the struggle of German Catholic theologians to find a way between the Roman and the Tübingen directions: secondly, of all our figures, he was the best known and the most read in the first half of the twentieth century. He represented the struggle of a few German theologians who would transcend neoscholasticism by employing patristic and idealist thought in their theologies.[1]

I. The Rhine and the Tiber

Born in the Rhineland near Bonn on March 1, 1835, he went at the end of his gymnasium years in 1852 to the German seminary in Rome, the Collegium Germanicum-Hungaricum, where in 1858 he was ordained a priest. He pursued graduate work at the Collegium Romanum (today the Gregorian University), and among his teachers were such great figures from the Jesuit Roman school as C. Passaglia, C. Schrader, J. B. Franzelin, and R. Cercia. Passaglia taught the history of sacramental theology and ecclesiology as well as special courses in the primacy of the papacy and the role of ecumenical councils. Cercia's lectures on grace were expanded by Schrader's courses on the natural and supernatural orders, and Franzelin lectured on the Trinity and Incarnation from an Augustinian viewpoint.

All were continuing the approach of the creative and erudite Giovanni Perrone, who had sought to arrange biblical, scholastic, and patristic approaches into a synthesis.[2] The approach was conservative, literal, and dogmatic but by no means shallow or reactionary. This "Roman theology" of the middle nineteenth century should not be confused with later neoscholasticisms that were suspicious of all other theologies whether of Alexandria in 330 or Germany in 1830. Perrone was professor from 1824 to 1863 and then rector and prefect of students until 1876; through these offices he influenced students from various countries. His *Praelectiones theologicae* in nine volumes appeared in the years up to 1842 (a popular *Compendium* offered the text in two volumes) and went through more than thirty editions. Here the church was pictured as a moral person, a worldwide society with an animating principle, grace. Under the obvious influence of Möhler, Perrone noted that in this Tübingen theology he could "recognize no pantheism."[3] Passaglia and Schrader (influential in preparing ecclesiological drafts for Vatican I) continued the patristic orientation begun by Perrone, but by the 1860s the tone of Franzelin, less gifted than his predecessors and more neoscholastic, prevailed. But ecclesiology too—the church active in persons and offices—drew from the Greek fathers, Petavius and Thomassin in the baroque age, as well as from Möhler of Tübingen. Despite being supported by the papacy, it offered a counter to an excessive scholastic formalism and an uncontrolled papal legalism. Through his teachers at the Gregorianum from 1840 to Vatican I, Scheeben learned to appreciate not only patristic and scholastic theologies but the great controversies over grace and free will.

Scheeben read widely in the Greek fathers, particularly Cyril of Alexandria. Kleutgen taught him neoscholastic theology, but he also had the opportunity to read in the library of the Germanicum the sources of "German theology," the Tübingen masters. Thus he was encouraged to reach back to theological sources, to pass beyond scholasticism to Thomas Aquinas. He absorbed in Rome a clear distinction between the natural and the supernatural world, a respect for a God who is infinite and active but whose life is mirrored in the human life of faith and grace.Scheeben was a scholastic *and* a patristic theologian, but like his Roman teachers he represented no creative system.

In line with Roman procedures Scheeben received doctorates in philosophy in 1855 and in theology in 1859. Returning to Germany as a young priest, he traveled to centers of the "Roman" direction in theology, Mainz and Würzburg, only to realize that his Roman education had limited his professional academic opportunities. Pontifical credentials were suspect and his theology was presumed to be ideological and lacking creativity. His youth had ended in a certain rigidity: he saw Hermesians everywhere, disdained J. E. Kuhn for being treated "like a pope" in Tübingen, and evaluated severely older scholars' treatments of Aquinas.[4] While serving as chaplain to Ursuline nuns and teaching at their school for girls he became at the age of twenty-six professor of dogmatic theology (and for a while of moral theology) at the Cologne Seminary in 1860.

Delicate in health and ascetic in personality, he stayed at the seminary until his death in 1888. He attended two important ecclesial events: the provincial council in Cologne in 1860 and the assembly of scholars in Munich in 1863. Both, like other events in the 1860s, led him to conclude that nature and grace composed the central theological areas.

II. Scheeben's Theological World

Nature and grace with their history of controversies, Scheeben stated in his first articles, raise the great issues of the nineteenth century. He attached himself firmly to neither the older, German idealist and historical school nor to the neoscholastic centers of Rome or Germany. He did not hesitate to judge Kuhn, Schäzler, and Schmid as well as Jesuit neoscholastics in the controversies over grace, and he disputed with such Tübingen figures as F. X. Linsenmann and F. X. Funk. He soon distanced himself not only from "Romans" north of the Alps like Schäzler and T. Granderath, but also from the Roman Jesuits such as J. B. Franzelin and J. Kleutgen who would eventually advise the Roman curia not to recommend Scheeben's *Dogmatik*.[5] Joseph Kleutgen himself recognized that Scheeben was not a docile product of Roman Jesuit scholasticism. Mentioning Scheeben's first article in a letter he wrote: "He talks about a supernatural logic, a supernatural ontology, etc.—what reasonable sense does that have?... Although the teaching is good, I am afraid that it will confuse more heads than it will illumine."[6] Scheeben had seen by 1864 that he had to deepen his understanding of Aquinas and free himself from Kleutgen. He wrote later of himself and Aquinas:

> St. Thomas took the right tack by not forcing these questions [free will and grace] too much, driving them to the edge as his followers later did...and so either side can call upon Aquinas for support. I have tried for a reconciliation of the opposing tensions on the basis of Augustinian and Thomistic views, an approach which has, at least, the value of not preferring one of these systems over the other. I have placed particular emphasis upon the essential difference between the divine movement on the natural and supernatural level and noted the various modes in which the physical influences God exercises upon the will occur.[7]

Scheeben did not come to Aquinas through Suarez, Molina, De Lugo, or Bañez but acquired a broad knowledge of Aquinas's writings and through his large works an early grasp of the Dominican's principles. Whether the Cologne theologian's resolution of the dialectic between

nature and grace did justice to Aquinas's balance or included other theological directions need not be decided here. His lack of interest in the
historical explains his joining of ideas found in Augustine, Aquinas, and
baroque scholastics, and his thought can point to an Augustinian-Franciscan dimension where intuition, process, and life rule.[8] He recognized
his own independence from scholastic schools, as he corresponded with
Franz Morgott: "It would particularly interest me what you, as an authentic Thomist, think of my Thomism, particularly of the many questions
in christology, and also (this too is important for christology), what you
think about my teaching on grace, my views of Molina and Bañez."[9]

How did the Cologne theologian evaluate the period of philosophy
and theology which had just preceded him? The great figures from Kant
to Hegel he viewed as rationalists, naturalists, and liberals. The early
Tübingen figures such as Drey and Staudenmaier worked in a laudatory
way, but during a time—the first third of the century—which Scheeben
viewed as one of decline, when in fact it was the age of romanticism's
renewal. We see here the birth of the false historical myth that the nineteenth century before the arrival of neoscholasticism either lacked creative
theology or was a time when Catholics unwittingly sold out to idealism.
This view would last for a century. According to Tübingen's calumniators
its Catholic dogmatic theologians, drawing upon Kant and Schelling, confused the lines of grace and nature.[10] Baader, Hermes, and Günther were
praised for their speculative energy, but they had limited success because
they neglected scholasticism. "Scheeben hardly had any real knowledge
of Hegel's or Schelling's philosophy...[but] did have an affinity for
the dynamic contained within idealism and he employed [some aspects
of modern philosophy in] areas of theology...making possible a transcendental science of the life of God with its uncreated ideas."[11] But
A. Kerkvoorde compared him to Hegel: "Like a Hegel of Catholic theology he would have wanted to make an amalgam of all doctrines, or
better, a higher synthesis penetrated by one idea."[12]

The Cologne theologian learned in his seminary studies something
of Tübingen's importance, and some scholars even see Tübingen as "the
preliminary school for Scheeben's work."[13] His preference for the living and the organic and his refusal to encapsulate Christianity in precise terms were rather uncharacteristic of contemporary and subsequent
scholasticisms.[14] In a review of Karl Werner's vast history of Catholic
theology after Trent, Scheeben expressed an anxious view:

> What we basically miss is the highlighting and consistent presenta-
> tion of the process where, in philosophical areas, the progress and
> maturing of theology is effected through the mutuality of national-

modern and universal-traditional elements. We note, however, the absence [of a critique] of the one-sidedness and the deficiencies marking the theologians of the 1830s and 1840s, even if we do not want to diminish the noble aspirations, the special talents and great merits of Hirscher, Drey, and Staudenmaier.[15]

R. Vatter has compared in detail Scheeben and Kuhn. "The principle with which Scheeben directed his historical presentation resembles the stance of Kuhn. Scheeben wanted through the study of the historical development of the teaching of the divine Trinity to arrive at a deeper understanding of the inner nature of this truth."[16] And yet, Scheeben presented grace as divine, ontic, physical, with few personal and transcendental dimensions. In the controversy between Schäzler and Kuhn he saluted Schäzler's critique of Kuhn's "one-sided" emphasis upon human nature (one must not portray the spirituality of human consciousness in an exaggerated way so that it appears to inform or beget grace). Still, Schäzler was "too crass a Thomist," unappreciative of the contributions of Molinism and almost minimalizing person and freedom, while Kuhn was correct in establishing a positive receptivity to grace even if he understood it in too moral a sense and therefore not in an adequately physical one.[17]

Scheeben's theology did have a transcendental mode, for it began with the divine self unfolding in process and life into various organically arranged finite realizations. Its divergence from earlier idealism lay in its substitution of emanation for history and, above all, in the reluctance to pursue a transcendental analysis of the human subject. An early enthusiasm for the supernatural led Scheeben away from the transcendental and historical theologies of Tübingen and Munich. The scholastics perceived correctly the axiomatic center of the theology of grace, while "modern theologians ignored it completely."[18]

III. In the Workshop of Theology

Scheeben's first publications in 1860 were a collection of patristic texts on the Immaculate Conception and a programmatic essay on the supernatural in science and life. He went on to compose three large works: (1) *Natur und Gnade: Versuch einer systematischen wissenschaftlichen Darstellung der natürlichen und übernatürlichen Lebensordnung im Menschen*; (2) *Die Mysterien des Christentums: Wesen, Bedeutung und Zusammenhang derselben nach der in ihrem übernatürlichen Charakter gegebenen Perspektive dargestellt*; (3) *Handbuch der katholischen Dogmatik*.[19] He published close to a hundred articles and reviews, some preparing for his books; their recurring themes are grace and ecclesiological issues surrounding Vatican I. Smaller pieces treat practical church issues such as relationships with Protestantism, celibacy, and diocesan assemblies.

The poles of his emanational theology were Trinity and human nature. How should one interpret an incarnational religion so that it remained such without being pantheistic? The great mysteries of Christianity were interpreted in terms of life, human activity, knowing and willing, joined to authority, organism, and the supernatural. Intent upon being incarnational, this theology seemed to explore neither idealism nor the history of revelation but unfolded a middle language: a kind of aesthetic metaphysics drawn from past theologies. While he mentioned that the deposit of revelation is not a jewel to be hidden in a vault, a consequence of Scheeben's failure to resolve the activity of human nature as it is touched by grace appeared in his view of religion and culture.

> Christian revelation is a treasure of divine truths which people grasp in faith, and make the object of knowing and thinking. . . . Christianity bears within itself an essential determination to bring to particular cultures its religious ideas and principles in order, through its divine energy, to change them, to penetrate, transform, ennoble and raise them from the natural sphere.[20]

Scheeben's view of the development of dogma, a normal and necessary service to revelation in broadening the circles of the church, was the "seminal" interpretation. An inner truth was unfolded by external factors and what came forth was not a new revelation but a deeper knowledge and a greater precision. Theology, conceptual and dogmatic, was to serve that development—by advising and by documentating popes and councils.

The life of the Trinity shared with creatures is the ground and theme of all theology and is realized in the interplay of the divine and the corporeal in Christ, Mary, the church, and the Eucharist. Theology explores the meeting of two personal grounds of activity, one divine, one created: the Trinity and the human personality. The themes and chapters of Scheeben's theology—divine life, Trinity, missions, grace and graced life, humanity as the image of God, Christ, Mary, and the church—are "concretizations" of the one life, formalizations of the one principle, God.[21]

Henri Rondet described Scheeben as poised "between the Charybdis of pantheism and the Scylla of moralism."[22] *Nature and Grace* was begun not with history or psychology but with God as it sketched progressive concretizations of the divine life in two distinct orders, natural and supernatural.

> Man receives from God not only a nature proportionate to his proper mode of being, but a higher nature (which is accidental, not substantial) whereby we are refashioned on the model of the higher,

divine nature...causing in the human being the dawning of a new light that makes him capable of a higher knowledge and love...in a new, special relationship with God, who draws near to us in his own essence and not only as creator of a nature foreign to us.[23]

The book's chapters reach the economy of salvation only at the end; before that they unfold an abstract metaphysics of human and divine orders with their own principles, activities, qualities and effects. Grace was not a holy state of mind but an objective and formal reality given by God alone. The human being faded before this powerful participated divinity (Scheeben's chapters on human virtues became concrete only in examples from the saints). *Nature and Grace* led to Greek patristic theologies that offer a certain openness beyond the physics of actual grace. In contrast to Kleutgen and other Jesuit neoscholastics, Thomas Aquinas was followed in topics like physical premotion, the completion of virtue by gifts, the physicality and distinct formal object of grace and the dialectic with freedom. On the other hand, a rejection of a natural teleology for humanity and the too stolid presentations of grace and nature could not recall the *Summa theologiae*.[24] By emphasizing the divine, Scheeben passed beyond the dominance in theology of actual grace to uncreated grace. Eugen Paul asks:

> Is he the prototype of those theologians who, if they did not establish, at least represented the demeaned "two-level theory" of nature and grace? Or does he belong to those who represent a transcendental unity of nature and grace? Does he understand grace in an extremely ontic ("physical") manner or was he concerned with the a priori dynamic of being in its ontico-ethical, personal but dual aspects? Finally, does he view "the primary concept of grace" to be habitual or actual grace?[25]

Regardless, the two models—process and distinction, idealism and Aristotelianism—would not be mixed. Synthesis would come only in the hypostatic union.

Scheeben reviewed the controversy over grace between Kuhn and Schäzler as well as Alois Schmid's attempts to mediate between them.[26] Both men, he thought, had exaggerated in the labels hurled at the other, but Schäzler had been particularly offensive in his epithets. Kuhn had gone beyond "the old Tübingen view" where grace was a religious force for activity, but he gave no substance or substantial role to the personality.[27] Was not Kuhn's insistence upon the active nature of the personality vis-à-vis grace also to be found in Schäzler's passive nature that in its receptivity is active? Scheeben offered no new theology but, as an outsider, tried to reconcile the viewpoint of each, although it was not clear that he had seen in these theological positions their real differences.

IV. "The Mysteries of Christianity"

Die Mysterien des Christentums, although its publication in 1865 occurred before that of the never completed *Handbuch*, was the last major work to appear in a final form. Despite its length this work, Scheeben said, was written not for theological specialists but for a wider public.

The work's great theme is life—the life of a supernatural order which differentiates itself into an "organism of mysteries." The book's order is not convincing and indicates the lack of creativity in theologians of this age struggling with the systematic even as they distanced themselves from both Hegel and Aristotle. The section on Trinity is largely concerned with internal theology but through a treatment of the missions of Logos and Spirit extends the divine being into Incarnation, framed by a modest context of salvation-history. His christology finds further realizations in the real presence of the sacraments and in Calvary as sacrifice. Eucharist is seen as the entry and paradigm for the other sacraments and for the church. After the chapter on the church, one other sacrament is treated in detail: matrimony—for incarnation is marriage. Detached sections, almost appendices, are then given to justification and to eschatology as beatific vision and the resurrection of the body. The work then curiously returns to grace as predestination, while the nature of theology is considered at the end.[28]

From the point of view of method, there are several difficulties. First Scheeben wished to address the difficult issues of his age, but the discussion of these problems remained artificial and *a priori*. Grace was a dominant theme of Scheeben's career, but his difficiencies in format hinder his presentation, and grace is treated in four different sections. Topics are grouped around the Trinity like rays around the sun of deity. Scheeben considered his work to be a system or a science, because new ideas and aspects can be deduced from fundamental revealed truths. This deductive interpretation of theology—here in its simple beginnings—would come to dominate neoscholasticism in the twentieth century.

The Triune God of Mysteries

"Mystery" is the title, theme, and mood of this theological work. The opening chapter on mystery is a kind of treatise on theological method, distinguishing and separating the beliefs of Christianity from past philosophies and theologies which have brought them too close together.

Christian mysteries are not derived from reason nor spewed forth by a God who is one with cosmos or consciousness. Not discordant with reason, Christian faith is centered upon truths revealed in a special way by God. *The Mysteries of Christianity* is almost a very sophisticated kind of catechism, for its topics are not introduced from sources or established by insight but from the general creed of Christianity.

Scheeben describes revealed mysteries as attractive, born of love, and drawing one to divine union. Thus he establishes an apologetic theology from an aesthetic point of view. The book also shows the tendency to treat the articles of faith as intellectual areas rather than as activities of God or experiences of humanity. This is then neither a system like Schelling's or Kuhn's nor a *summa* from Aquinas or Alexander of Hales. Without critique or dialectic a positivist tonality presents blocks of traditional and scholastic thinking arranged around the major *revelata*. Contemporary authors are rarely cited and, if so, usually positively, thus not disturbing the tranquility and safety of the theological pages.

The idea of the Trinity need not be derived from rationalism or pantheism. "Our initiation into the mystery of the Trinity engenders, above all, a supernatural, elevated and tender love for God, a love of friendship."[29] But Scheeben fails to show why the idea of the Trinity would bear in men and women excitement, much less love. His arguments about Trinitarian life remain bland, standing outside of psychology and history. Jesus' preaching seems to give no key to why the Trinity exists or acts. Scheeben's extensive speculation on the Trinity, with little originality, gains some life through its emphasis upon the missions of Incarnation and grace, of Son and Spirit. But here too a lofty conclusion—our filiation—is left vague: what does it mean in life (and in Jesus' teaching) to be an offspring and not a slave? Moreover, Scheeben's close derivation of our filiation in Christ to the natural sonship of the Logos to God is not necessarily traditional, orthodox, or true. "The very notion of adoptive filiation presupposes natural sonship. We could not properly regard ourselves as adoptive children of God unless natural sonship were present to our minds as the ideal to which we are to be conformed through adoption by God and in grace; and God Himself can have the idea of creating adoptive children from no other exemplar than from his own Son."[30] Throughout the pages of *Mysteries* his imagination posits relationships, resemblances, and theandric actions, inspiring and exciting forms fraught with implication, but they all remain concepts of an abstract metaphysics.

Scheeben's orientation was strongly supernatural. Whenever possible creation yielded to the influence of God and of grace. His fear of grace being derived from the order of nature led him to separate the two realms sharply. Human knowing is not faith; human life does not ground

Christian life.[31] Now this could be true *in the abstract*; but how does it reconcile with divine presence in billions of men and women with their own identities?[32]

Channels of the Divine: Christ and Church

Scheeben's christology is an exploration of the God-man, an extraordinary mystery, but what is described is the metaphysical reality of the one person with two natures but nothing of his daily life. "The union is absolutely miraculous and supernatural and hence mysterious if only for the reason that two extremes which are separated by so immeasurable a distance as the finite and the infinite combine to form one whole, and that the lowest joins with the highest."[33] The biblical activities of Jesus are not discussed but only the metaphysical facets of a special being. A mediator at Calvary gained grace by a priestly sacrifice ("latreutic death"). Platonist and Aristotelian metaphysics are mixed with poetry.

From Scheeben on, soteriology, sacramental theology, and ecclesiology were constructed in light of an interpretation of instrumental causality. This mechanical theology had considerable impact on subsequent Catholic theologians.

> By his satisfaction and merit the God-man is the moral cause of man's restoration to the sonship of God; that is, he moves God, he begs God to forgive us . . . . This moral causality is a great mystery in its own right . . . the *gratia capitis* . . . . The grounds on which Christ's unexampled moral causality rests demand that we admit a physical causality, or better a hyperphysical causality.[34]

Scheeben's emphasis on physical causality described Jesus as having a humanity which is an "instrument," "conductor," or "organ." This theology overlooked that in church and worship instrumental causality acts through free, historical human beings. In addition, Scheeben had to face the difficulty of how a limited instrument could channel grace in a mode free of the limitations of time and space. He did occasionally admit that such activity (receiving communion, faith) must be broadly interpreted in spiritual, i.e., moral, terms.[35]

Eucharistic consecration and ordination are the paradigms of a causality of grace. The real presence and the activity of the divine are stressed while the human is reduced to a ministerial role; the finite cannot directly or effectively produce grace. "This power can be viewed as an investiture of the material element with the power of the Holy Spirit descending upon it through the sacramental word or the ecclesial prayer of ordination; it can be interpreted as a kind of marriage of the created substratum with God and a pouring in or 'mixture' of the divine substance in the created."[36]

The church is a great and stupendous mystery. In language recalling Möhler's *Einheit*, church and tradition are composed of "a diversity of organisms communicating the charismatic influence of the Holy Spirit in diverse ways."[37] Church is a mystery in its being and organization as well as in its power. Although maternal and priestly, the visible and organizational nature of the church is never analyzed and seems to be a static conductor, generally good and perfect, existing apart from history and sin like the paradigmatic and active figures adorning the interior of German baroque church. Membership links the believer with networks of grace and mystery almost automatically, and the impression is given that the virtues, gifts, and graces that come to an individual come not precisely *through* the real, human ecclesial agencies but as a reward for being in some contact with the church. Electricity is used as an analogy; a live wire always produces electricity apart from other circumstances.[38]

His theology of the papacy, also a "supernatural mystery" and the supreme instrumentality after Christ, passes rapidly from pastoral office to an infallibility which (some influence of Möhler survived) included offices and factors beyond the papacy.

> The pronouncement of the pope is an official witness of the existing agreement, and the pope himself is the spokesman of the community, and only in this sense is he the spokesman of the Holy Spirit, who abides in the community. . . . Infallibility lives not outside but within the total organism of the church. . . . The church is not a machine but a living organism in which the fullness of life in the head does not exclude the proper life of the heart and other members, but rather the one principle of life, the Holy Spirit, maintaining the head in truth, also influences directly the other members with its light.[39]

Scheeben did not enumerate these "other members" nor describe their dialectic with the pope; bishops, leaders of local churches, are not infallible, and their relationship to the pope is one of grateful acceptance of his teaching and authority. There is little discussion of the vast network by which the church is administered and by which decisions are reached at various levels. So a theology of ecclesial organism has been inserted into a pyramidical model of hierarchy without noticing or resolving the tensions. Teachers have meager roles: the laity witness by their faith—an echo of authoritative teaching—and their lives invite others to enter the church. "The recourse to the confession of faith existing in the people is for the church teachers always only a secondary help, and not primarily a rule or source of its teaching."[40] Scheeben spent the final year of his life, his energy diminished, working on his *Dogmatik*; the scope was larger but there were no indications that theological method and the results would differ from *Mysterien*.[41]

This theology of mysteries was not a pastoral correlation of culture with revelation but a conceptual service to bishop and pope. One gains the impression that all teaching tended toward the infallible, just as all sacramentality tended toward the hypostatic union. Equally important was the large role ecclesial epistemology had in this theology. The *Dogmatik* begins with an ecclesiology which will unfold revelation as mystery. Faith appears later in connection with Christ. This signals the future dominant textbook arrangement, where the power and language of Vatican theology is a necessary prelude to God and Trinity.

V. Amid Ecclesiastical Controversies

Rome had left its impact on Scheeben. At Munich, he sided with the Würzburg and Mainz conservatives; he felt the nunciatur was dealing too mildly with the other side and viewed positively the appearance of the *Syllabus* of Pius IX in 1864.[42] And yet the Cologne scholar was not a papalist or neoscholastic. He evaluated various positions, was not inclined to write a theology simply repeating Aquinas, and found a model in the irenic theologian at Munich, Alois Schmid. Eugen Paul describes him as pursuing a "moderate ultramontane position."[43] At the time of Vatican I he wrote many articles defending the definition of infallibility and even founded a periodical *Das ökumenische Concil* for this purpose. Essays spoke of the "suicide" of intellectuals who had sold themselves exclusively to science (e.g., Döllinger and F. H. Reusch) or listed the reasons expressed in Germany for not following the council. The third volume of 1871 was given over to a defense of the dogma of infallibility, while as late as 1881 Scheeben was still in the midst of the debate in Germany over church authority.[44] Originally the theologian had not been one of those who strongly wanted the definition to emerge from the council, because he wanted peace for the Catholic church in Germany.[45] This was not to be, for shortly after the council the Berlin government in their *Kampf* to control alien Catholicism closed the Cologne seminary. Without teaching obligations Scheeben expanded his journalistic activity and his work with the newly founded Görresgesellschaft. In the 1870s he viewed Görres as the model for Catholic scholars opposing the Kulturkampf.

As the years passed, Scheeben did not attain a positive view of his own era: speculation was in decline; dangerous new sciences accelerated the sophistication of warfare. But he did see accurately some dangers which lay ahead. Was not the desire for an unreasonable freedom the background for a militant Protestantism and an aggressive secular science? Moreover, the tension between German Catholics and Rome (yet another result of the modern quest for emancipation from the primal authority of God?) could eventually be used to support the militarism and centrism of the German Reich. A strong, authoritative papacy seemed to be needed.[46]

VI. Between the Times

The Dominican apologete A. M. Weiss praised the *Mysteries of Christianity* as "the most original, the most profound, and the most brilliant work which recent theology has produced," while at Tübingen, W. Mattes described it as an outpouring of "poetry and daydreams."[47] In 1946, Cyril Vollert, as he was concluding the arduous task of translating *Mysterien*, evaluated Scheeben's popularity as a sign of the renewal of theology, of interest in Scripture, the fathers, and Aquinas.[48]

In subsequent chapters we will witness the struggle of four theologians against a policy of retiring into a ghetto and for a positive conversation between the Catholic interpretation of Christianity and natural science, education, and government. Scheeben's theology, however, was written more from the perspective of a spirituality than as a publicly challenging work on religion. (He observed that the worldly spirits criticized by Paul and Jesus would be uninterested in his pages on the mysteries of Christianity.) To find faith attractive one must be humble, concerned not with human but divine wisdom, empty of ambition or envy. Ultimately the Holy Spirit must inspire. This melange resulted from his selection of no single perspective: neither the Greek fathers nor Thomas Aquinas served as mentor and standard. His synthesis had no imitators and inspired the most divergent evaluations. Julien Bellamy wrote in 1904 that Scheeben had "some depth, new approaches and vast erudition, but also certain subtle and risky opinions," but fifty years later G. Philips evaluated the same theology differently: "The theological thought of Scheeben had a proverbial obscurity. Widely and randomly ecclectic, its harmonization was imperfect. Despite the extraordinary erudition, it clearly suffered from an absence of critical methods consistently unfolded."[49]

Scheeben's work was the beginning of a transference of Catholic dogmatic theology from the university to the seminary. He was haunted by specters of the past which he globally censored: pantheism, fideism, psychologism. In form and goal Scheeben was modestly creative (strict Thomists and scholastics kept their distance from him). He understood and appreciated contributions from the Tübingen school, and in his own way he was a transcendental theologian, albeit more in touch with divine transcendentality than with human.

In a land and century of philosophers and historians, Scheeben was neither. For this Catholic theologian the plan of God was the deepest theme of all world history, but time (which Schelling and Hegel had observed was similar to human consciousness in its active complexity) was absent from theology. A certain aestheticism and extrinsicism results from a theology seemingly conceived without any reference to the culture of the times. The papacy of Vatican I seemed immediate and real to him, while the Kulturkampf, which violently barred him from his life's position, seemed remote and uninteresting. In the 1930s this theology was drawn into the sphere of "kerygmatic theology" at Innsbruck, and at the same time Scheeben's works in the United States moved subtly into the world of inspirational reading. Because of the prominence in translation of marian and devotional works and the role of terms like "bridal mother" and "Trinitarian marriage," in America Scheeben was frequently thought of as a writer in spirituality.[50]

Karl Eschweiler's study on the two paths of Catholic theology around 1900 established Scheeben as the polar opposite to the rationalism of Hermes, since Scheeben's theology unfolded speculative mysteries, Trinitarian life, and ecclesiastical authoritarianism. Eschweiler saw in Scheeben's thought a dualism fashioned by the mysticism of divine participation and the positivist logic of dogmatic and ecclesiastical propositions. But the many analogies, metaphors, and images which explained supernatural faith never introduced the thought-forms of modernity.[51] Eschweiler's views of Scheeben were perceptive, but his choice of directions in German theology after 1860 was, as we saw in the previous chapter, utterly skewed. Scheeben was always an outsider, a theologian belonging to no major school, a composer of abstract systems filled with quotations. He did not represent a major line. What Eschweiler glimpsed was an ecclesiastical mysticism produced by a profound (though perhaps hardly perceived) fear of modern process and subjectivity.

Bernhard Welte more accurately evaluated Scheeben as symptomatic of the fissures in the second half of the nineteenth century of a separation between nature and grace.

We see this disassociation between nature and supernature in the polemic of Schäzler against Kuhn, but its strongest and most impressive expression lies with Scheeben.... He had a brilliance of thought and conception, occasional penetrative thinking, and something of the inheritance of the Tübingen theologians survived in him. If his theology was an attractive system, it was still thoroughly removed from history, even absorbing whatever the historical material it employed.[52]

Because of the large audiences his writings found up to 1960, Matthias Joseph Scheeben has at times been compared to John Henry Newman. Yves Congar found him an ecclesiologist of some originality. "Under the motif of a christology of Christian mystery, trying to get beyond the narrow limits of apologetic consideration of the church where the tract limits itself to the hierarchy, he sought to reach a true *theological* treatise of the church—that was the line of the Roman school of Scheeben."[53] Heribert Mühlen found there stimuli for a personal theology of the Spirit after Vatican II. Thus, Scheeben had an ambiguous role in Roman Catholic theology after his death. His very independence led him to be forgotten by 1900, but after World War I he represented a modestly creative alternative to neoscholasticism. Eventually he faded away, a theologian whose speculations were distant from any cultural context, an abstract spiritual writer, someone who in the birth of the world of Vatican II was mute.

4

Between Idealism and Neoscholasticism: The Fundamental and Apologetic Theology of Alois Schmid

MUNICH HAD BEEN a center for the Roman Catholic renewal which between 1815 and 1835 coincided with the advent of romanticism and the climax of idealism. As we have seen, the theological school of Munich survived through the years from 1840 to 1880 in scholars like Martin Deutinger, Ignaz Döllinger and Jakob Frohschammer. An interesting theologian of the latter third of the nineteenth century was the Munich professor Alois Schmid. The years of his career covered the period from Schopenhauer to Freud. His education occurred in the era of the great post-Kantian thinkers and their Catholic disciples. Neither a disciple of Tübingen nor a neoscholastic, Schmid pursued a career linked with the school of liberal, culture-oriented philosophy and theology at Munich. Martin Grabmann observed that he stood between Tübingen theology and neoscholasticism and that he had been a speculative thinker who struggled for some independence during the decades after 1870.[1] His writings allow us to see someone working at the intersection of modern and neoscholastic thought patterns. Perhaps this mediating career explains why he became the historian of apologetics and the innovator of fundamental theology.

Alois Schmid was born in the Allgäu in 1825. Educated first by the Benedictines in Augsburg, in 1844 he began his study of philosophy at the University of Munich. Arriving there only three years after Schelling had left for Berlin, he was impressed by Görres's system of world history and by Döllinger's lectures on church history even as he pursued specialized courses in aesthetics and epistemology. A student for the priesthood at the Georgianum, the Bavarian seminary attached to the university, he completed his studies with a prize-winning dissertation on "The Origin, Growth, and Collapse of the Diocesan Synod." This was published in 1850 in two volumes and is an almost unique history of the synod joined to a kind of local ecclesiology arranged around the nature and rights of such a local council.[2] For the solemn inaugural disputation the young professor chose to compare Thomas Aquinas and Nicholaus of Cusa on the finite and the infinite. Schmid was Martin Deutinger's successor at Dillingen after 1852 (Deutinger being the last major Catholic disciple of Schelling),[3] and there most of his philosophical works were written. The most important was a study on Hegel (1858) from a historical point of view. Under the guiding motif of *"Logik"* Schmid succinctly described the development of this philosophy in seven periods ranging from those of Frankfurt and Schelling's influence to the final period in Berlin. Setting aside any polemical tone (although the Catholic Hegelian Anton Günther had been only recently condemned) and inspired by Franz von Baader ("ahead of all others in pursuing Hegel's logic in its development and seeing its defects"), he wanted to understand Hegel's meaning and intention. Noting that few had taken the time to look at Hegelian philosophy in its historical context and in its totality, he concluded that, while areas of speculation were rich and valuable, the system as a whole was abstract, even closed and deceptive in what it claimed but did not produce. [4]

In 1866 Alois Schmid was called to the University of Munich for the professorship in dogmatic theology and he began at once to specialize in apologetics. Retiring after fifty-three years of teaching, he died in 1910. Schmid was a Catholic theologian who worked within the times (and there were fewer and fewer of them after 1860). He was placed in the group of "mediators" who would synthesize scholastic and idealist approaches. This enterprise reached its climax in his evaluation of the Kuhn-Schäzler debate and in his book surveying the two directions of Catholic scholarship in 1870. At his death a colleague observed:

> Because of Schmid's various connections with modern philosophy from the eighteenth and nineteenth centuries as well as with the prominent representatives of scholasticism, he is without doubt one of the most remarkable philosophical figures in the nineteenth century. A comprehensive presentation of the epistemological-methodological standpoint of Schmid along with its links to nominalism and Scotism, to Descartes, Hume, and Kant, to Fichte, Hegel, Schelling, Baader, Hermes, Günther, and Gioberti, to Kleutgen, Schäzler, and the neoscholastics would show not only philosophical but historical-cultural interests on a large scale.[5]

I. Sources and Directions in Schmid's Theology

Schmid grew up in a time which included both transition and reaction. His past mentors as well as his students and colleagues interest us, for they sketch a picture of the schools of Munich and Tübingen at this time as well as a portrait of the resurgent scholasticism that formed him. These three worlds led him to work amid what he called "the two directions" in theology.

Schmid and the "Age d'Or" of the University of Munich

"Three men were members of our university from its move here until the 1840s," Schmid wrote in 1879, "men who were universities in themselves: Schelling, Franz Baader, Görres. Each possessed an intellectual capacity, in breadth and depth, which far exceeded the limits of any particular discipline. Each, thanks to his particular universality of spirit, was in his own way of incomparable greatness."[6] For Schmid, Schelling's final system was the unfolding of a theory of God and humanity in process through the format of Incarnation and Trinity; in short, a philosophy of Christianity. He noted the significance of Schelling's development: in 1804 the introduction of a fall, and in 1810 the exploration of freedom and evil in the godhead. For Schmid process and history in speculative thought could not be avoided, and he noted that the Middle Ages had no significant theory of history. Schelling's momentous separation of the purely rational from a positive philosophy of history and existence laid the foundation for the philosophy of world history and for Christianity as the completing segment of religious history. "Here Christian revelation was not simply source but content in philosophy," not just Christian dogmatics but a higher transcendental history illumined by Christianity.[7] As had previous Catholic critics like Möhler, Döllinger, and Deutinger, the young Catholic theologian in 1879 questioned whether Schelling's theogony did justice to Christian faith and whether it permitted revelation to break through necessity and myth-making. The positive philosophy remained an idealism where revelation had been absorbed into a larger system of divine processes.

Franz von Baader was admired precisely because he rejected idealist pantheism. Baader's own system was neither a rigid theism nor a pantheism but a theosophy "grasping everything in a developmental mode, in an intuitive leap over every intermediary."[8] Baader omitted the rational and the empirical in our knowledge of a God of process. Schmid judged negatively (if imprecisely) Baader's energetic ecumenism which failed to do justice to the claims of the Roman Catholic church and exalted Protestantism. The second half of the nineteenth century was less adventuresome than the earlier time when Benedikt Staatler, Baader, and others formulated ecumenical theories.

For a third teacher, Joseph Görres, Schmid had only praise. Not bothered by the Rhinelander's youthful period as an anarchist and barely touching upon his writings on nature, art, and politics, Schmid praised Görres's offering of "a theism as the only true philosophy, a Christian supranaturalism as the only true theology, and a Catholicism as the true (because the only fully true) Christianity."[9] Görres succeeded where Baader and Schelling failed because he perceived that creation came not out of the godhead but out of nothingness. The active Trinity and a sinfully fallen humanity were not linked by the same process. The divine will and revelation remained properly supranatural. Schmid concluded his tribute to the Munich school, at which he had been a student and was now a professor, in a striking way.

> This was the time of youthful, creative romanticism which came out of the desolation of the Enlightenment (the leveler of every trace of poetry and history). It began with a captivating philosophy of nature, and after the difficult years of revolution moved to the historical powers of positive Christianity and Catholicism.... It was a beautiful time of courageous wrestling and working; it is gone like a dream of youth. It was—and is no more![10]

Tübingen Influences

If the philosopher and theologian Schmid described the three transcendental systematicians, Schelling, Baader, and Görres as great but past teachers, he also acknowledged his debt to the theologian of history, Johann Adam Möhler. His study of Möhler's development and career was a lengthy and mature retrospective on the Tübingen theologian. Möhler, too, had belonged to the Munich theology faculty but only for a few semesters, as his life was cut short in 1838. "More than anyone else J. A. Möhler broke the power of the Enlightenment. A revivification of the study of the fathers and the church's creeds brought the lost deposit of the theology of the early church into a new form."[11] In history and ecclesiology the dynamic interplay of *Geist* and historical revelation was Möhler's framework; historical studies of theologians from Tertullian to Anselm assisted him in appreciating both spirit and revelation. "Christian revelation bears the proof of its divine nature in itself on the basis of the witness of the Holy Spirit in the interior of each individual human being."[12] The theologian-historian had accepted as format the idealist dialectic but without banishing positive revelation and an illuminating, sanctifying grace. One need not fear speculation concerning an immediate knowledge of God that is rooted in God's image in our reason or in the histories of the divine and human subjects where revelation occurs. The Catholic Tübingen school, distinguished by their insistence on the supernatural character of revelation and grace, did not fall into the ontologistic excesses of the great philosophers they had examined: Hegel, Jacobi and Schelling. They certainly could not be lumped together with Hermes and Günther. Schmid discussed Tübingen themes of history and doctrine in the apologetic vocabulary of late nineteenth century, and there we glimpse the distance between him and the Tübingen generations of Möhler and Kuhn. The earlier subjectivity of theology was appreciated as well as Drey's and Möhler's use of sweeping motifs for a "construction" of revelation in consciousness and history, even if Schmid then spends dozens of pages in surveying Möhler on the issues of papal administration, cannon law, and the history of ecclesiastical institutions.

Thomas Aquinas and Neoscholasticism

Schmid, the "mediating theologian," strove over decades to sustain the dialogue between modernity and neoscholasticism (curiously, he viewed both theologies as phenomena of the past). Some argue that he was the first to use the word "neoscholastic" at this time, but his usage implied a pluralism incorporating not only the Roman schools but ontologism in Belgium and personalism in France.[13] Early works from his philosophical period at Dillingen include, besides the book on Hegel, a comparison of Aquinas and Scotus on conscience and a study on Aquinas's metaphysics of God;[14] they unfolded a growing acquaintance with medieval sources, which were, however, studied for their responses to modern issues.

In some ways the perduring formal theme of Schmid's thought was epistemology, and there were two reasons for this emphasis. First, the critical philosophy of idealism had been increasingly interiorized into questions of knowing; second, Kleutgen, influenced by Suarez and other baroque scholastics and critical of Descartes and Kant, had led the way in treating the scholastics largely in terms of their epistemology. An article written for Frohschammer's *Athenäum* in 1863 contrasted the modes of conceptual expression found in theism and pantheism.[15] Thomas Aquinas's theory of analogy was a resource to be used against pantheism —a pantheism represented not only by Hegel and Schelling but philosophies of religion from the post-Hegelian period. The article moved from epistemology to language as Schmid instructed both neo-Schellingians and neo-Thomists on the diversity which had existed among theological schools in the Middle Ages, where the Aristotelianism of Aquinas was taught with the Dionysian neo-Platonism of Eckhart. His survey of Catholic theology in 1862 (neoscholasticism was one of the "two directions" he spoke of) rejoiced in the rebirth of the medieval tradition. This new scholasticism was found throughout Europe and was particularly furthered by the Jesuits, drawing on their baroque scholars. But the new form was not the same as Aquinas's Aristotelianism: the order, the separation of philosophy from theology, the absence of psychology and natural science reflected post-Tridentine approaches. Schmid recommended to the zealous young neo-Thomists that they should pursue in their research, care, modesty, and awareness of the spirit rather than the letter of the text, pay attention to history and principles, and observe the differences between Aquinas and his commentators.[16]

II. The Mediating Theologian

Inspired by Görres, surrounded by neoscholastics, and teaching in the Wilhelminian Reich as a Catholic, Schmid displayed no clear theological identity. He was an independent—but also an eclectic, combining struggles and theologies, and this is reflected in Schmid's most important work charting the "two directions" in Catholic thought.

Between Kuhn and Schäzler

Schmid began his study of the controversy over nature and grace in this way: "The points around which the entire controversy centers are the scientific concept of freedom, the idea of nature and personality, and the concept of grace."[17] While he rejected the contrary positions on grace and freedom in Molinism and Baianism, and interpreted J. E. Kuhn in a positive light, he commented on some weaknesses of the Tübingen theologian even as he evaluated Schäzler's conclusions as exaggerated and shrill. Although Schmid understood and sympathized with some of the aims of modern theology, he gave his allegiance mainly to past theologians, particularly to Aquinas. "We, with Schäzler, venerate the scholastic view of ideas and words in nature, personality, in the natural and supernatural, but we draw a strict line between different conceptualities needed for the areas of philosophy and theology . . . and we evaluate Kuhn differently."[18] In Kuhn, Schmid objected not to active consciousness but to Kuhn's bestowing upon it too active a receptivity for faith and grace. Nonetheless, since there are many theological schools with respect to grace, this theme is far from exhausted.

There were links from a theology of grace and nature to issues of politics and praxis such as the legitimacy of dialogue with post-Kantian philosophy, the independence of science, and the freedom of the Catholic intellectual. "These various questions agitating the present times clearly concentrate themselves in the basic issues concerning the relationship of nature and grace."[19] The conflict's apologetic dimensions are obvious—

how transcendentally dynamic is the human spirit, how free is fallen humanity, how independent is *Wissenschaft* before theology?

In terms of the dogmatic nature of *Natur and Übernatur*, the book's polemical side against Kuhn can hardly be understood as contributing to science. In the view of Schäzler, Kuhn teaches modalism in the Trinity, Nestorianism in Christology, Baianism in faith, and then sometimes pelagianism and semi-pelagianism; and even offers a free rationalism rejecting any positive revelation and authority. . . . As to whether Kuhn's theology really contains these errors in an objective and formal way, we can only deny it.[20]

Nothing fans anger more than another's detached attempt to resolve conflict. Schäzler saw Schmid's articles only as the writings of an opponent: he could not attack the Munich theologian's knowledge of history and Aquinas, so he fought in the area of church authority, arguing that Kuhn's errors were readily apparent and that Schmid treated dogmas as though they were subjects still open to theological exploration.[21] Schmid replied with a book on theological freedom and authority. He distinguished between speculative and practical freedoms in the church, noting that there was such a thing as legitimate theological freedom and in "border-areas" respect was due to past teachings but the possibility of theological exploration did exist.[22] In a further article considering not only the two protagonists but recent interpretations by Scheeben and Kleutgen, Schmid made a number of interesting observations about Aquinas. Both neoscholastic and modern intellectuals could miss the inner dynamic of Aquinas overcoming both dualism and monism, whether the issue were grace and personality or Incarnation. An "organic-physiological" Christian theology could not be set aside. "Only where there is a physically real contact can power and grace pour into the redeemed creature from God's spirit through the God-man Christ."[23] This, he argues, is Aquinas's intention: "Thomas arrives at a strictly real, organic-physiological view of human nature, grace, and sacraments only in the later, mature period of his thought. Here is the true, complete Thomism for a mysticism of supernatural life developed in his spirit."[24] But in this area, where Schäzler's mind could not do justice and where Kuhn strove to retain the personal and psychological, Schmid ended with questions whose answers might lead to the deeper, complete "physiology of grace" of Thomas Aquinas.

Schmid's harmonizing approach became more popular than Kuhn's or Schäzler's; Scheeben and others agreed with its stance. But these articles indicated Schmid's strength as an analyst while revealing his weakness as a theologian. Schmid comprehended the history and needs of modernity but kept his distance even from tempered expressions such as those of Kuhn, and his theology became more and more an exposition of Aquinas and Augustine in the midst of other past theologies learned from history books.

Between the Two Directions

A detached mediation appeared in Schmid's exploration of Catholic intellectual life from 1845 to 1860. Published just one year before the Munich assembly division and eight years before Vatican I, *Wissenschaftliche Richtungen auf dem Gebiete des Katholicismus in neuester und in gegenwärtiger Zeit* [25] looked first at the formal structure of Hermesian, Güntherian, theosophic (Baader), Tübingen (Staudenmaier and Kuhn), and neoscholastic patterns of philosophy and theology. A second part of the book presented controversial questions over which these schools labored and disputed: (1) mediacy and immediacy in the human spirit and faith; (2) knowing and its interpretation by ontologism; (3) freedom for science in terms of faith and church authority; (4) the relationship of apologetics to faith; (5) the reconciling of rational certainty with the certainty of faith; (6) the necessity of tradition but also its relationship to language. The book was a tour de force, organizing numerous opinions, figures, and movements. Schmid was not sympathetic to the traditionalist and ontologist figures in Italy (Gioberti, Liberatore), France (Gatry), and Louvain (curiously, he located Kleutgen among the ontologists as representing a psychological direction). The confines of the German neoscholastics' treatment of science and knowledge were narrow; Schmid took the medieval thinkers (not only Aquinas) seriously and employed their ideas as a standard to measure current alternative positions on revelation and reason. The thinkers Schmid found congenial were theosophic idealism (Baader) and Tübingen (Kuhn). Baader's thought on revelation was analyzed in detail because his "theosophic form" represented the synthesis of Catholicism and idealism. The central issues were the underlying history of religion and the activity of reason.[26] Baader's "relative supranaturalism" avoided "the dualism of natural and theological," gave validity to the sphere of consciousness of the thinking subject," formed a kind of "mystical faith in grace" and gave faith "an ultimate preceding authority." Finally Kuhn had fashioned a theology largely out of past theologians who employed, more or less, a modern philosophical perspective as a positive orientation, and Kuhn's inclusion of Thomas was not just a from of neoscholasticism.

Schmid saw no need to withdraw from modernity. Medieval theology too knew of critical and transcendental philosophy. "There is no more risky assertion than that Cartesianism is simply philosophical Protestantism; that the very principle of modern intellectual history cannot be reconciled with Catholicism and is in its root Protestantism."[27] Catholicism should not eliminate the freedom of science, although many Catholic writers from a neoscholastic or ecclesiastico-positivist orientation, because of their excessive enthusiasm for an authoritative and ecclesiastical mentality, gave that impression, thereby injuring the goal of a mature and free Catholic intellectual life.

> Scholasticism, even in that most distinguished system of Thomas Aquinas, is only one individual member in the great organism of historical spirit reaching through the pagan, patristic, medieval, and modern worlds.... Ideal power will be bestowed upon the neoscholastic direction by the insight that the flourishing of science comes by going beyond modern pantheistic and rationalistic systems (which die precisely by struggling to be without presuppositions or boundaries) and finding the way back into a living harmony of theology and philosophy.[28]

The future of culture did not lie solely with Germany; Catholicism hoped for a new synthesis of the Germanic attention to the knowing subject and the romantic attention to tradition and scholasticism.

Schmid's book on the two directions illustrated the move taking place at this time from speculative Christianity or systematic theology to apologetics, for it was apologetics which gave the framework to arrange the positions of the various schools in the second part of this work. The formulation of the issues which faith presented to philosophy had become somewhat narrow, apologetic, and ecclesiastical; concerned less with a universally appealing system than with a personal, mental identification with doctrine and church. But theologians from 1870 to 1900 found in the survey of scientific directions the problems which would dominate the foundations of theology and faith for the next period: (1) the act of belief as distinct from its content; (2) reason as a rational source of proofs rather than as *Geist* creative of world; (3) *motiva credibilitatis* and *praeambula fidei*; (4) rational proof and revealed content; (5) church authority and university science.

Schmid's work displayed what its title claimed: the existence and legitimacy of two streams within Catholic life. Furthermore, out of the variety of philosophies and theologies there emerged a new set of theological interests. Summing up his previous writings on Baader and Aquinas, on epistemology and academic freedom, on reason and faith, the book pointed ahead to a particular kind of foundational theology cultivated from

1870 to 1960, an apologetics of the epistemology of faith supporting the objectively supernatural in history.

III. The Scholar and Vatican I

The turbulent years extending from the Munich assembly of 1863 to Vatican I involved Schmid not just in the issues of theology's pluralism and faith's epistemology but in the question of the individual Christian before the authority of Rome. Schmid had addressed the relationship of scientific freedom to supernatural revelation in the *Wissenschaftliche Richtungen*, singling out the inflammatory topic of the culpability of a Catholic believer or scholar who left the Catholic faith. He came to the conclusion that in the modern age an individual, albeit for objectively false reasons, might with existential legitimacy come to the decision to leave the church (after all, the church had condemned the blind faith and obedience of the traditionalists).[29]

This controversy began shortly before Vatican I and was discussed at conciliar deliberations. The powerful figures Scheeben and Kleutgen disagreed with Schmid's position. Public opinion came to believe that Kleutgen had argued for a condemnation of texts on this topic of the loss of faith in the council's *De Fide Catholica*. Though no author was mentioned, were not some of the condemned views drawn from Schmid?[30] For the next twenty years Schmid (and the theological world in general) presumed that his views had been implicitly condemned by conciliar documents. Courageously, in his *Erkenntnislehre* (a theological epistemology published in 1890) he still opted for individual freedom of conscience, although he conceded that in every complete apostasy that freedom would be joined to some, perhaps light, sinfulness. When the *Acta* of the council appeared in 1892, the Austrian neoscholastic Theodore Granderath argued that Schmid's theology had not been condemned, and the Munich theologian at once presented his views anew with "Die Wissensfreiheit im Lichte des Vatikanums," published in *Historisch-politische Blätter* in 1892.

During the many years of apparent theological divergence from official conciliar teaching, Schmid had avoided difficulty with church authority because he belonged to the minority at the University of Munich which prepared a theological position paper supporting the decrees of Vatican I. Opposing their colleagues Döllinger and Johannes Friedrich, they had argued that the drastic negative consequences of the proclamation of papal infallibility anticipated by the majority of professors would not occur and that a theology asserting the church's preservation by the

Holy Spirit rendered it unlikely that the ecumenical council was fully in error.[31]

IV. Apologetics

Apologetics dominated Catholic theology from the late nineteenth century until the Second World War, but we lack surveys of its history, forms, and cultural motivation.[32] The figure and work of Alois Schmid offer a particularly interesting access to the emergence and formalization of Roman Catholic apologetics in the second half of the past century.

The Ascendency of Apologetics

The meeting place between German theology and culture at the end of the nineteenth century was not a new synthesis correlating culture and revelation but apologetics. Josef Finkenzeller notes "As much as philosophy and its related fields suited Schmid's personal gifts, soon after his acceptance of a professorship at Munich he began to work for the independence of apologetics and its separation from dogmatic theology."[33] Apologetics (which Schmid also called "fundamental theology") became at Munich in 1878 an independent *Fach*, a specific area within theology. When Schmid retired in 1903 after fifty-three years of teaching he continued to lecture for a few years on "Controversial Questions in Apologetics." He linked apologetics to theology as one of its foundations. The preliminary grounding section of dogmatics, apologetics as fundamental theology was "a bridge-science" ("*Übergangswissenschaft*") from the profane sciences to dogmatics. The apologetic point of departure included science and philosophy, but its process aimed at theology's interpretation of revelation.[34]

Vatican I and Döllinger's excommunication had heightened the divisions between the two theological directions in Germany. More important, the German culture which Catholics addressed was less and less Lutheran and more a liberal demythologization—not the reform of pastors but the academy dissolving revelation into myth. Schmid wrote that the nineteenth century was the century of discoveries, of innovations in transportation and business, of the unexpected in religious and cultural life. The population had shifted toward the cities; new classes in wealth and education emerged. A kind of migration of peoples had taken place, ending previous social structures and refashioning the individuality and freedom of people. Breakthroughs in natural science resulted in a materialistic positivism and specialized research, binding everything from mind to microbe in networks of causal chains. And too, for other areas of society science was a paradigm, bringing both fragmentation and evolution. Thus the historical claims of revelation were questioned by general historical criticism, by philosophy reduced to epistemology, and by new sciences such as paleontology and archaeology. The transcendental *Wesen* of Christianity was being examined negatively by a line of thinkers reaching from Feuerbach and various neo-Hegelians to Nietzsche and Harnack. Not system but apologetics seemed the suitable genre and the defense of revelation and faith the essential task.

The rise to dominance of neoscholasticism was aided by the paucity of original and synthetic Catholic writers and teachers in the German universities after 1848. The pugnacity of neoscholasticism and the postivist secularity of the universities made it natural for Catholic thinkers to turn to apologetics, and by 1880 a flood of works were in print, in volumes of hundreds of pages, each attempting to be unique in the genre. Increasingly apologetics became not a defense of the ground of divine communication in history but a proving of religious facts and beliefs whose expression was controlled by the papal magisterium. Names like the Jesuit I. Ottiger, the Dominican A. M. Weiss, and A. Michelitsch—all issuing or reissuing their large tomes—represented the direction of theologians who eschewed the intrinsic openness of apologetics and who pursued logical proofs and an easy and uninformed rejection of every modern approach to life.

Schmid and other Catholic theologians of the time had the task of a double mediation: (1) between an idealist system grounded in Christian motifs and an avowedly Catholic apologetic theology; (2) between medieval and modern theology and philosophy. Paul Schanz at Tübingen, the successor of Kuhn, was the most successful apologete of this era; his three volumes of 1888 were viewed as a standard for the genre and were published in translations in Europe and America. This vast work gave considerable space to the phenomenon of religion, to natural science and causality, and to Protestant apologetics and theologies. [35]

A second prominent apologetic theologian was the Würzburg professor F. S. Hettinger (1813–1890), who labored on a fundamental theology in various formats and editions from 1862 to 1898 and early in his career began from post-Cartesian issues, taking Günther and Hegel seriously and modeling his ideas upon J. S. Drey.[36] Herman Schell's *Apologie des Christentums* (1896) was more than an apologetics. A creative theology of religion and revelation not only addressing but couched in the conceptuality of German nineteenth-century thought, this work was one of the few Catholic theological efforts of its time which could be called original.

Schmid's approach was more speculative than that of Schanz, less intricately involved with science and the history of religion. He resembled Hettinger in his attention to epistemological questions and his use of

Drey, but his structure was clearer, more compact, his speculative gifts more self-assured. Schell stood apart, for the Würzburg theologian, almost alone, was facing creatively and profoundly the dialogue between orthodox Christianity and German culture at the end of the nineteenth century, a task Schmid glimpsed but could not assume.

Alois Schmid's Apologetic Project

Not easily accessible and rarely cited today, Schmid's apologetical viewpoint is of importance in the history of modern theology in the nineteenth and twentieth centuries because it exemplifies the dominant role of apologetics in the modern era. Schmid's theology was more speculative than the numerous volumes issuing from neoscholastic presses and more engaged with modern philosophy than Paul Schanz's later dialogue with science.

A University Discipline

In his *Apologetik als spekulative Grundlegung der Theologie* (1900) Schmid held that apologetics should be a university discipline with a respectable, positive task linked to faith and reason: "the science of the divinity and credibility of a positive-supernatural revelation. . . as a critical foundation (*'Begründungswissenschaft'*) of dogmatic theology." [37] An introduction preceded two main sections, locating apologetics in the activity of knowing and believing, with epistemology surfacing as the model and content of this area of theology. Dismissing much apologetical literature as an argumentative concatenation of proofs from vividly supernatural events, the introduction looked at the principles, methods, and types of apologetics after it had offered a valuable history of apologetics.

The *Apologetik* then unfolded its own exposition. Part One presented a dynamic framework. Schmid's specific goal was to establish the scientific nature of apologetics (scientific not in the sense of the natural sciences but in terms of a German university discipline) and then to separate a Catholic apologetic, emphasizing historical revelation, from Protestant approaches based upon experience. The subjective principle of every science was the human person with its potentiality for action; the objective principles of apologetics were found in a revelation which was both positive and supernatural, and in Christianity as presented by ecclesiastical statements.

How were the structures and grounds of knowing brought to serve as a springboard to faith? Of course, Schmid never found a theological bridge which melds the two together—the era of Schelling and Günther had passed. Sometimes Schmid moved into what we might call the middle ground of apologetics, philosophical critiques of erroneous positions. "The modern era is a time of fundamental errors; a critical, fundamental theology must meet these errors with means of proof which are historical and philosophical."[38] If the goal of apologetics was proving the truth of Christianity, then apologetics could claim principles which were more than arguments from emotion, experience, or aesthetics. The forms, issues, and problematics of reason were not autonomous but needed to be drawn from and directed back toward the objective. Neither world-creating reason (Hegel) nor faith-creating feeling (Schleiermacher) did justice to what Christianity saw as revelation.

The first part of the book, then, was a speculative consideration of the possibility and necessity of a truly supernatural revelation and sought to preserve the freedom, mystery, and historical character of a revelation which was distinct from the activity of reason. Truths, events, and even miracles pointing to the truth of Christianity were analyzed, so that an epistemology leading to faith might be glimpsed. But the final few pages on miracle and prophecy seem slightly unworthy of the preceding methodological analysis and appear to have lost contact with the reader or believer. There is too much dependency on ecclesiastical tradition, too little insight into how Jesus' preaching and miracles actually attracted followers. The second part examined at some length the two criteria by which speculative apologetics established concretely the presence of revelation, e.g., miracle and prophecy. These pages also were preceded by an interesting historical *tour d'horizon* as Schmid looked at these criteria employed in different religions as well as in different periods of Christianity, e.g., gnostic and mystic approaches, Alexandrian, medieval, Protestant and Catholic stances.

The History of Apologetics

The introduction to the major work on apologetics had a lengthy historical section which showed Schmid's considerable acquaintance with the literature of apologetics. He ranged from confrontations with Judaism in the first centuries through medieval to sixteenth-century Counter-Reformation apologetics. Brief sections on the Renaissance and Reformation were followed by dozens of pages on the argumentative tracts of the baroque and the Enlightenment with the latter period treating separately England, France, and Holland. Schmid offered separate sections for Protestant and Catholic apologetics after 1700 (the array of figures and movements makes these pages of value today). In the eighteenth century, Catholic theology was concerned with the challenge to Rome's authority by France and Austria; speculative theologians such as Sailer, Gerbert of St. Blase, and Stattler were mentioned only briefly. It was Protestant apologetics which had been addressing the new ideas from the thought of Lessing to that of Kant, and the Munich theologian described the variety and creativity of Protestant approaches, including K. H. Sack as a central figure.

Theologians at the edge of romantic idealism such as S. Mutschelle and M. Fingerlos, P. B. Zimmer and J. Salat, as well as Hermes dealt with the foundations of Christian faith in a new intellectual world. Still it was J. S. Drey who was selected as a transitional figure. Drey's *Apologetik* (1838–1847) was the bridge from theological speculation to apologetics, composing a "mild traditionalism" where a true revelation enters incarnationally into active consciousness and history. Apologetics assumed in the early nineteenth century new forms and relationships to philosophy and dogmatic theology.

Surveying the Catholic centers of Europe, Schmid grouped together theologians as different as H. Klee and V. M. Gatti, M. J. Scheeben and G. Lahouse. He arranged the history of apologetics after Drey around a typology:

> Since the 1830s and particularly in the second half of the nineteenth century Catholic theologians have enriched the science of apologetics. In the area of *apologia* significant achievements have come forth in Germany from Hettinger, Bosen, Weiss, Schanz, and Schell, and outside of Germany from Deschamps, Lafore, Causette, Bougaud, Duilhé de Saint Projet, Orti y Lara, Franchi. Many Catholic theologians have also developed apologetics as *fundamental theology*, and in various ways. They have to a large extent followed Drey in the direction of *a historical-philosophical science offering a ground for dogmatics* (Schwetz, Stöckl). Others have grasped apologetics as fundamental theology in a different way, namely, that of a *general dogmatics* which itself grounds special dogmatics and serves all of theology (Kuhn).[39]

This last group Schmid divided into theologians who focused upon philosophical proofs or argumentation from religious history and others who developed interior persuasions and proofs. Ultimately apologetes separated into two groups, depending upon how deeply they entered into the content of revelation or how they worked within rationalist philosophy or traditional metaphysics, within the history of religion or biblical science.

Apologetics' Mission

As the year 1900 approached, apologetics was being presented as an independent discipline drawing on philosophy and critical biblical studies.

Not dogmatic theology but its ground, it maintained its independence from new overbearing sciences and from a succession of epistemologies and psychologies.

The correct method of apologetics lay in a dialectic between object and subject; it was "historical-critical" as well as "philosophical-critical," so that the revealed truth might be explored and defended by philosophy. Schmid struggled to emphasize the objective pole of this dialectic, for he feared the encroachment of late-idealism's philosophies of secular subjectivity and he mistrusted Catholic and Protestant theologies where experience or reason bestowed human faith. "Mystery" was where the two poles met. But this central motif raised three sets of difficulties. Could the revealed mystery be real for human reason (or was it ultimately a myth, a symbol, a faith-held doctrine)? Could the mystery enter into our history? Finally, could these mysteries, if revealed in history, be shown to be more than reason's speculative depths?[40]

V. The Currents of an Age

We began by looking at Schmid's acknowledged lineage at Munich going back to the great figures of Baader, Görres, and Schelling. In his last work, the *Apologetik*, surveying the early nineteenth century, he focused not upon Fichte or Hegel but upon Schelling. Schelling's exposition of the Trinity and Incarnation in his philosophy after 1800 was a kind of interpretation of the newness in Christianity where the ideal became real. "Schelling," he noted, "judged severely the ordinary rationalism of the Enlightenment."[41]

Ultimately what had stimulated the numerous European Catholic thinkers to become involved in apologetics was precisely the evaporation of the older speculative philosophy of religion (in the line of Schelling and Hegel), the diminished prestige of historical and speculative theology in the style of Tübingen, and a new approach to theological issues more focused upon a critical study of Scripture and history. New scientific methodologies in natural science and history were an unavoidable partner in apologetics. There was a new urban bourgeoisie with interests other than transcendental speculation. "The great questions of the development of the cosmos and of organic life, of the development of the cultures and races of humanity, of Christianity and the church vis-à-vis family, society, church and school. These are questions which are leading us into the twentieth century and which will occupy thinkers more and more."[42]

In 1906, four years before his death, Schmid looked back at his work and the age. He defended the middle position he had chosen for himself. "The older, peripatetic scholasticism . . . needs to be enriched by numerous elements and insights from the philosophy of the present time."[43] If the great medieval thinkers knew something of the critical and transcendental facets of ontology, Schelling and Hegel had gone beyond the subjective apriorism of Kant, offering in harmony a dynamic interplay between subjective and objective experience. Schmid never ceased to defend his liberal view of the variety of philosophical and theological schools and their legitimate dialectic. Both objective and subjective principles explained revelation and grace. Apologetics, far from being a haughty extension of neoscholasticism, was a fundamental theology: an analysis of an objective revelation (with a further objectivity in miracle and prophecy) present to the complexity of human knowing.

Is it too much to say that Alois Schmid represents not only an important force in modern apologetics but a philosophical and theological breadth which few subsequent theologians reached? His knowledge of history was considerable and this made his views balanced; while the subjective side—credibility, faith, certainty, conscience—were prominent in his writings, they did not predominate. In reading him, one sees not only the rise of apologetics but the neoscholastic and ecclesiastical atmospheres which would move that discipline from being a dialogue with culture to being an argument against modernity.

5

Addressing Science and History:
Paul Schanz at Tübingen

DURING THE YEARS leading to the twentieth century, it belonged to Paul Schanz to continue the tradition of the Catholic Tübingen school, to link the generations of Drey, Möhler, and Staudenmaier with the rapidly changing world of the Wilhelminian Reich. Schanz continued the theological format of history and revelation but within the context of natural science rather than idealist *Wissenschaft*.

I. Heir to Tübingen

On the eightieth anniversary of the founding of the *Theologische Quartalschrift* Professor Schanz looked back at the Tübingen Catholic faculty's tradition. The Tübingen school was a collective personality living amid changing theological perspectives: 1760 to 1830 was a time of decline; 1830 to 1860, a period of the flowering of German speculative theology; 1860 to 1900, years of "a more or less complete return to scholasticism."

> The dividing line is 1870 because the Vatican Council would express the principles upon which Catholic theology and truth should grow . . . , re-activating the old bases of faith and knowing, natural and supernatural vis-à-vis the excessive control of modern philosophy.[1]

Nevertheless, the Tübingen characteristic of fashioning theology in an open and creative atmosphere remained, and in that tradition Catholic theology, like every theology, required a dialogue with a living, contemporary philosophical tradition and with Protestant theologians. This had been the project of Drey and Möhler. Questions of dogmatic, moral, and propaedeutical theology (an area which will become apologetics or fundamental theology) were worked out in the language and concepts of the times. In contrast, neoscholastic centers offered only a defensive evaluation and made no pretense to be open to the philosophical, scientific, and cultural movements of the time.

The natural sciences and not post-Kantian metaphysics were, for Schanz, the world addressed by faith. History and transcendental idealism had been superseded by natural science; already in his seminary years, compiling notebooks of information on physics, he had seen that the natural sciences were the product and image of the age. Even the issues of history came not just from world history or religion's evolution but from the scientific nature of the precise research involved in the new biblical and historical criticism. Schanz noted:

> One would have misread thoroughly the signs of the times if one denied that the modern natural sciences exercise a marked influence upon the life and thought of people and are a stream which had penetrated into many circles of society. Experimental science, the center of an intellectual effort different from past metaphysics, is something new.[2]

But one should not yield to the ideology that nature and revelation were two opposed areas. The long course of Christian thought had argued the opposite; great thinkers had perceived a harmony for nature and revelation, for scientific and religious knowledge, even if today scientist and believer often seem intent upon mutual misunderstanding.

How did Paul Schanz continue in his late nineteenth-century career the earlier theological approach of Tübingen? Born in 1841 in Swabia, he left the *Gymnasium* at Rottweil in 1861 to study philosophy, theology, and natural science at the University of Tübingen. His doctorate came in 1866 with a dissertation on "Iranian Religion according to Greek and Roman Writers," and the same year he was ordained a priest. He became a tutor at the Catholic seminary at the university, the *Wilhelmsstift*, where he studied science and mathematics, and at times substituted for Johannes Evangelist Kuhn. After research trips to Berlin and Paris, he spent some years teaching mathematics and science at the Rottweil school, during which time his books on Nicholas of Cusa's mathematics (1872) and on Copernicus (1876) were published as well as two studies on Galileo (1878).

Because his work on critical hypotheses concerning the Gospel of Mark had been well received, in 1876 he was called back to Tübingen to be professor of New Testament exegesis. Despite the professorship in Scripture, his entrance address treated the topic of "The Christian World-view in Its Relationship to Modern Natural Sciences."[3] Schanz's grasp of the issues and perspectives brought by the natural sciences to the biblical message were complemented by patristic research after 1875. A survey of the exegesis of the fathers concerning some questions on natural science was followed by studies on Augustine's and Thomas Aquinas's theology of creation and their interpretations of the hexaemeron. Between 1877 and 1887 the Tübingen scholar also wrote on the composition and context of Matthew, arguing for the priority of this gospel over against Q as the first discernible source of the synoptic sayings of Jesus. The theological motifs in James and Paul, law and grace, were brought together dialectically. Climaxing his study of the New Testament in light of modern problems were commentaries on all four gospels. Schanz employed an exegetical method that was historical, philological, and critical. The exegete, he believed, even while being conscious of working within a historical and ecclesial tradition, must face the new and difficult problems raised by individual writings and passages. Schanz's biblical studies have been evaluated as "the best exegetical performance of Catholic theology in the nineteenth century, capable of being placed next to M. J. Lagrange as a pioneering work for Catholics."[4]

II. Amid Theological Methods

Johannes Evangelist Kuhn requested that Schanz, despite Schanz's professorship in exegesis, succeed him in the chair of dogmatic theology. It was hardly foreign to the Tübingen mind to join studies in New Testament with theology: history is the dynamic trend of both. In the line of Kuhn and Drey, Schanz attained a perspective on culture and theology which was foreign to neoscholasticism but which was also not absorbed by a secular theory of history or by laboratory research. Christianity was a historical religion, founded by a historical person, not a theory or system but a fact. Revelation presented to faith a double assignment: to assimilate the results of research into the history of early Christianity and its documents; to uncover from the subsequent centuries of theologies the underlying "principles and forms."[5] Christianity was indeed a religion which claimed not a foundation from philosophy but from an absolute revelation in Christ. "Early Christianity is the source and verification of the Christian religion. The history of Christianity is the unfolding and development of the Christian religion: the history of dogma [is] the unfolding of teaching and organization."[6] While theology recognizes the distinction between the faith of tradition and the knowledge of the human spirit, it knows how to employ secular science and culture in order to explain revelation.

History was not far distant from evolution: moreover, the evolution of species (treated by Schanz frequently in writings dealing with natural science and apologetics) suggested an evolution of dogma. The Tübingen theologian observed how Loisy's and Harnack's positions on history formed a dialectic. The German searched beneath layers of verbal forms and theologies for an essence or a kernel of Christian revelation, while the Frenchman, turning to modern science, saw that development was also transformation. History was a special means by which Christian revelation spoke to people even as a personal address implied change and development.

> The assertion that the Catholic Church does not recognize the existence of development and condemns that idea is incorrect. It would be more accurate to say that the church has not come to the full consciousness of what "development" might be. What Vincent of Lérins, modern theologians (with the exception of Cardinal Newman) and the Vatican Council have presented concerning the development of dogma touches only the intellectual and theological phase of development but not the full emergence and forming of doctrine itself. It is *the concept of development* which now must form and interpret itself.[7]

Schanz found balanced and seminal ideas in Loisy rather than in the German Protestant professors. He concluded: "It is impossible to deny the justification for a historical treatment of Christianity and impossible to understand Christianity without taking into account its development." Neither frozen immutability through all ages nor the facile and ceaseless reduction of the substance of Christianity was the answer. Both history and the primal Christian event should receive their due. Why merge one into the other or sweep both away in a tide of empiricism? A middle way which "recognizes fully the rights of revelation and authority but leaves the development of both to human institutions" was needed.[8]

With the move to dogmatics, the studies on Mark and Galileo were set aside. His apologetical system in three volumes appeared in 1887 and 1888. Then, showing an extraordinary productivity, Schanz in the five years after 1892 wrote seven historical-theological studies (all on the sacraments) from the perspective of patristics and discussed issues raised by recent Protestant histories of dogma. Schanz's rectorship of the university in 1899/1900 gave him an opportunity to address the issues of freedom and Catholic identity in the Reich. Upon his return to research, the theologian composed not a systematic theology but revised his apologetics with new material. In 1905, two years after the *Apologie des Christentum* appeared in an expanded version, Schanz died at the age of sixty-four.

III. A Theology Forged from the Issues of the Age

The Tübingen university remained a center of thought where history and system met, where Protestant and Catholic colleagues examined each other's works in progress. The Catholic faculty refused to yield its heritage to the new scholasticism or to leave its Catholicism for Germanic Protestantism. Schanz wrote articles and reviews surveying and criticizing the currents of the age. Döllinger once observed that Schanz had two eyes: a systematic one and a historical one.[9]

The Challenge of Neoscholasticism

The rise of neoscholasticism marked a decline in understanding revelation and dogma historically. The proliferation of neoscholasticism in metaphysical monographs or seminary texts not only avoided history but came to view it in a hostile way. One could compose a fascinating history of the Tübingen theologians' attitude toward neoscholasticism for the century after 1840. Largely they escaped its monopoly and weakness, and perhaps because of the scholasticism's bold neglect of history, Schanz's writings after 1880 emphasized the school's identity.

The Thomistic monopoly, Schanz wrote, implied an inevitable denial of cultural history. The history of interpretation and a historical sense were ignored. Worse still, neoscholasticism effected a decline in using the writings of the early Church. "Even the neoscholastics must agree [that dogmatic theology is not possible without history of dogma], even if individuals still believe that they can treat the most important articles in their controversies with Protestants according to the old methods of exegesis and with a view of the history of dogma which are now generally avoided."[10] In the last analysis, this scholasticism's conflicts with the directions of Schelling and Hegel, Drey, Möhler, and Staudenmaier were aberrations, denunciations largely lacking information. It had been through the support of the papacy and religious orders that "this striving for restoration" had gained considerable and growing power. And paradoxically, movements in the development of science—an anti-Christian spirit in modern philosophy and the expansion of the natural sciences—had only furthered the scholastic revival.[11] Understandably Catholic thinkers might long for an earlier time when these areas fell into a simple harmony with theology. The scholastic easily forgot life and made philosophy the preserve of a few scholars. But every theological point of view should be appreciated, not just that of Aquinas. Even the best neoscholastics glossed over differences in historical and dogmatic positions and presumed that Aquinas was always correct or prudent.

There was an inevitable abstractness in the neoscholastics' exposition of Aquinas: a forgetfulness of the human person acting, an isolation of grace in a qualitative world neither human nor divine, a separation of grace and faith from life.[12]

For decades, in the pages of the *Theologische Quartalschrift* Schanz and his colleagues evaluated innumerable neoscholastic books and manuals. Schanz distinguished between types of neoscholasticisms, and also between the thought of Aquinas and its varied interpretations. If the scholastics would justify Aristotle in every issue, e.g., *creatio ex nihilo*, still the commentaries by Aquinas on Aristotle remained unread. The fundamental contribution of Drey and the Tübingen school was the historical context of dogma and this would uncover the differences in medieval and later scholastic theologians. In fact, rigid Thomists lacked a deep knowledge of the Dominican theologian. In many issues in the philosophy of religion and apologetics the scholastics disagreed among themselves over Aquinas's stance and the correct position.[13] Schanz bemoaned the tendency to compose lengthy commentaries on Aquinas which were superficial or little more than spiritual reading, or to write books of hundreds of pages commenting upon what Aquinas said in a dozen pages. Not infrequently what was offered was "a mere textbook restatement of scholasticism."[14] While the neo-Thomists would venerate Aquinas, they altered the order in which he treated material, bringing disparate areas of the *Summa theologiae* together and obscuring the formal side of the work. Schanz criticized a German edition of the *Summa* of the 1890s because it failed to situate Aquinas in the history of doctrine or to give any idea of the order or development of his thought.[15]

The exaggerated and bombastic claims for scholasticism as the sole mode of viewing reality injured the entire cause of Catholic thought. Schanz illustrated his critique by cosmology. "What we need to find is the agreement between old and new cosmologies. Augustine, Albert, and Thomas Aquinas have expressly demanded that one should look in nature, not for a miracle but, much more, for that which happens in nature according to the laws immanent in nature's way."[16] If crass or secular empiricism was an error, so was suspicion of the empirical based upon a fideism or upon an idolatry of one past rational system. Great theologies described creation as a fact of God's sovereignty, and perhaps the meaning of the "seven days" was the emergence of a world in development, a more astonishing mode of coming into existence. One should find in Thomas a theological relationship to Augustine, Basil, and the other hexaemeronists and not simply a platform for Aristotle.[17]

Schanz must have felt a certain isolation from 1885 to 1905: he was the heir to the Tübingen tradition but also the critical witness of an "almost complete" restoration of scholasticism, a Catholic theological movement which challenged his faculty's very existence.

The Dialogue with Protestantism

The Catholic theologians of the previous generation—from Zimmer in 1799 to Deutinger in 1869—drew largely on Schelling and Hegel, and Möhler and Kuhn took pains to study contemporary Protestant theologies even if they ended by disagreeing with them. In the next generation, fewer and fewer fundamental theologians studied appreciatively their Protestant counterparts. Indeed, Roman and German neoscholastics had begun by linking Reformation theologies and modern philosophy. Schanz, working alongside the Tübingen Protestant faculty, supplied the tradition of dialogue with other Christian theologies, although it was not as important a partner for him as scholasticism and science. In 1893 the Tübingen apologete wrote a series of articles surveying the recent history of Protestant theology.[18] He pointed out that German Christians had seen for much of the nineteenth century that neither their history nor their life could be pursued in isolation. "Recent Protestant theology stands under the destiny of modern philosophy . . ., combining the Reformation principle with modern philosophy, and so bringing subjectivity to its full extent."[19] Schanz saw Kant and then Schleiermacher as the most influential figures: both renewed Protestantism and continued idealism. Idealism influenced the entire century: the marriage of subject and object, of spirit and process. This explained why Protestant theologies replaced the anthropological and ethical theology of the Reformation with the utilitarian morality of the Enlightenment. While Catholic Kantians (even Hermes) preserved in some way objective revelation, liberal Protestant theology became a dogmatics of subjectivity and neglected the objectivity of revelation.[20]

Schleiermacher could be called without exaggeration epoch-making, and his influence upon Schanz was significant (although Drey and Möhler recognized his Protestantism and limitations).

> Schleiermacher has in his sights less the span of real religion than the conditions of piety for particular mystics or small religious sects. This approach is psychologically impossible as well as historically inaccurate. Moreover, this kind of religion cannot form a large community, cannot become a historical force. In religion, religious conceptuality and the formation of society are inseparable.[21]

Kant's influence had even increased: "The broad influence of this theology is such that . . . one sees a right (Kaftan), a middle (Hermann and Ritschl), and a left (Bender)."[22] Schelling and Hegel had unfolded that extra-Christian dimension—in philosophy, culture, and religion—which made Protestantism nervous. Schanz concluded perceptively:

> In Protestantism religious knowledge is determined more and more by the latest, mutable directions of the humanities. At the same time, faith in Christ and in a church is more and more shaken. A significant opposition between nonbelief and modern belief for educated people emerges. Finally, where there is a large number of Protestants who are still Christian believers, this happens through communities, the majority of the articles of the creed and the sacraments. The old antinomy remains: free research or creed.[23]

IV. Apologetics for Science

For Schanz, "Apologetics, as a proper discipline, is, indeed, rather new. But in its essence and task it is as old as religious truth itself."[24] History offered the styles for apologetics. A new apologetics differed from the traditional approach, whether "traditional" meant that of the second century or of the Enlightenment. A plethora of new issues and problems poured out of the natural sciences, history, psychology, the dialectic of the immanent and transcendent, and they influenced not the gospel's message but the questions addressed and the formats presented to faith.

Apologetics after Vatican I

A Catholic apologete surveying around 1900 the numerous apologetic methods employed in Europe, but wanting to develop an original approach, faced two issues: the insistence by neoscholasticism of its monopoly and the theological shift of Vatican I from the content of historical revelation to the certitude of faith. The question is this: "To what extent can the new apologetics be reconciled with the dogma of the Catholic church?"[25] Schanz questioned the Vatican's conviction that every non-scholastic mode of theology or philosophy would be suspect and that Catholicism had to meet the cultural movements of the turn of the century like a Don Quixote in ill-fitting armor with rusted weapons.[26] Vatican I did not proscribe every form of modern thought but only their exaggerations: fideism and materialism in terms of the knowing self; pantheism and evolutionism in terms of the revealing God. The council did not publish one required outline for apologetics and dogmatic theology. Moreover, it insisted upon both reason and faith, historical fact and experience, belief and the personality.[27]

Paul Schanz became an apologete for apologetics. His numerous book reviews evaluated a variety of directions in fundamental theology and philosophy of religion. Most important was his passing beyond the German world to the immanentist apologetics of France as he advocated setting aside the traditional furniture of miracles and prophecies in order to look at the structure and expressions of the human person. Maurice Blondel's writings, for instance, were a dynamic quest for that infinite which the human cannot produce. Without an anthropological-existential correlation, Schanz warned that the fact and content of Christian revelation ran the danger of appearing extrinsic and external, and faith became words about the mythical and antique. Subjectivity could not be avoided when one spoke of faith in the modern world. "The supernatural is present in the mind's longing for truth but also in the will's search for a higher power and in the heart's need for love."[28] Defending the legitimacy of a more immanentist and less rationalist apologetics did not mean accepting every shift in the new (largely French) approach. Apologetics could and must give up those traditional methods which were weak and immature to search out sources for knowing God which had not occurred to past philosophies. For Catholics, the limits of apologetics should be given not by a monopolistic philosophy but by revelation.

A Christian Apology

The best-known work of Schanz, and arguably the most widely used apologetics of the time, was *A Christian Apology*.[29] In some ways it was the theoretical and popular climax for Catholic theology at the end of the nineteenth century. It appeared in 1887 and quickly underwent three revised editions, eventually increasing its size in the important revision of 1903 by over a hundred pages.

Apologetics' task was to argue intelligently for the historical origins of Christianity and the church by defending them against attacks on their historicity or truth. The newer contributions of an immanentist and psychological approach (with links to Augustine) could be used without ignoring the objective world, particularly since the natural sciences were fashioning our worldview in so many ways. While the theological content of the *Apologie* was not distinguished, the scope of the presentation, rich and modern, recognized the natural sciences, the theories of history and society, and new biblical criticism.

The three volumes of the work followed a traditional pattern, treating religion, Christian revelation, the Catholic church. Opening pages situated the activity of apologetics within specifically Catholic themes: the natural and the supernatural, the object of faith and the motives of credibility, and the relationship of these to the knowing person. The first volume was dominated by the need to address science and particularly the topic of evolution. Here the book's apologetic audience was not so much late-idealist nonbelievers but other schools of Roman Catholic theology. Next came a history of apologetics which only briefly mentioned modern trends and presumed other surveys. Religion was presented not as a Stoic duty or as a Kantian imperative but as a history of revelation suited to the activities of the human person. Unfolding the powers of knowing and living (so prominent in idealist philosophy) were chapters on intellectualist theories locating the proofs for the existence of God in the structure of consciousness, e.g., ontologism and traditionalism ("idealism" now means monism or pantheism). But transcendental philosophy was sparsely used. Nevertheless, the first volume, however, pursued an anthropological apologetics more than a cosmological one: the design of the universe, the search for virtue, the complexity of the human person deserve better treatment than the mere presentation of brittle arguments from causality. A treatment of causality and creation (Schanz said that the age of the human race is uncertain) ended in the terrestrial dispersal of the human race with its unity and history.

The second volume described world religions which are not removed from life or culture but which serve, Schanz observed trenchantly, the social process. Some modern thinkers have perverted the history of religion, making it profane or demonic. "As the doctrine of evolution serves natural sciences to render the knowledge of God unnecessary, so the history of religions works to remove the supernatural factor from Christianity and religion."[30] Six chapters presented the panorama of world religions, past and present, with Christianity emerging as the climax of religion and as a special revelation. What, as the twentieth century approaches, would be revelation's relationship to reason? What was distinctive in Christianity located within the spectrum of religions? After considering the traditional apologetic elements—miracles, prophecy, Scripture—Schanz unfolded arguments for the distinctive presence of the supernatural in Jesus.

The third volume aimed at showing the truth of the Catholic interpretation of Christianity. Schanz's theology of the development and history of dogma, rather distinctive in comparison with other Catholic apologetics, depicted a Christianity which is the "Kingdom of God." The first section treated the New Testament's passage from Kingdom to church. The second developed the four marks of the church, and the third took up the subject of authority in Scripture and in ecclesial teaching. Infallibility was sensitively located within the infallibility of revelation, the Apostles, and the graces of the entire church, and doctrinal authority was also related to the Scriptures.

Schanz's exegetical and patristic studies served him well as he assembled this work. In the tradition of Möhler he explored the relations of the Christian churches with each other. While a false irenicism should be avoided, much of the truth taught by the Catholic church is taught by Protestant churches. Long concluding chapters discussed the primacy and infallibility of the pope. The work ended with "Church and Civilization," a litany praising the church's visible personality in moral, political, intellectual, and cultural areas. All this Schanz unfolded in a harmony of nature and grace made concrete in human gifts and powers, in nature and the human family, in the interplay of reason and faith proclaimed by Vatican I, and finally in Jesus as the Alpha and Omega.

Catholic reaction to the new system was very favorable, ranking it above the many apologetics being composed at the turn of the century. Not a few Protestant reviews were laudatory:

> That such an all-encompassing and valuable apology already appears in a third edition is a sign of the vital interest in defending Christianity in Catholic circles. But Protestants too can rejoice in this apologetics of the Christian worldview, especially in its first part. Even when Schanz, in more than one place, shows himself to be a Catholic theologian with links to Thomas, Vatican and papal writings, still, by and large, he displays a beneficent openness, a scientific independence and respect for the achievements of Protestant science and apologetics.[31]

When we compare the work with apologetic texts reaching large audiences a half century later, the approach seems richer, more in touch with modernity.

Science and Theology

In Galileo and Darwin, Schanz saw two illustrations of the tension between science and faith.[32] For Heinrich Fries, author of studies on Paul Schanz spanning three decades, the apologete's attitude toward Darwin and Darwinism was a particularly apt example of his apologetics in action.

> If some of the views and conclusions of Schanz are today outdated (and they are so!), still his scientific ethos, his ability to distinguish, his responsibility and his sense of the cultural moment, his objectivity, his scientific accuracy and, not last, his courage for free exploration coming out of his correct understanding of the Christian faith are of permanent validity and inspiration.[33]

Schanz distinguished between the thought contained in the writings of Darwin and subsequent Darwinisms where he found among the theoretician's followers exaggerations and inaccuracies. He understood that

Darwin's work was not a philosophy but a theory based upon observation about limited areas of biology. Schanz saw in the variety of nature not chance form and chance occurrence but constant forms, themselves involved in a mutual network.[34] To survey numerous theories of the transmission of inherited forms, however, was to conclude that the inheritance of forms was a fact but not an all-encompassing principle. Darwinism was "the attempt to bring mechanism to the area of organic life."[35] The factor of natural selection was central, but it occurred not through ceaseless struggle, accident, and violence (otherwise we could not recognize a species) but through the bestowal of minor alterations upon a stable variety. While Darwin illumined natural science, his principles did not fully explain empirical nature with its constancy and order.

> Darwin's theory of descent is never capable of serving as an explanation for the organic world but only as a presentation of a historical fact; it gives a historical reconstruction but no causal explanation. The principle of survival of the fittest can really only explain how, within that competition individuals and species are trapped, ravaged to be placed on the rungs of a ladder of organic species—but he has little to say about the positive moments in the formation for the empire of forms of the more perfect and more suitable (as Lamarckianism has little to say).[36]

The Tübingen theologian did not conclude that evolution automatically led to materialism and atheism, or to a conflict with revelation. It could be a mode of creation, and Darwin could be a Copernican turn, a Galilean breakthrough. One need not be terrified of evolution, as were so many short-sighted faithful, and Darwin and Galileo should make the church careful about exaggerating hasty views on new theories.[37] Science brought both believer and nonbeliever to the borderline situation, and science's worldview offered to both different orientations for revelation and faith.

V. The Old Faith and the New Age

The intellectual depth of Schanz was striking: he did not simply hammer out a chain of arguments aimed at defeating extraecclesiastical attacks. Mystery remained: revelation did not remove the fact that God was the source and abyss of mysteries[38] or that the world of nature too was filled with numerous mysteries. The shifts in philosophy of science and the birth of new sciences addressed Christian theology. Uncritical exegesis was inadequate just as was hasty scientific research. Revelation was not theodicy or the philosophy of religion, and it did not provide missing forces for nature.[39] Faith and biology were not on the same level, and yet their common ground could not be freed of controversy by a fideism ignoring science.

In Schanz's perception of the age, a Catholic theologian must acknowledge that science has a certain autonomy and that revelation must be interpreted not in terms of life in the abstract but through life in a particular world fashioned by science and culture. It was not right to make Christians choose between their world and their church, between what research uncovered and faith disclosed. Unfortunately, alienation between science and faith, "the old faith and the new age," was happening.[40] "Experience and faith, reason and revelation can never be contradictory. When an appearance of contradiction appears, the problem lies either with the natural scientist who has drawn unsupported conclusions from the data of nature or with the theologian who has interpreted the words of revelation incorrectly."[41] The believer could not adequately respond to the new science, the new history, the new biblical criticism by giving easy answers to a caricature of Christianity; but too there must be a clear distinction between hypotheses and verifications. In the year 1900 Schanz looked at "the cultural movements of the age." He sensed a time of fragmentation, of uncertainty, for anyone who tended toward anxiety and pessimism. The dominant force of the age was now science, but it had produced "a psychology without soul, a religion without God . . ., an overestimation of intellectualism and naked materialism, unbelieving criticism and superstitious mysticism."[42] Some, he said, prophesy a great time for the Catholic church in Germany in the twentieth century, but he preferred "the sign of the times" rather than prophecy and saw difficulties so considerable that only the constant efforts of talent and community could get beyond them.

Schanz was not a major theologian; if his depth and purpose as an apologete exceeded much of the second-rate apologetics before and after him, it was still, in genre and execution, limited. He harmonized too quickly. His abilities enabled him to absorb diverse material and to write easily if not powerfully, while his natural gifts as pedagogue and academic adviser encouraged a wise reluctance to engage in endless public controversies. Nonetheless, Heinrich Fries concluded,

> Next to Herman Schell he was the most significant apologete of modern Catholicism—and that is something. As much as the words "apologete" and "apologetics" are today unpopular, one must see that the real task of response, accountability, and defense are included in the Christian faith. The forms and problematics change . . . but Schanz brought it about that faith had a creative encounter with his particular times.[43]

6
Herman Schell: Idealism
at the End of the Century

OUR NEXT FIGURE stands head and shoulders above an Alois Schmid or a Paul Schanz. Reminiscent of Johannes Evangelist Kuhn, yet anticipating Karl Rahner, Herman Schell was after 1880 without true peers. He fashioned a theology which synthesized Aristotelian, idealist, and patristic strains even as it drew them further to interpret numerous theological and cultural issues of the late nineteenth century. Driven by a desire to relate Roman Catholicism to modern culture and employing aspects of modernity from both the early and the late nineteenth century, Schell was the most creative German Catholic theologian in the last third of the century. And yet, the work of this creative theologian has remained little known, largely because some of his writings were placed on the Index. Nevertheless, theologies before and after Vatican II in the areas of grace, church, and world show similarities with Schell's thought, and his theology of the Trinitarian missions seems poised between Thomas Aquinas and Karl Rahner.

I. A Life in Theology

Herman Schell was born in Freiburg in Breisgau two years after the revolutions of 1848 and died in 1906 just as the encyclical *Pascendi* was being prepared at the Vatican. His entry into the seminary attached to the Freiburg University in 1868 led to a study of philosophy and theology in diverse traditions. The Tübingen heritage of historical and idealist speculation had come to Freiburg in the person of Franz Anton Staudenmaier and was continued by his disciple and successor, Friedrich Wörter (1819–1901). As professor of dogmatic and apologetic theology at Freiburg from 1858 to 1897, Wörter's lectures on grace in Augustine and Pelagius displayed a historical approach while his dogmatic theology continued the stance of Tübingen.[1]

Another important influence on Schell at Freiburg was the philosopher Jakob Sengler. Born near Frankfurt in 1799, Sengler left the shoe-
maker's trade for the university world and in 1824 began studies in
theology at Tübingen with Johann Adam Möhler. After working in religious pedagogy and sketching a new approach to catechetics, he went to
Munich in 1828 to hear Schelling, whose early book on university faculties had influenced him. Sengler entered the Munich circle of Baader,
Görres, Schubert, and Oken, and by 1830 he had gained I. von Döllinger,
C. H. Weisse, and I. H. Fichte as contributors to his new periodical,
Kirchenzeitung für das katholische Deutschland. Sengler measured himself against the great figures of philosophy in *Über das Wesen und die Bedeutung der spekulativen Philosophie und Theologie in der gegenwärtigen
Zeit* (1834–1837), but even then this work implied that the great idealist systems were dissolving and that philosophy was moving toward
something new. Schelling's dialectic of concept and reality had ended unfortunately in Hegel's conceptualism; now "the mediation between Hegel
and Schelling (Schelling's positive philosophy of freedom and experience) was being taken up anew by Weisse and the younger Fichte."[2] This
metaphysics remained within "*Spätidealismus,*" where a universe based
on various triads linking finite and infinite worlds recalled the system of
Franz von Baader.[3] Professor for Catholic thought for a short time in
Marburg, in 1842 Sengler accepted a position in Freiburg after failing to
be the successor in Bonn of his friend Fichte. A multi-volume *Die Idee
Gottes* (1845/1847) and an *Erkenntnislehre* (1858) appeared.

Sengler credited his thought as being "the result of the totality of
modern philosophy."[4] He noticed that the early Schelling had shown how
one had to begin with the active transcendental world of subjectivity; the
Essay on Freedom of 1809 emphasized the life and will of God, while the
issues of freedom, existence, and religious history reflected Schelling's
lectures in Munich and Berlin after 1827. But Sengler criticized Schelling
for his identification of the world with the Absolute and for confusing the
phenomenological with the ontological paths of knowing God and world.
In creation, primacy should be given to divine freedom: "The world is
not, as Schelling and others following him say, the also-not-capable of
being; it is rather what-must-be."[5]

For Sengler (as for Schelling) being proceeded from the unity of the
Absolute, from the undifferentiated being of God, unfolding in a will to be
real and external. This expansion and activity have three moments behind
which stands a radically free "primal personality." This Schell would later
name "*causa-sui.*"[6] Christianity developed this withdrawn and abstract
Trinity into persons with proper activities, but unfortunately, in Sengler's
view, theologians like Thomas Aquinas had offered too abstract a concept

of God ("form" and "substance") and a Trinity which had activities but not true persons.[7]

Sengler's idealism was complemented by a move into more anthropological and phenomenological directions after 1850. The human person was special: not simply a product of the intersection of nature and spirit and not just a transcendental facet of the Absolute but a knower and agent in the world. Citing Meister Eckhart he wrote:

> In the most inner ground of the human being is the mysterious link of the soul with the ideal nature of all things. Since the human being is a microcosm, its ideal nature contains the ideal ground of all things and views in it the ideal, eternal connection of all things. This intuition then touches the eternal intuitions of God. Thus the human spirit in its ideal intuition is drawn into this divine intuition and looks out of it into God and into the world.[8]

Thus in 1870 Sengler could teach Schell in a sympathetic way of the entire span of high idealism ("these treasures must be preserved and employed for new constructions"[9]) and point to the anthropological and existential shift in Schelling beyond Hegel, the union of system and of supernatural event. At the same time, criticizing the mythical transcendental cosmologies of Baader and Günther, Sengler saw how transcendental philosophy was in the process of becoming empirical psychology. The insufficiencies of Trinitarian theologies which were merely the elaboration of myths or physical forces implied a reconsideration of godhead and absolute self-causation.

Constantin von Schäzler (just laying down his weapons from the controversy with Kuhn) taught the young Schell the history of dogma. Despite a tendency to neo-Thomist rigidity, at Freiburg his neoscholasticism was still touched by the history of theology and had not yet reached its Roman, authoritarian stage. What attracted Schell was Schäzler's philosophical and linguistic accuracy along with a commitment to translate Greek and Roman philosophical terms into carefully nuanced German. Possibly Schäzler's study on the Incarnation was the model for Schell's work on the Trinity. The young seminarian also heard lectures outside of theology: the famous zoologist A. Weismann presented him with a theoretical discussion of evolution and Darwinism.[10]

Schell was asked to leave the Freiburg seminary in 1870 for disciplinary reasons (it was said that he had missed Compline for a few glasses of beer). He continued his studies in Würzburg with the permission of the bishop there; as he entered another significant school with personalities ready to mark his career, Sengler advised him to seek out Franz von Brentano. Würzburg was a leading German theological faculty (some seminaries closed by the Kulturkamp established schools in exile there). Heinrich Denzinger, the faculty's historian of dogma, was a man of vast erudition in the history of Christianity; he was also a critic of Günther and subsequent attempts to link transcendental philosophy with faith. By 1854 he had arranged ecclesiastical decrees into an influential collection, the *Enchiridion*, which became not just a theological resource but a theological method.[11]

The important influence, however, came from the philosophical faculty, from that gifted advocate of neo-Aristotelianism, Franz Brentano. Among Catholic intellectuals of the past century, Brentano stands out in originality and influence. He had an important impact on Schell and later in Vienna on both Edmund Husserl and I. Meinong. While his work on Aristotle led Heidegger to philosophy, his writings on psychology pleased both Sigmund Freud and G. E. Moore.

Brentano, born in 1838 and nephew of the romantic poet Clemens Brentano, became acquainted with neoscholasticism in Münster through F. J. Clemens and with the new, positive approach to Aristotle through A. Trendelenburg in Berlin, under whom he wrote his famous work *Von der mannigfachen Bedeutung des Seienden nach Aristoteles* in 1862. Residing for a while in the Dominican priory in Graz, he met Heinrich Denifle, who encouraged theological studies in Munich and in Würzburg, where he was ordained a priest in 1864. He helped complete Möhler's church history, set aside an early interest in Kant and Schelling in favor of scientific theory and logic, and wrote a position paper for the German bishops against infallibility.

A popular teacher, he lectured on history and dogmatics, but his career ran into difficulties: by some he was seen as a Jesuit *manqué*; for others, he was a too liberal philosopher of religion. Brentano was drifting away from formal religion, and he left both church and priesthood formally in 1873. Although he was able to find a position in Vienna, his marriage in 1880 without ecclesiastical dispensation from orders forced his retirement from teaching. He spent his last years in Italy and Switzerland and died in 1917. Eventually the philosopher came to understand dogmas such as the Trinity as marginal to Christianity (it introduced process into the concept of God), while at the end of his life in a book on Jesus (written against Catholic apologetes including Schell), he sought the "lasting significance" of Jesus in the purity of the moral challenge of the New Testament's ethical teaching.

Experts see Brentano not simply as an Aristotelian mentor but as a bridge from idealism to psychology. A conviction that Aquinas's thought on divine existence and being could be maintained by insights from post-Kantian philosophy occupied him from 1868 to 1891. Modern subjectivism should be overcome but also expanded through Aristotelian psychology.[12] In Baader and Schell the motif of "act" as thinking and willing was primary and prior to being. J. Koch writes: "The metaphysical element whose fundamental meaning emerges in the idea of God as *causa-sui* is the gift of the theist school, particularly of Jakob Sengler; the empirical element, the filling of the formalism of act with the content of interior experience is drawn from Franz Brentano."[13] Not only was Aristotle revered, but Plato too was heralded in the Brentano school of which Schell was an early member. Idealism was becoming psychology, for the experience of the psyche was not just the point of departure but a dominant measure and perspective of the entire philosophical system.[14] The young Schell could have heard lectures on "Deductive and Inductive Logic," Kant, the full range of the history of philosophy, psychology, and metaphysics. He attended a special seminar concerning the existence of God with an approach uniting psychology and theodicy.[15] A dissertation topic was suggested by Brentano, who had a charism for recognizing and leading gifted students to completed dissertations; it had two facets: a critique of Eduard von Hartmann's philosophy of the unconscious and an Aristotelian evaluation of various authors on psychology ranging from contemporary writers to Thomas Aquinas. Although Aristotle was ancient, the topic, the unconscious, was new. Both Sengler and Brentano worked with Schell on "The Unity of the Life of the Soul as Developed by the Principles of Aristotelian Philosophy." The theme was quite contemporary, for some Aristotelian scholars were arguing for a duality of souls, while others like von Hartmann drew upon modern psychological approaches, often monist if not materialist, to oppose this dualism. When it was published in 1873 it drew considerable attention to the twenty-two-year-old author. Detailed comparisons indicate that Schell (who throughout his life would consider himself a disciple of Brentano) absorbed an interpretation of Aristotle in a personal and dynamic but not essentialist mode and so was introduced to the content of neoscholasticism without accepting its ideology. Critique and analysis led to a prominence for self-consciousness: "While the distinction of matter and form does not explain the nature of things, the differentiation of the elements of consciousness do explain their being."[16]

Schell was among the first Catholics to study the new tendencies of epistemology to changing into psychology. At the turn of the century he was lecturing on Kant, Nietzsche, and Asian religions and selecting life as a theme of his philosophical theology. Thus the late idealism of Sengler moved into a phenomenology of active personality; the unconscious brought forth the empirical. But neither theology nor psychology needed to relinquish the transcendental approach, for a richer understanding of consciousness leading to psychological phenomenology was, as Vincent Berning concludes, "the bridge from Sengler through Brentano, Aristotle and even a kind of Thomism to Schell's complete system in *Gott und Geist*."[17] Even from an Aristotelian analysis, consciousness provided the place for the subject's activity and thus a dialectical relationship with the world and its ground.

Schell was admitted to the Würzburg seminary, promoted to doctor in 1872, and ordained the next year. As was the German custom the young priest was expected to work in parishes prior to further study. Brentano's departure from the university and the priesthood may have made diocesan superiors reserved toward Schell, for only in 1879 did a new bishop, Franz Joseph Stein (who had taught Schell pastoral theology), give Schell permission for further study—but in Rome. Schell worked at the Jesuit Gregorian University; the doctoral dissertation had the Trinity as its subject. G. B. Franzelin and Domenico Palmieri represented philosophical and theological scholasticism at the Roman school (Schäzler too was in Rome at this time). Schell also met Kleutgen, who was just retiring as Leo XIII intensified his support for the neoscholastic revival in *Aeterni Patris*. But Schell was not enthusiastic about Kleutgen's books and was cool toward a medieval philosophy that was almost becoming an ideology.[18] Thus the most creative theologian of the era was drawn early in his life into the idealist and neoscholastic directions of Catholic intellectual life in a particularly rich way: to Kuhn, Sengler, Brentano, and Palmieri.

The thirty-year-old theologian returned from Rome capable of distinguishing and synthesizing the intellectual worlds of late idealism (Freiburg), Aristotelianism and Catholic positive theology (Würzburg), and the active neoscholasticism and positivist theology (Rome). Schell was again serving in parishes from 1882 until 1883, when the second dissertation was completed, "The Activity of the Triune God." Some faculty members at Würzburg were hostile toward him, and Schell investigated attaining the doctorate in Freiburg but then chose to pursue the degree at Tübingen. His *"Promotion"* in theology occurred in November 1883, and the large dissertation was published in 1885, receiving positive reviews.[19]

Upon the death of Denzinger, F. S. Hettinger (1816–1891) left the professorship in apologetics for that in dogmatics. He had published two works in apologetics, but his questioning of "progress" in a book of 1863 shows that his relationship to the Tübingen school and his apologetical dialogue with his own age had their limits.[20] He was intent upon preventing Schell from becoming his successor in apologetics. Having blocked his promotion in Würzburg, Hettinger now wanted to discredit his Tübingen *Promotion* with a testimony from the dean, F. X. Linsenmann, that Schell was "not adequate" in canon law.[21] Nevertheless, the younger scholar had some university support, and in November 1884 Ludwig II appointed him to be extraordinary professor for apologetics in Würzburg with the added obligation of lecturing on the history of Christian art and archaeology. Four years later he was named ordinary professor for apologetics with added courses in the philosophy of religion and the history of Christian art. He was nominated in 1890 for the professorship in dogmatic theology upon the death of Hettinger, but the bishop of Würzburg refused his approval.

II. Schell's Theological World

We have described the links between Schell's education and the philosophy and theology of the first half of the century. Motifs of will and freedom in God, of divine person as activity, a kind of theological ecumenism evaluating positively the history of Christianity and the world religions—these reflect, albeit faintly, Schelling as mediated to him by Sengler and Kuhn, while Schell's psychological approach to Christian doctrine and philosophical subject comes from Brentano.

Romanticism and Idealism in the Early Nineteenth Century

Schell received little direct influence from the writings of Schelling and did not always understand him well. The importance of a positive philosophy of act Schell received from the idealists, while his idea of God comes essentially from the influence of Kuhn.[22]

There was in Schell an emphasis upon the inner life of God. A triune concept of God and an absolute concept of creation go together, inwardly and consequently. Both have the same foundation. Spirit is inwardly active as life and process. The world, however, is not the essential content of the divine act of life. The creation of the primal world is free and without presupposition; any monistic derivation of the finite from the substance of the infinite is simply unthinkable. The divine act of life has its essence and object in the realization of the infinite perfection in an eternal spirit-life. The processing divine persons have one, eternal, and inseparable life through the Spirit. By means of their self-communication the reality of the finite world is included in the divine thought and act. The ground of Christianity is the Trinity, which itself resulted from the self-causation of God.[23]

Some neoscholastics inaccurately called Schell "a Schellingian," but this overlooked Schell's criticism of the content of the world between the two Fichtes and his confrontation with von Hartmann, who transformed idealism into an anti-Christian psychology of religion. In general,

Schell did not condemn idealism but evaluated the approach of speculative theism as needing the corrective of revelation in history. "Idealism is
one-sided, merely an opposition to naturalism. It explains the world from
ideas and ideals (*Idealen*), employs images and necessary concepts dis-
connected from spirit which is always active thought and will."[24] From
his perspective at the end of the nineteenth century the great systems
of idealism with their emphasis upon divine process and transcendental
history had become a closed monism, fossils in which one saw a frozen
mixture of the Absolute and the created.

Neoscholasticism

Schell taught not in 1840 but in 1880. If he had learned much from
the Tübingen school, he lived in the midst of two Aristotelian revivals:
Roman Catholic neoscholasticism and German academic neo-Aristotelianism. Schäzler inspired Schell to study Aquinas and the baroque disputes
over grace and freedom, but he learned Aristotelianism in its content,
goals, and interpretation not from the neoscholastics but from Brentano.
Schell's dogmatic theology criticized neoscholastic misunderstandings of
potency and act, of human personality, of static substance, and of global
final causality. Aquinas on grace was interpreted strictly with the proper
emphasis on divine activity; modern theologians had to strive for a middle
position between Molinism and Thomism, one which respected both grace
and freedom.[25]

And yet, for Schell, Thomism passed on not simply Aristotelian influence but Platonic and Dionysian motifs. The neoscholastics in their lack
of perception and their zeal for monopoly turned Thomism into a mixture
of different superficial scholasticisms that lacked theological depth and
ignored the finite autonomy of spirit. Excessive interest in "concepts" and
"correct propositions," joined to a retreat from culture and science, can
only lead to a "cemetery."[26] The issue ultimately was freedom and pluralism. Schell's thought implied a rejection of neoscholasticism because
a psychological idealism and not a static metaphysics was to be the underlying form. His theology would mirror the two directions of the age.
While he was a knowledgeable student of Aquinas (much more so than
many neo-Thomists), he found in Kuhn and Sengler openings to both the
modern and patristic worlds.

III. A Time of Productivity

The book on the Trinity, *Das Wirken des dreieinigen Gottes*, of 1885
calmly rejected the nineteenth century's derivations of God and Trinity

from consciousness but was seen as "the brilliant . . . , genial response of Christianity to the new problematics of modern speculation on the ultimate sources of life and life in the culture of *Geist*."[27] A *Katholische Dogmatik* was published from 1889 to 1894 with four sections in three volumes. Next, a first apologetics, *Gott und Geist*, appeared in two volumes from 1893 to 1896. The 1890s saw Schell's career at its height. The leading expert on Schell, Vincent Berning says: "A new spirit entered the theological faculty with Schell, and with him a new age in the history of modern Catholicism in Germany broke forth."[28] A popular teacher, a writer whose ideas were sparked by the meeting of contemporary culture and science with Catholic faith, and a successful university preacher before city and academy, Schell was an accessible person who enjoyed students, colleagues, and friends. As a teacher he was aware of his students' lives; his theology, even in its most metaphysical form, was never just speculation. He served as chaplain for the city's orphanage and visited the parishes where he had worked previously. A leading Jewish writer of the time recalled meeting Schell:

> A small man with the face of an Alemannian farmer and childlike eyes. A broad-rimmed hat modified a little the clerical image but gave it not a worldly, but an extra-worldly atmosphere. . . . He could thunder like Jehovah and be mild like St. John: his voice could blast like a sounding trumpet or make an entrance like the flute playing of a pious shepherd. He had many voices; if one were open to the poetic and the literary, inevitably one heard too the crackling fire of the passionate theologian.[29]

He enjoyed good relationships with most of his colleagues on the faculty, and figures like Sebastian Merkle and Albert Erhard shared his desire for the renewal of Catholicism, as did the Thomist dogmatician Friedrich Abert (later archbishop of Bamberg) and Schell's successor, F. X. Kiefl.

Schell was rector when the dedication of new university buildings took place. His inaugural discourse as rector in 1893, "Theology and University," addressed the role of Catholics in the German universities. "Catholicism itself in its name and essence is a university of truth (in an open-ended sense) for the entire world, not just for the education of Catholics but for all cultural levels of humanity."[30] For some years it had been asked whether theology professors linked to a church should be included in a university. Being Catholic and being German, however, meant taking part in the university life of Germany; Catholic universities could be a value, but they could not replace the theology faculties at state universities, for the kingdom of God existed not simply for eschatological souls but for the world.

IV. Toward the Twentieth Century

How were Catholics faring in Wilhelminian Germany? On the one hand, they were urged to overlook the weakening injustices left behind by Prussian hegemony and the Kulturkampf. In some religious and intellectual circles being German seemed to preclude not only Catholicism but orthodox Christianity. On the other hand, a mode of thinking which reproduced forms from medieval and baroque centuries was urged upon them by an aggressive Vatican. Books were published to show through statistics and sociology that Catholics were more and more marginalized in education and the professions. A Munich newspaper wrote: "Catholics, despite their protests, are being moved with mathematical certainty little by little out of the most significant and influential positions in the cultural and business life of the nation. The consequence will be that they will become poorer. Then as a result of the poverty they will be unable to send their children on for further education."[31]

To highlight this crisis before the new Germany and the new century, Schell wrote *Der Katholicismus als Princip des Fortschritts* (1897).[32] A best-seller, the book raised the question: Did Catholicism exclude progress? There were chapters on church policies, hierarchical triumphalism, the furthering of a purely passive laity, the preference for childish devotions over liturgy and doctrine, and the mistake of separating seminaries from universities. Schell's book and addresses pursued the risky course of uniting theology with political and cultural issues. Rome came to view this as dangerous and from that time on it seemed to view German Catholicism as a complex of philosophical theology, politics, journalism, and social issues.

Christianity was a reality in history, not a dead religion, but a fact which gave rise to theological interpretations and systems.

> Catholicism means a peaceful covenant of reason and faith, of research and revelation without any devaluation and humiliation for the logos. For Christianity is the religion of spirit and logos! The true spirit of religion and holiness no more and no less than the spirit which proceeds from the word of truth. This is the great significance of the divine Trinity expressed in the *Filioque*, standing over against any irrational-supranatural mysticism in East or West; then too against its rationalistic form, and against its tendency to aloof superstition or to aggressive disbelief.[33]

Christianity was "the wisdom and power of God providing completion for the human race," and all its branches had a share in this. Catholicism, however, is "full and total Christianity."[34] For Schell Protestantism had an inevitably protesting, hence anti-Catholic facet, while Catholicism was not necessarily anti-Protestant, but was, in its ideal, a true, serene resolution above all oppositions and one-sidedness.

In Catholic circles in the 1890s a pessimistic tone and a dualistic intellectual position were common. Schell identified that dualism with a "Scotistic and nominalist" position dividing the spiritual from the secular, the natural from the supernatural. This helpless theology would argue for a withdrawal by the church from German institutions. This, in turn, neglected the basic Christian view of a general ministry and priesthood of the baptized in the world, and made Catholics defensive not just about the infallibility of the pope but about essential aspects of their church and faith. Recent ecclesiastical decisions, far from recognizing the decline of Catholic cultural presence or furthering opportunities for its growth, had retreated into a false glorification of the ecclesiastical. The hierarchical preference in the church was for servility, Byzantine politics, uniformity, even boredom, none of which contributed to serving the gospel.[35]

Freedom and progress occupied Schell's book. "Freedom for research, freedom to think," was a slogan of the times. Obviously there could be false freedoms: freedom and progress might engender error, even moral evil, and some dangerous and foolish causes were defended in universities in the name of an absolute freedom. Schell argued for freedom by showing that one could not come to the truth in a human way without a freedom of spirit. Learning was a child of freedom in research and thinking. Some church circles ("the most extreme scholastic theology")[36] implied that free research into the empirical, the social, the human was to be feared—a position quite alien to true Catholicism and one which Protestant polemicists bemoaned in the church. "One of the facts of life among the ultramontanes—a particularly notorious one—is to insist that not only Roman Catholic theologians but philosophers, lawyers, physicians, natural scientists, and every specialist allow their concepts to be corrected by an infallible pope as soon as the results of their scientific work appear. Cultural freedom rarely touches on revealed truth, and science implies freedom to think and to learn."[37]

Schell made three concluding pastoral suggestions.[38] First, corresponding to the general priesthood of the baptized, the laity must be given more and significant positions in education and leadership. Their deeper role in the church would give new insights into the faith and effect an interplay of the natural and the supernatural. Second, theology should be permitted free development, while theology and seminary should not be isolated away from university and city. Thirdly, Catholics should not just work along with culture and politics but should actively influence them. Catholicism should be known by its deeds as "a principle of progress."

To answer his critics Schell wrote a second book in 1898, *Die neue Zeit und der alte Glaube*.[39] Cardinal Manning had been cited as an inspiration in the first volume, and now similar movements in France, Ireland, and the United States inspired him to devote an opening chapter in the next book to Archbishop Ireland and Isaac Hecker of the United States.

The accusation circulating for almost a century after 1869—Catholicism was a faith of second-class citizens (Protestant countries lead in finance, education, and culture, while Catholic, Mediterranean countries with their relaxed if colorful ways were empty of the achievements of modernity)—was answered not by citing famous physicians and artists from the Renaissance but by furthering a Catholic intellectual life. Theology should show how the Catholic essence and principle was compatible with progress without becoming an atheism or an ethical humanism. Schell saw the horizon of modernity (the gift of the Germanic peoples) to be healthy and fruitful. "Everywhere idealism is the precursor of realism: the productive construction of worldviews hastens ahead of predictions."[40] Religion, Christianity, and church proceeded outwards, the self-realization from an inner depth, from a truth which was always too great and multiple for one expression.

In contrast, ultramontanism was a negative propaganda, implying that the church was authoritarian and that Christianity was world-denying. Life in the modern era was not a cosmic fall from the gifts of the Middle Ages but a recognition of a new approach to what had been affirmed even then: "God as the inner idea of all intellectual and cultural values, as a life born of truth and unfolding toward completeness. . . . The kingdom of God is the ideal, striving in an ideal expanse for totality . . . furthering the spiritual personality in self and neighbor."[41] The goal of Catholicism was to appropriate Christianity for humanity as a principle of progress grounded in revelation; to introduce the kingdom of God in this life and in the next; to avoid the extremes of modern life—not just atheism but dualism and pessimism.

> Catholicism can never yield to the separation of religion and epistemology, faith and knowledge, subject and object. In its essence, it is the mutual penetration of both. So it is not necessary to defend the *objectivism* of religion and revelation by forcing away the inner dimensions of religion. Catholicism can do justice to the entire religious ideal, to all of what is human, to the interior and the external, to law and freedom, to God and creation. It can include the past but also the present with its proper claims, and even that dimension with greater claims, the future.[42]

Catholicism had not stood utterly outside of European history since Descartes and the Enlightenment: it had movements similar to Protestant pietisms and modern theologies. The Würzburg theologian insightfully recognized that Roman directions after the eighteenth century fashioned a kind of orthodoxy which was paradoxically also a rationalism. This avoided, yet imitated by distortion, the conversation between Catholicism and modernity. Catholicism was concerned with the ideal in the future, with the means not only of overcoming disbelief and sin but of expanding truth and love in freedom.[43]

V. Storm Clouds

Schell's book was seized upon by the liberal press who portrayed him falsely as the leader of a modernistic revolution against the papacy. Fixed by publicity's spotlight, he was identified with the various movements grouped together as *"Reformkatholizismus."* Conservative Catholics published responses, one of the sharpest coming from the pastor of the Würzburg cathedral.[44] The Catholic bishops kept silence (publication of the first book without ecclesiastical *imprimatur* had aroused the ire of Schell's bishop in Würzburg), but reactionary Catholic circles—Austrian Jesuits and the neoscholastics M. Glossner and E. Commer—saw the creative and outspoken development in Schell's book on Catholicism in the coming century as the long sought-for opportunity to injure the Würzburg theologian and his followers. The Vatican's office for anti-modernist rumor and campaign under Umberto Benigni (whose power grew in the last years of Pius X but who was removed from office by the next pope, Benedict XV, in 1915) assembled a dossier for action.

By 1898 Schell's career began a spiral downward. Opposition increased, more from Rome than from Germany, more from bishops than theologians, more from Jesuits and Benedictines than from the diocesan clergy. The Prussian bishops expressed their fears to Rome, while the bishops of Trier and Würzburg (while visiting the Vatican) reported that their seminarians might no longer believe in the eternity of hell as a result of Schell's lectures.[45] On October 5, 1898, Leo XIII issued through the Munich nuncio a letter which reached Bishop Friedrich Schlör in Würzburg at the end of November. It complained that Schell's lectures expressed heterodox opinions (the nuncio added passages from *Die neue Zeit und der alte Glaube* and the *Dogmatik*). The bishop and the theologian agreed to a response by Schell, but in December 1898 the Congregation of the Index was already acting (this was done without the pope's approval—he was ill). The two books on Catholicism and the future were placed on the Index, and the early apologetics *Gott und Geist* and the published volumes of the *Katholische Dogmatik* were soon added to them. To objections about the procedure, Rome replied inaccurately that they had received no answer from Würzburg and that German bishops had initiated the affair.

Tyrrell and von Hügel followed Schell's case, while in Paris Loisy perceived the situation as one mirroring the strong conservative tendencies of French ultramontanes.[46] The Bavarian minister Georg von Hertling, while visiting the Vatican, reported that Schell's books were placed on the Index from theological, not dogmatic grounds—there were members of the evaluative commission who viewed his work favorably. Schell was not required to repudiate particular errors but only to accept the measure of the church. As a particular sign of favor (for not only accusers and process but issues and conclusions were kept secret) Leo XIII permitted the disclosure of areas where Schell's theology was judged erroneous: the self-causality of God, his questioning of the nature and permanence of mortal sin and the eternity of damnation in light of the love of God and human freedom, his promotion of the quasi-sacramentality of death and suffering, his qualifications concerning the necessity of baptism and extreme unction were mentioned. To illustrate the nature of the theology in question we can mention Schell's theory of how grace was present in the nonbaptized. He pondered the idea that after Calvary (and by its power) death itself was a kind of sacrament. In and through it dying people could participate in the redemptive grace purchased by Christ.[47] In general, Roman fears were directed toward either an idealist theology of God or a generous and ecumenical view of the power of God's grace.

Germany, secular and Protestant, watched to see how the leading Catholic theologian would behave. How could a man so moderate in his discussions with opponents now be summarily and extra-legally condemned? Schell could not be argued into conflict with Rome and on the first Sunday in March 1899 he announced from the pulpit of the university church in Würzburg that he submitted to the decision of the Congregation of the Index. He then preached a sermon on Jesus' prayer for the unity of the church in the gospel of John. In the lecture hall Schell never addressed his censors, and he suffered as village pastors implied that he was no longer suitable to preach. "Disappointing the liberal public and press who hoped for a second Döllinger and a permanent enemy of the papacy, Schell found extraordinary support. Thousands of letters and telegrams from all the areas of Europe and the Americas arrived stating their support and admiration, and many of the best-known scholars of his time stood with him."[48]

In the following years the Würzburg theologian undertook a number of trips and accepted important invitations for lectures—for example, on Christ and culture, Descartes, Harnack, faith and natural science, Leo XIII and contemporary thought (laudatory), and the significance of the world religions. From Würzburg he composed from 1901 to 1905 an apologetics, *Apologie des Christentums*, but the third volume of the apologetics, on the church, was not completed.

Shortly after his election as pope, Pius X received Schell in a private audience in October 1903. The pope was kind, did not mention the Index or Reform Catholicism, and discussed with Schell the difficulties of certain issues in apologetics.[49] Schell interpreted the meeting as reassuring, but others later recalled the pope's behavior as distant and cool. Enemies, however, were relentless, asking whether he had really rejected the indexed errors.[50] After the publication in 1903 of the popular book on Jesus the Savior, *Christus*, the attacks began again, not only in Rome but at the local level in Paderborn and Mainz. Rome told the bishop of Würzburg to request further submissions (neither the original issues nor the attackers were to be known) and speculated that perhaps Schell should be removed from the university. Schell signed the *"Protokoll"* of a meeting discussing twelve controversial points but rejected on principle the right of the bishop to conduct such an examination. At Bishop Schlör's papal audience in Rome in the autumn of 1905, the pope made no mention of Schell, but then a few weeks afterward a letter came from Rome expressing the pope's pain that Schell was demeaning the deposit of faith. Schell angrily complained to Cardinal Merry del Val and the prefect of the Index that the ignorance of the doctrinal issues by Roman theologians and German bishops was outrageous. The tiring, uncertain procedures along with the hostility of colleagues and of anonymously published articles in both scholarly and popular journals left Schell exhausted. He had for a few years suffered from heart disease, and at the end of May 1906, a few days before Pentecost, he suffered a heart attack in his rooms. His rosary was found near his body, and on his desk a small statue: Galileo holding a globe in his hand.

That rigid neo-Thomist Ernst Commer wrote two lengthy works on Schell. The first received an endorsement from Pius X, who wrote that the virtue and scholarship of Schell's life could not be doubted but that his teaching was not "incorrupt" but held a "poison of new things."[51] Opening pages praised Schell for a depth of education and speculative gifts; his weaknesses came from originality or from an eclecticism linking the influence of Kuhn and the Tübingen school with a weak knowledge of the fathers and Aquinas.[52] There were errors in every area of his theology. Theology did not need freedom for creativity. Church teaching was grounded in Plato and Aristotle, for they inspired both the church fathers and the scholastics; in neoscholasticism Aquinas and Albert the Great had found another victory. "And so the church has a fixed deposit of teaching expressed philosophically through the inheritance of the classical age in purity, and a fixed formulation through the Latin of the church, although philosophical research has not reached its final destiny, still the search for principles has ceased."[53] Schell's system is marked by injuries to reason or contradictions to revelation. Commer never analyzed specific ideas, for instance, God or eschatology; their original language and their desire to be insightful in a contemporary way condemned them. Any accommodation with contemporary life was a reproduction of "Americanism" (with its dreaded democracy), and succumbing to French modernism, a sell-out to Protestantism.

> Schell preached to the world of the indifferent laity: by wanting to reconcile Catholicism and Protestantism, he sacrificed much to the camp of nonbelievers and aroused unreal hopes. He wanted to show new goals and new ways; they led, however, not to the treasures of Catholic antiquity . . . but to the bitter waters of German subjective idealism, back to Kant (the philosopher of Protestantism), to Deutinger, Baader, and their followers, from faith downwards to skepticism.[54]

Commer had his own theological method: obedience to the Holy See and a deeper devotion to neoscholasticism, and this former student and friend of Schell concluded outrageously: "Schell, in your teaching there remains little that is Catholic."[55]

But Archbishop Friedrich Abert of Bamberg, theologian and lifetime supporter of Schell, wrote that if Schell—he called him "the most popular theologian in modern times"—erred in his theology it was out of love. Clearly his works were written out of a deep faith; he did not hesitate to submit his own judgment to the church's, and his views on sin, hell, and salvation, if novel, were composed out of love for sinners and the unbaptized.[56]

Schell was the most prominent Catholic theologian of the late nineteenth century, and the Vatican measures against him left theology itself in disrepute. The pope interfered in German plans for a monument to Schell, fearing that its planning committee might become a cell of reform. Of the theological age leading up to Herman Schell, Bernhard Welte wrote:

> This tension between orthodoxy and creativity, between scholasticism and the thinking subject permeated the entire period. And yet there were still some original, independent and great figures. If the most prominent name in this period is John Henry Newman,

in Germany the most significant is Herman Schell.... One recalls that both of these men were pushed to the edge of church and theology in their time. And neither Schell's theological impulses (an alternative to modernism) nor the magnificent and more influential thoughts of Newman were appreciated and absorbed by the schools and figures of theology at that time.[57]

After the Great War Catholicism began anew a dialogue with post-Kantian philosophy, and only when Catholic dogmatics had gained some maturity in the decade leading to Vatican II was Schell remembered.

VI. Dogmatic Theology

Having followed the course of Schell's career, we want to look more closely at the governing insights of his thought. The *Katholische Dogmatik* described the task of theology for a contemporary Catholic and non-Christian readership. "Today's age is not satisfied with questioning a few basic truths but wants to examine critically the totality of religion itself. Apologetics must become dogmatics and dogmatics must be done in an apologetic way." [58] The impetus for dogmatic theology comes from devotion to truth, speculation, and freedom. Theology is not a display of concept-games at the expense of revelation but the careful elaboration of revelation. Theology has an obligation to display its disdain of fantasy by speaking not only to scientists but to preachers. Schell described his method as truly "scholastic in that it addresses the truths of faith by philosophy (granting rights to both idealism and realism), idealist in the goal towards which it strives, and realistic in the path on which it moves forward."[59] Scripture, Aquinas, and the history of theology were widely discussed, although contemporary figures other than Catholic neoscholastics were rarely included. The first volume surveyed the modes of knowing God, from the philosophical to the mystical. Volume two treated the Trinity, "Cosmological Revelation," and the finite beings of spirit—angels and human beings—amid fall, sin, and grace. The third volume's two parts treated Christ, church, and the eschaton.

The pattern of the *Dogmatik* was a progress from human subjectivity to the cosmos, and then from God to Christian revelation. The subject emerged out of a transcendental analysis with insights drawn from Kant and Schelling but including categories from late idealist personalism. Person, so described, was the ground of the activities of consciousness. But the meaningfulness of being and the activity of spirit existed primordially and infinitely in another self, in God whose life extended (in

modes disclosed by revelation) into Trinity and salvation-history. Berning evaluated Schell from a methodological stance as the creator of a
complete dogmatic and philosophical systematic that was based upon the
Christian late-idealism of Sengler, Günther, Kuhn, and Brentano, with
Thomas Aquinas independently interpreted and reservedly employed.[60]
Less explicit but nonetheless present was the new world of natural science. "From the interiority of the life of spirit come the forms arranging
the world out of a mass of ciphers into number, out of various sounds
into discourse, out of scattered pages into a book. All the categories of
this world . . . give out of the depth of essence and from the value of
their content numerous pointers toward spirit within which they alone are
intelligible and worthwhile."[61] The human self was spirit analogously,
for only in God was there true transcendental realization, full resolution of necessity and freedom, of person and its objectification. In God
any potential dualism is overcome by the eternal self-causality, and how
this overcoming occurs we learn positively from the revelation of the
Trinity.

Every conceptualization of God had to be set free from two static
schoolmasters: scholasticism and Kant. The correct idea of God was the
battleground and goal of modern thought. God was the all which is first,
the goal of spirits, light from light.[62] God was the source of all realities
treated by religion whether it be Trinity or church. Dogmatic theology
was the scientific exposition of the idea of God in revelation through the
entire saving work of grace. Precisely through the true conceptualization
of God, Christianity addressed modernity.

The root of a theology of infinite personal activity was God as *actus
purus*, or better, as *causa-sui*, the divine self-causation. "Self-causation is
nothing other than a determination of the natural idea of God by which
it becomes receptive of the threefold personality and of the dual intra-
divine processes. Without it the theistic idea of God and the revealed one
of Trinity are quite foreign, if not mutually irreconcilable."[63] The Trinity
is not a divine puzzle or a metaphysical mechanism but revelation's elaboration of the *causa-sui*. "The *Trinity* is the *Aseity* of the living God as
explained by revelation. . . . Only what explains itself can serve as the
ultimate ground of explanation for everything else." [64] If some criticized
here a mixing of the revealed with the metaphysical, Schell thought he
had found in the *causa-sui* a single principle linking divine consciousness and reality, and the best named ground for the life of God. Günter
Bleickert concludes:

> The *causa-sui* was for Schell a logical necessity for his thought,
> a postulate, a formal concept; to some extent it was an "empty

formula" in the highest sense and as such open for the mystery of the Trinity which . . . remains mystery. For the human striving of thought could not deduce the Trinity, a gift solely from divine revelation. There could be here no inference of a rationalistic dilution of the mystery of the Trinity; just the opposite, the concept of *causa-sui* was interpreted out of the fact of the self-revelation of God as Trinity.[65]

Causa-sui led to the Trinity as to its unfolding. Implying divine life from transcendental ontology was an approach and dream which had hypnotized Günther and others, but Schell avoided the risk of "deriving" revealed truth from the forms of consciousness, something which Rome in the nineteenth century was quick to censure. Far from being a revealed but irrelevant mental process, the Trinity was viewed as the ground of reality. Trinity could even assist faith's response to modernity. Not an impersonal deity nor the old Father God of religions, the Trinity was absolutely primal, with each person sovereign in its activity and perfection. No Arianism was to remain; the Augustinian model survived only as a conceptual model drawn from psychology. The believer recognized in life the bridge to the Trinity and saw there the primal ground of reality. "As the triune God, this self-realization in its absolute independence and relationlessness is positively conceived in a supra-cosmic sublimity, the most inward life-community of the infinite with the finite; being in the fullest sense as content and goal of creation; active . . . in the divine mission; the royal goal of the work of grace . . . in the world, the church and the soul."[66]

The similarities and differences between Trinity and human life emerged out of an analysis of personality. "While God is the total fullness of reality, truth and goodness in an eternal realization, possession and enjoyment . . . , the human being pursues a gathering in thought and love of the totality of the real, seeking to evaluate, value and understand it."[67] The activities of the human personality—knowing and loving, the empirical and the transcendental—were ultimately realized in the historical and the concrete. In man and woman the mode of existence in the *causa-sui* in God became free causality in time. But the human being was finite: an image which does not fully posit itself. Ranging from patristic and medieval thought to the best theologians of recent times, Schell dared in a work of philosophical depth to gather and to penetrate the doctrinal elements of the Trinitarian understanding of God and to offer, at the same time, an *Apologie* for the teaching on the Trinity.[68]

VII. Apologetics

The texts promulgated by Vatican I in 1870 contained in their language and form an approach to theology which was extrinsic and propositional. This stance left unconsidered the personality and the social history of the believer or nonbeliever. Mind and will received empirical data (miracles), arguments (a scholastic logic), and actual grace (a transitory, efficacious divine movement rather than a principle of new life). Positivism and psychology, history and evolution, revolution and post-feudal politics had put the church on the defensive, but the Catholic response to quite influential relativisms, subjectivisms and evolutionisms (rightly judged unacceptable as ideologies) remained isolated from how European society thought and lived. The conflict was over the basic stance toward the cultural epoch. Should the Christian apologete make an effort to understand modernity? Could a historical era be intrinsically evil? Or should one expect that in every era human consciousness will provide insights and approaches for faith and theology? Vatican I intensified an official Roman jeremiad against modernity which lasted for ninety years.

In the quarter century after 1880 Schell saw things differently. Kant and Descartes had to be criticized, and pantheism and monism as well as recent psychologies and positivisms combated, but Catholic theology could not become a frozen textbook suited to a church where late romanticism offered a shallow reproduction of ecclesiastical baroque. Apologetics was not a collection of syllogisms but a "discussion of different worldviews."[69] Heinrich Fries writes:

> Schell's age received its intellectual geography from the natural sciences, from the worldviews influenced by these sciences, and from the philosophical systems of Schopenhauer, Eduard von Hartmann, and Friedrich Paulsen which one called monistic, pantheistic, materialistic, positivistic. In Protestantism, "liberal theology" dominated with its historical and biblical criticism as well as a view of Christianity among equal religions. Evangelical faith itself was a *"Kultur-Protestantismus"* with its own tasks in the world. So we understand why, in the face of monism and materialism, his apologetics bore the title *Gott und Geist* and why his book on Christ spent so much time on questions of the history of religions and cultural philosophy.[70]

The Catholic theologian did not concede to the halls of science or liberal Protestantism that a perspective involving faith was artificial or unfree. In a Munich lecture, Schell addressed the relationship of Christ and culture. Culture is work and artifact, the ideal effected through human effort.

While some voices in culture flee Christ, the gospel offers insights and hopes to cultivate values and personality.[71]

Apologetics was theology; not logic or rhetoric, but a way of looking at the central issues of Christianity. Theology was apologetical when it found for its own use terms, issues, and thought-forms in an open dialogue with others. For Schell, the reactionary view of theology treated the human being like a bird: "The bars of the bird's cage are the dogmas; the owner watching that the bird does not fly away is the church's teaching office; the possibility to hop from the bar to the base of the cage and back is the freedom of the theologians. It is a freedom as limited as the bird's."[72] Apologetic theology, however, did not intend to remain in "the peaceful precinct of the sacristy."[73] Apologetics had nothing to fear from the psychology of consciousness nor from the empiricism of science. Theology out of its organic life inevitably gave birth to apologetics as a philosophical, critical-speculative foundational science. "So we hold on to the intellectualist foundation of the old apologetics and respect in its principles of intellectualism the *philosophia perennis*. But because reason is the power of truth, it can and must do justice to all the ideals and demands which the mature spirit of natural science, the history of practical life, and the seriously considered meaning of religious views of life render valid."[74]

Could there be Roman Catholic thought outside of the monopoly of neoscholasticism? Schell observed that Harnack dismissed all apologetics, while the neoscholastics insisted upon their one form of apologetics. Schell intended to do justice to both sides of life, the empirical and the transcendental; and to both apologetics, immanent and extrinsic. The human personality responded to faith not by an abnormal obedience to the mysterious or the bizarre but by a "hearing" born out of human life existing between the world and revelation. Bleickert notes the tension between church and apologetics:

> Schell's apologetics aimed largely at his society. The client was the church; the accuser was the "new age." Schell worked with all his powers to display the ideal form of the church, above all, to defend it before the world. But the church (or more precisely, its official representatives) was concerned with a tough assertion of its organization and a defense of a faith which was not only traditional but defensive and reactionary. Since curial officials always intervened on behalf of the neoscholastic party, they avoided completely any dialogue with idealism, something which in Germany had been normal for a long time. The Vatican met modern questions—the views and doubts raised by philosophy and natural science—with the old

answers of a theology which had been developed in the conceptual horizon and linguistic field of scholasticism. The faith should be interpreted and defended—but only in the language of a school of the past.[75]

Schell had conceived of an apologetics in five volumes titled *The Divine Truth of Christianity*. When the first two appeared as *Gott und Geist* in 1895 and were put on the Index, the next two volumes on religion and revelation, and on Jahweh and Christ were presented as part of a new work, *Apologie des Christentums*, published after 1901. A final volume on the church was not completed. *Gott und Geist* began with the personal, active movement of the human self to the divine presence. God was not a distant object but the primal act of thinking and the primal personality of love. This biblical revelation—the union of human spirit with God's Spirit—was present not only in prophecy and miracle but in holiness and wisdom. The second volume opened with a biblical theology of God as a life-giving spirit and then moved to a theological phenomenology of Jesus Christ as the transcending critique of the monisms of the age which melded the finite and the infinite. The *Apologie*, however, moved away from subject and life. The first volume did not appear particularly modern; its philosophy of religion was a survey of different kinds of religion, followed by a list of the forms of consciousness touched by religion, for example, fear, morality, feeling. The second part, "a philosophy of revelation," followed a traditional path in looking at the need for and criteria of revelation, at miracle and prophecy as criteria, and then at mystery as a new approach to revelation.[76] Nevertheless, Schell was attracted by the immanence-apologetics of France developed by L. Ollé-Laprune, F. Brunetière and M. Blondel, because they rendered Christianity credible, or at least attractive, to the modern person through a meditation on the dynamics of life and love, spirit and will.

Schell was ultimately an apologete. His mission was to address Germans living at the end of the nineteenth century not at the time of the Reformation. What was at issue was the image of God, the work of God in salvation.[77] Schell became known far beyond pastors and theologians. His work was logical, inviting, and clear. His friend and successor Kiefl said: "Schell was not a dogmatic theologian; but no greater apologete has there ever been."[78]

VIII. Christ, the World, and History

Let us go briefly beyond dogmatics and apologetics to glimpse in some areas of theology the dialectic between the history of dogma and the personal, psychological approach.

The human world: "The world is in some sense like God in as much as every work is like its artisan."[79] Schell never relinquished his respect for secondary causes before the All-cause. He spent a great deal of time on facets of nature and grace, showing himself to be a Thomist, a disciple of Kuhn and a critic of Molinism. The divine activity is interior and exterior, surrounding the finite agent in personal, determining, prior, physical, planned modes.[80]

Schell's theology did not remain with the divine but offered new views of life in grace, the fall, the nature of original and mortal sin, the perdurance of alienation from God. The treatment of original sin was creative (it was to be an issue raised by the Vatican congregations). Sin was basically a rejection of God as the personal cause of the order of grace for created persons. The precise evil deed recorded in Genesis and in religious mythogenesis was a symbolic form of an action which is complex and partly developmental. Original sin itself was the rejection of the order of grace. It continued in a fixed aversion from this order, resulting in uncontrolled sensuality, in illness and death. It could be called a sin (and not just an inheritance) because we live de facto within this *aversio*, but it was neither the sin of Adam imposed upon us nor our personal cooperation in this sin; nor was it a physical defect or an ethical difficulty. Rather it was "a mis-relationship to the divine order." Mortal sin, however, was sin with a voluntary commitment, and every such sin was the sin against the Holy Spirit, the free turning from God. "Mortal sin occurs wherever the will immediately contradicts and excludes God and does this with full self-determination by mis-acting in terms of a created good."[81] Schell noted how weak theologies offer a picture of inner, religious failure and lead to irresponsible, crass physical explanations while emphasizing the injustice of creatures being punished because of Eve and Adam.

Schell's idea of God and his appreciation of development and evolution led to a new eschatology.[82] The end was a vast theophany in appearance, presence, community; the Trinitarian missions have reached triumph and fulfillment. The various theories of evolution could not be avoided. Does the human personality alter its relationship to good and evil beyond death? Is punishment eternal? The Index selected these views on human salvation not because they contradicted church teaching but because their tone and manner was new and potentially disturbing.

Jesus Christ: Jesus is a statement of divine anthropology. The incarnation of God is the highest goal in a hierarchy of specific goals of the plan of creation. "What the Logos is in an eternal, supra-historical, and infinite mode, the Son of Man is in a finite and historical mode. He is revelation,, word of the Father, source-ground of the Holy Spirit, way to the Father in the Spirit of Filiation . . . the ideal human being."[83] The Trinitarian life is made concrete, visible, and expressive in Jesus.

Activity discloses being. Emphases upon causality in God and activity in the Trinity have the salutary effect in christology of highlighting the reality of Jesus' human and divine life precisely through activities. The mission and self-giving of Jesus are metaphysical and ministerial, for he is the sacrament of God's attitude toward us. A certain duality in Jesus is necessary. The hypostatic union does not diminish freedom, and so Jesus' life is not a play, nor is his obedience arbitrary.[84] Jesus' consciousness is human, not a showplace for divine pyrotechnics. The Logos is present in an intensity of insight: at the depths of consciousness "the human ego is aware of an absence of constraints."[85] The head is destined to have members, the master to have the disciples. In the exemplary image of the Crucified and Risen One the kingdom of God is uncovered as a way to God as Father.

Schell's christology was aimed at several audiences: against liberal Protestant exegesis, he wanted to show that Chalcedon had done justice to the humanity of Christ; from his knowledge and meditation on the history of religions he realized that Roman Catholic christology had to be open to new ways of presenting Jesus. As we saw, his final book, *Christus*, presented these new directions to a popular audience.

The church: A society realizing "the essential form of the kingdom of God"[86] in its teaching and its liturgy is the gift of the missions of the Trinity. Vitalized by the Holy Spirit's charisms, this community owns both interior and exterior aspects of religious and social life. The church lives in a covenantal relationship to a God whose role is absolute while the church has a limited, relative being before the Spirit. The church as an institution has a variety of roles; these include a hierarchy given by Christ, but this hierarchy exists to serve the activity of the Spirit, and the church's organization is also a sacrament and service. The teaching office of the church does not control revelation but witnesses to it authoritatively. "Apostolicity" is not truth in written traditions but perduring authority. "The Spirit in which the church administers its threefold office is presented by all the Gospels; so the church is in some way also the gospel. The spirit of a serving and forgiving love is not treated as a means for enjoyment of power or of lordship over a people who are not its equal or who are spiritually immature but as the means for immediate communion with God."[87] Church and papacy exist within a dual set of relationships: to the Trinity and to the community.

The papacy is not dependent upon the universal church's whim, nor is it tied to an ecumenical council in session. Nonetheless, the subject of infallibility is both pope and ecumenical council. The pope acts within, not next to the church. Ecclesial roles are realizations of the Triune missions but do not replace the scriptural word.[88] Not all teaching is dogma, and before the Roman magisterium theology need not be piety or catechism. In 1904, years after his ecclesiastical troubles began, Schell wrote on the partnership between "the teaching church" and the "learning church." Differences between charisms and offices appeared soon in the early church but there need be no competition or exclusion among them. The Pauline ministries, charisms and gifts find their structures in the human cultural background, in the issues of knowing and believing. "Between that which is ecclesially decided and that which is not only not decided as teaching but can and must perdure as the religious form of piety and life, there is a broad area (of Christianity) capable of unfolding on its own religious directions for human theory and praxis. And one must not assume, on behalf of one particular direction, that this particular textbook, meaning, or form of piety excludes all others, or alone is Catholic."[89]

The Christian people have different roles: the ordained administer the sacraments while the laity participate in a general priesthood but "not mechanically and without differentiation,"[90] for the laity too can baptize. Schell complained in the 1890s that Catholic lay people discussed religious questions outside of a church context because there they were not threatened by the Index. He criticized the one-sided view that the laity should be involved only in secular affairs—politics, finances, charity—while the church's life was reserved for clerics. All were called to Christian life, all to the communication of the Word, all to the discipleship of Christ. Both society and church would benefit from a penetration by Christian ideas into all the areas of culture. Even more, Schell urged an active contribution by the laity in resolving theological questions.[91]

The church lives from Trinity and Spirit. This vertical dimension safeguards revelation and grace, but there is also an organic and historical dynamic considering new ways of human existence and a world beyond Europe. Karl Mühlek concluded: "Herman Schell's ecclesiology distinguishes itself from those of his age by a theological-anthropological accent, and from ecclesiologies of today by an inclusion of the Trinity . . . . In general Schell's theology of the church was oriented much more toward our times than toward the past, more similar to Vatican II than to Vatican I."[92]

IX. A Modern Theologian

Vincent Berning has traced in detail Schell's contacts with politicians like Robert Schuman and Heinrich Bruning, with the youth movement of Quickborn, and with those interested in liturgical renewal.[93] Schell built theological bridges and openings—but for whom? Roman Catholicism was racing into a defensive posture. Even the large number of friends, colleagues, and gifted doctoral students could not hold back the curtain of obscurity which fell upon him. Schell's difficulties with church authority led some to lump him together with turn-of-the-century "modernists" (just as Möhler and Kuhn had for some decades been joined with Günther and Hermes). The "modernism" in his writings consisted simply of a conviction that Catholicism can address modern culture. Many concluded that Schell's books were condemned not because of their content but because of their author's espousal of a view of Catholicism which was open to cultural change and vital theology—in short, "progress"—and such an openness was dangerous to the neoscholastic fixation upon what was supposed to be perennial. Schell's tragedy was born of his own insights; he saw that theology could not simply be apologetics but must be followed by a new synthesis. The immediate rewards for his genius and work were imprecise condemnations and, after his death, an unjustified image as a cause of the anti-modernist measures of the pope.

At Schell's death Carl Muth, founder of the Catholic journal on culture *Hochland*, predicted that the verdict on Schell would be revised, while the important philosopher of religion Friedrich Heiler considered him "the most significant Roman Catholic dogmatic theologian of the past century, one who joined popular appeal and religious enthusiasm to a comprehensive knowledge of dogmatics and the philosophy of religion."[94] If ten years after his death few books defended him, at the end of Vatican II his writings and thought reappeared, and the fiftieth anniversary of his death occasioned Josef Hasenfuss to begin this revision: "He was born too early. Now after *Ecclesiam suam*, Paul VI's address opening the second session of Vatican II, and the pastoral constitution *Gaudium et Spes*, his basic ideas appear in an essentially different light. If he had been able to present his theology of a Christian personalism today rather than in 1900, he would certainly have become a star in the sky of theologians."[95] Heinrich Fries, writing in the 1950s, asked: "What would have happened in Germany if Schell's theology had had a different destiny and thereby different potentialities?"[96] Schell's intellectual breadth and theological career, as witnessed in his condemnations, reached from Vatican I to Vatican II. And yet, Schell's theology was modern, idealist, and creative in the style of the late nineteenth century. His speculative wrestling with divine subjectivity is not original and his awareness of historical consciousness limited, but he remained a theological writer in dialogue with modern currents within the parameters of the Catholic church and the traditions and theologies of the past.

7

Carl Braig:
On the Boundary in Freiburg

WITH CARL BRAIG our narrative of modern theologians reaches into the twentieth century. But the Freiburg theologian is something of a phantom. Little information on him exists in print, nor except for one or two pages on his thought in a few recent books have his ideas and writings been studied.[1] His memory has been kept alive since his death largely through two autobiographical allusions to him by Martin Heidegger, who said Braig understood Hegel and Schelling in a time when metaphysical polemic had obscured their theological implications. Presumed to be a philosopher, Braig was in fact a dogmatic theologian. The creator of the term "modernism," he both defended papal authority and criticized neoscholasticism. Braig's writings focused on Christology and on two currents challenging it: the liberal history of dogma and philosophical psychology. Both were occasioned by the philosophical and theological movements of the times. Although he was the Catholic respondent to Eduard von Hartmann's Schellingianism and Adolf von Harnack's Hegelianism, his impact faded rapidly.

In the view of the Freiburg theologian, Christian theology and philosophy faced two central issues: the perduring approach of modernity in interpreting the human self and the entrance of history into religion, revelation, and doctrine. The rejection of the Christian church by some intellectuals had its seeds ultimately in the philosophical issues of the late nineteenth century.[2] Braig's books and articles — the product of lectures before audiences ranging from university students to nobility — provide an apt conclusion to our survey of theologians at the turn of the century.

I. The Education of a Theological Critic

Born twenty years earlier in a small town in Württemberg, Carl Braig began his studies in philosophy at Tübingen in 1873. There he heard J. E. Kuhn as well as representatives of the next, third generation

of the Catholic faculty such as F. X. Linsenmann in moral theology and
F. X. Funk in church history and patristics. A prize-winning essay on aesthetics became the basis for a doctoral dissertation in philosophy, which
he finished in 1877. That year he entered the seminary at Rottenburg and
was soon ordained a priest. His first publication, in 1881, took as its theme
the natural knowledge of God according to Thomas Aquinas, an enterprise
influenced by the crowning point of the second decade of the neoscholastic movement, Leo XIII's *Aeterni Patris*. Nonetheless, the young scholar
did not hesitate to state what he saw as limitations in Aquinas: a too narrow reduction of thought to abstract Aristotelianism and a neglect of the
Platonic.[3] If Braig was attracted to Aquinas in the years of Leo XIII, he
soon moved toward contemporary German intellectual life. In the winter
semester of 1880/81 he has the opportunity (as a substitute) to hold some
of Kuhn's lectures on dogmatics. But Paul Schanz, and not the young
Braig, was to be Kuhn's successor for dogmatics and apologetics. Disap-
pointed, Braig left Tübingen and for almost ten years served as pastor in
the small city of Wilbad near Karlsruhe. There was leisure not only for
study but for travels: to Berlin, Vienna, and Prague in 1883, and in 1887
to France. In Toulouse the rector of the Institut Catholique, F. Duilhé de
Saint-Projet, impressed him and in 1889 Braig's translation of his popular
and papally praised apologetics appeared.

The German edition of the French work was much more than a translation, for it was preceded by a book-length introduction and concluded by
pages of commentary, sources, and footnotes. The edition was accepted as
a dissertation for a doctorate in theology given by the Freiburg University.
At this institution four years later in 1893 Braig became extraordinary
professor for "philosophical and theological disciplines in propadeutic
theology,"[4] and in 1897 at the age of forty-four he was *Ordinarius* in
dogmatic theology. Chosen pro-rector (the grand duke was permanent
rector) for the theologically fateful year 1907/08, he retired in 1919 and
died in 1923.

At Freiburg the university world of theology and philosophy attracted various movements and was more pluralistic than either Tübingen
or Münster. F. A. Staudenmaier and J. B. Hirscher had brought there
Tübingen theology, which was continued by Friedrich Wörter, Braig's
predecessor.[5] Neoscholasticism was not absent, but it was represented
by only a few students and faculty whose forerunner had been Kuhn's
opponent, Constantin von Schäzler, *Privatdozent* from 1863 to 1873 before leaving Freiburg for Rome. Toward the end of the century there still
lingered the influence of Schelling in Jakob Sengler or Franz Brentano
as well as the impact of neo-Aristotelian schools. Finally there was the
emergence of the Freiburg school of neo-Kantianism.[6]

Braig's philosophical works include studies of Aquinas's theodicy, positive appraisals (Leibniz) and critiques (Kant) of modern philosophers, an incomplete philosophical system,[7] and studies on philosophical psychology. The theological works can be arranged around three areas: Christ and God[8], an apologetic consideration of the nature of Christianity,[9] and freedom in the church.[10]

II. Examining the Philosophies of the Self

In an early essay on Aquinas, Braig examined the enterprise of proving the existence of God. After employing Aquinas's *Summa contra Gentiles* and surveying neoscholastics like Kleutgen, Gutberlet, C. Pesch, and Heinrich, he interpreted with some originality the modern shift to forms and categories of knowing. "The emergence of language is caused by thought, and the development of thought is joined to speaking. Language is a work of art prior to art."[11] Antiquity sought proofs for a deity in an objective cosmology, while modernity spotlighted person and attitude. Braig rejected proofs claiming the rigor of mathematics and physics by asking what kind of God is being proved. The attitude and stances of the knowing subject influenced knowledge, and knowledge of God could hardly exist apart from them. "Morality, rationality, and religion are one in the ground of the soul."[12] The idea of God had to lie behind "proving God." The feeling for truth, duty, and sensitivity to beauty explained the human drives toward the divine but also bore witness to erroneous views of God.

So Braig pursued an approach as modern as it was neoscholastic and Aristotelian, one attentive to the powers of the personality, one where affection and intuition engaged the world. In short, the Platonic and Augustinian facets in Aquinas could not be abandoned. "Aquinas will show himself to be a true disciple of Aristotle through the genius of Augustine and Plato."[13]

During his first years at Freiburg philosophical lectures too were his responsibility (his inaugural address was on "The Freedom of Philosophical Research"), and Braig began to compose a multivolume course in philosophy, *Die Grundzüge der Philosophie*, with three of the planned ten volumes (logic, noetics, and ontology) published after 1986. The strict neo-Thomists criticized its ontology as unorthodox from an Aristotelian point of view, since it overemphasized activity and spirit in God. Braig wanted to balance the static morphology of Aristotle with insights from Leibniz and Lotze. If being means activity and consciousness, modern points of departure could be retained without accepting subjectivism or monism, and yet the earlier approaches to synthesis of Jacobi, Baader, and Kuhn were clearly no longer satisfactory. The Heideggerian scholar John Caputo has analyzed this rather bland system in detail and uncovered some surprising perspectives. Resemblances to Braig's student, Heidegger, in style, terminology, and content emerge. There is the same attention to but independence from scholastics and post-Kantians. Being has a primacy both as reality and as an actuality within creation and history (perspectives important for the distinction between *Sein* and *Seiende*).[14]

Ontology and apologetics had come together in 1882 in Braig's critique of Eduard von Hartmann.[15] Hartmann drew terms and patterns for his philosophy of religion from Kant, Hegel, and from Schelling, on whom he wrote two books.[16] An interpretation of religion and Christianity, within which Catholicism was fast becoming "moribund" (the Kulturkampf was in its final preparation), argued for a new form of religion, a panmonotheism aimed at the ethical and religious needs of the heart.

> If our attempt succeeds, namely showing from the categorical structure of spirit not only the subjective necessity of religious consciousness but also the objective truth of its unavoidable representative presuppositions, then the remainder of religious dogmatism will disappear from dogmatic theology and the difference which has existed up to this time between the philosophy of religion and dogmatic theology will be extinguished.[17]

Braig's response began by considering his sources in Strauss, Hegel, and Schleiermacher, and continued by contrasting him with Ritschl and G. Planck. In terms of Christianity Hartmann offered the same monism as had the past idealists: an attack on the Incarnation by dissolving it in psychological structures. Did not the increasing discoveries of research into religion by the schools of comparison and history support Hartmann's pessimism as he waited in vain for a new idealization of the human drive toward the absolute?

When what was termed "monism" eliminated every dialectic, when every contrast between spirit and matter, between the visible and the invisible was erased in psychology, history, science, and religion — this was "modernism"! Thus Braig named a theological epoch.[18] Nourished by an absence of sin and a confidence in secular process, modernism was the absorption of all that had to do with religion into psychology or language. Philosophies of personality in their "exploration of depth" or "press of the infinite" claimed to be modern religion.

Although neither had intended such an austere development, did not this subjectivism even in religion come ultimately from Luther and

Schleiermacher? Kant was the primal catalyst (more so that Hegel) in giving direction and content to theories dealing with religion and Christianity. The deeper dynamic of Luther's reformation was the turn to the independent self. Braig saw in Kant the most influential contributor to the new concept of religion. Here the advocates of the new concept of religion were preparing not a modern Christianity but agnosticism. The basic issues of modernity remained: the awareness of the depth and activity of knowing, "something we consider to be more difficult and profound than its depiction in either Aristotelian or critical thought."[19] The search for monoform conceptuality could bring its own intellectualism and dogmatism, while the philosophical absorption of every aspect of religion into a theory led to exaggerated choices of "either/or."[20] The suitable philosophy for the age awaited discovery.

The gap had widened between late idealism and Catholicism. Dialogue was not easy to pursue with critics who militantly argued for an all-encompassing reduction of religion and revelation. While monism and psychologism stimulated Catholics to write the systems of apologetics appearing almost yearly, their scholastic language rendered them inaccessible and unattractive. Braig correctly saw that the subjective turn characteristic of modernity at the end of the nineteenth century came not so much from the productive ego of Fichte as from the new psychologies. Heidegger spoke of learning positively of Schelling and Hegel and of a Catholic engagement with them, but Braig's works did not treat the earlier great generation frequently. He alluded to a period he called "the new romanticism" — the age when a Joseph Görres brought "new impulses" to philosophy and theology — but he was critical of the attempt by the great idealists to transform Christian revelation into their speculative thought. The origins of liberal Protestant theologies and new philosophies of religion could be traced to "the announcement that modern philosophy has grasped the essence of religion in its roots."

> We treasure the philosophical efforts of human thinking but not in the manner of those who identify the mysteries of nature with mathematical cleverness. If we have to choose between the prophetic word of the Old and New Testaments and the philosophers' molding of God and Christ into a ground for religions faith, we would not hesitate for a moment to choose the former.[21]

What was Braig's attitude toward neoscholasticism? He stood self-consciously in the tradition of Tübingen. Certainly he was critical of modern philosophies and their current flood of subjectivism and historicism, but he could not conceive of developing philosophy or theology apart from one's own times. The neoscholastics generally found his writings too modern, too unconsciously if not literally different from Aquinas and Aristotle. To be critical of extra-Catholic forces was not to wish back the Middle Ages. "My advice would be: let us not only study the philosophy *of* St. Thomas; let us also study philosophy as Thomas Aquinas did, treating our opponents calmly and objectively." He denied that the program of *Aeterni Patris* involved living in the "shadowy lands of empty formulas."[22] F. Stegmüller summed it up: "He found scholastic philosophy to be in no essential point untrue but in some not unessential points to be incomplete. As scholasticism itself has been eclectic and as Thomas fully reshaped Aristotle, so he would expand the insufficiency of scholasticism and give it further form through figures like Plato, Augustine, and Leibniz."[23] Curiously, however, modern philosophers other than Leibniz were largely absent. The dynamic quality of Braig's ontology was precisely what the neoscholastics rejected: transcendental subjectivity, employment of modern philosophy.[24]

Braig is significant in his independence. He understood Aristotelian and medieval philosophy, patristic and biblical theology but was not partisan, and he refused to limit the expression of Christianity to one program. He comprehended well (if with increasing lack of sympathy because of their impact upon Protestant theologians) the great modern philosophers. His philosophical and theological stance was one of research motivated by the need to address the controversies and dangers of his own time. He could recommend as an alternative to modernism "the old, perennial philosophy"[25] (which meant much more than neoscholasticism). If he basically agreed with Rome's recommended return to Aquinas, he, nonetheless, noted the limitations of the papal letter and advocated independence and freedom in philosophy. Philosophy could not be bestowed by authority. A sentence is true not because Augustine said it, but because its truth is seen. "We study philosophy to pursue this equation, to develop our reason as independent and self-active."[26] Braig dared to find scholasticism as well as Harnack's historicism unacceptable. Insightfully he summarized the quandary of the age:

> The former [scholasticism] confused verbal figures and structures with principles and effects; the other takes schemata and shadows emerging amid the views of an imagination entranced by hypotheses and presumes they are facts and realities. Both constructs are vacuous because they have nothing to place in the position of the living, because they mix the movements of the reasoning subject with objective fact.[27]

III. Who Is Jesus Christ?

Braig's lectures on Christ touched three areas: the person of Jesus Christ, his teaching, and the foundation of the church. The theme was "the presentations of modern and modernistic critique. . . , the 'depths' of the liberal view" of Christ and of early Christianity. Surveying a spectrum of theologies, his approach uncovered the origins and reductionism of liberal theology in the modern philosophy of the evolving, creative self. "History has become the catalyst where historians led by Harnack find a theory to explain all of religion as simply as electricity explains the working of technology. The basic mistake of modern history, of modern science, is to make the human subject the measure of being."[28] Those who reduced Christianity to human constructs of a single psychological insight denied an incarnation in spirit and matter. Ultimately the issue was history and heresy — how does the Christian gospel express itself anew while remaining much the same? Is only Harnack to decide which is which?

> What Christ revealed to the world is not a new concept of a God in three persons but that, in and through his person, God. . . has presented eternal truth to all his children of all ages, and indeed for the purpose of giving an opening to the sinful, longing humanity for its inner needs and guarantees, for its hope. Therein we have not a new meaning but *the* meaning of world history, shown at every stage as the intermingling product of infinite and finite factors. The proof for this truth is the incarnation of the eternal logos. . . and the church.[29]

IV. Between Subjectivity and History

In his address upon assuming the pro-rectorate of the university at Freiburg, Braig looked at his theological world not in terms of Christ but from the perspective of early Christianity. The meaning of Christ was a battleground of modern philosophies as much as of theologies. But had not a similar situation existed in the early church? The central issue remained the very nature of religion. Liberal theology would reduce Christianity to monotheism and monism, a monism which reduced the Trinity to God as Father and eliminated human sin in favor of secular progress. Nor should one be distracted by the lavish praise heaped by some secular scholars upon Jesus' teaching, for this did not take seriously the person of the teacher. With the cross as a warning against a religion of reason, Christianity survived and expanded in its first decades not in the train of emperors and scholars but through the symbol which had been the wood of redemption.

In 1902, Braig wrote an article for a volume honoring Grand Duke Friedrich of Baden.[30] His contribution contrasted the methodology of Adolf Harnack in his recently published *Das Wesen des Christentums* (the book went through more than five editions between 1900 and 1902) with two earlier theologians of Catholicism: F. A. Staudenmaier and René Chateaubriand. Braig opened by noting that the French romantic's famous apologetic, *Génie du Christianisme*, had been published exactly a century before, in 1802. Braig's essay was a comparison of what he called the critical-historical method in Adolf Harnack with a method in theology that had deeper links to tradition and to New Testament revelation. By the end of the century Harnack had replaced philosophical figures like Hartmann and had become, as a more theological figure, a frequent object of Braig's critique of modernism interpreting Christianity.[31]

All three Christian thinkers, however, were searching for the inner essence of Christianity, a *"Wesen,"* a *"Geist,"* a *"Génie."* They differed in their employment of a historical method for interpreting Christianity. One can hardly imagine a greater distance than that between Chateaubriand and Harnack. Braig objected to the method and goal of Harnack's book, which ranged from the historical Jesus to a renewal plan for German Protestantism. The first section presented the well-known principles of kingdom, fatherhood, and justification in love and applied them to individual life. Braig concentrated on this section, omitting Harnack's analysis of historical Christianity with its contrast to Graeco-Roman and Jewish forms. Harnack seemed to have abandoned Eastern Orthodoxy and Catholicism, both East and West; in the nineteenth century their successor would be a new realization of the Reformation in Germany.

Harnack hoped through his vast researches to find some inner essence of Christianity, to find a gospel within the gospel: to find what is most basic and simple and yet to discover that which is most free and convincing. Braig complained that historical research claims to find what in fact lies outside history. If for Harnack no individual aspect of the gospel would survive critical examination, why would one conclude that beyond all revelatory forms there lies an Absolute? Braig criticized this method: "Data touching objective truth are replaced by a blueprint for the subject seeking truth: a confusion of the object of knowing with the potentiality of knowing."[32] Harnack's absolute judgments about history were objective actions but those judgments too were products of a subjectivity. The glance of the researcher created the value of the object, and the theoretical plan was limited because it could not discuss its objects with others and isolated because it was fully dependent on a particular school, neo-Kantianism. The Protestant theologian's search for the single reality behind the enormous "mass of things" was like the physicist who failed to verify his general theory by what electricity actually does.

The product of Harnack's research qualified as pre-Christian. The fatherhood of God and the close similarity of Jesus to all human beings — these truths would not need revelation. Paradoxically, in liberal Protestantism at the end of the nineteenth century a historical criticism supported what is ultimately a metaphysics of religion. For it was not the historical text of the New Testament which argued against a real, temporal incarnation of the Logos but a claimed metaphysical and psychological process. A "Protestant principle" dominated both metaphysics and history.[33]

Two romantic apologetes — the French Chateaubriand and the German Staudenmaier (the missionary of the Tübingen school's theology to Freiburg) — argued that there is an objective content to Christianity. To look at one, Franz Anton Staudenmaier, is to see a person who considered anew Catholic dogmatics under the positive influence of the giants of German idealism. From 1837 to 1856 while teaching at Freiburg, he worked on a number of systems in the style of Hegel and Schelling. Staudenmaier belonged to the period of the *Romantik* and owed a debt to Goethe, Schlegel, Schelling, and Schleiermacher. Indicative of his wide range of interests were a pioneering, 120-page review of Schleiermacher's *Glaubenslehre*, his inaugural lecture on the nature of a university, and his influence in liturgical issues. Schelling was studied, Hegel employed, but both were critiqued. Hegel had proclaimed that idealism was the spirit of its age expressed in thought, and Staudenmaier agreed: "It is vain to withstand the spirit of the times. . . . We must recognize it, penetrate it, but not in every way adopt it."[34] Braig chose to counterbalance Harnack, not with Staudenmaier's early system, *Der Geist der göttlichen Offenbarung* (1837), but with a more popular work, *Der Geist des Christentums* (1835). To disclose the *"hohen Geist"* of Christianity, Staudenmaier started from "what appears to be clear subjectivism." The book used a framework of the church year, tradition, and art. Staudenmaier too began from life, from the activity of the Absolute in our spirit. "The Son reveals to us the Father; the Spirit explains the Father and the Son. The truth from Father and Son through the Spirit unites us with God and is at the same time life. The teaching of Christianity is therefore the deepest truth and the truest philosophy."[35]

Braig commented that: "Staudenmaier's mode of expression is often incomplete, awkward, and expressed in the 'grammar' of a false philosophy, namely idealism."[36] The subjective, idealist side of Staudenmaier originated in a respect for authentic mysticism, and this romantic idealism was not that of a subjectivistic and skeptical historicism. Both Freiburg

theologians were comfortable with aspects of modern philosophy and philosophy of religion. Braig objected to turning the preaching of Jesus into
an ethical christology, a series of moral lessons about human life, or into
a theology, an explication of the being of God toward us. What is the
essence of Christianity? It is the "total content of the gospel of Jesus
Christ.... With its own principles and logic, it is also empirical and
historical, necessarily owning content as well as form."[37]

V. Modernity and Theological Freedom

With an antipathy toward both a confining neoscholasticism and an
exaggeration of freedom in modern thinkers, Braig espoused a clear and
somewhat positivistic defense of church authority. There was something
unexpected about this, for, although he abhorred the enterprise of seeking a mastery over Christian revelation by critical or historical methods,
he included roles for the human subject and social development, and he
argued that theology was a cultural and historical enterprise (faith had its
emotional and experiential side). If Schelling and Hegel were criticized
by name, their thought-forms, employed by Staudenmaier's generation,
were understood and passed on. But Braig eventually came to see a dangerous direction in the cluster of issues that surrounded the two poles
he had singled out, subjectivism and historicism. Was it wrestling with
late idealist theoreticians of dogma and religion more than with philosophers which convinced him of the dangers of what he (and then the papal
documents) called "modernism"? "Free science" and "science without
presupposition" were slogans used in attacking Catholic intellectual life.
We should recall that theologians like Braig were attacked not only
by secular or liberal Protestant writers but by rightist Catholics who were
hostile to any dialogue with modern philosophy and politics. Braig found
it easy to show that every intellectual stance had its presuppositions,
but he did not think that a Catholic university (the issue was still hotly
discussed forty years after the Kuhn-Schäzler debate) would offer the
right atmosphere for all the sciences.[38] The young professor's inaugural
lecture had looked at freedom in philosophical research from two perspectives, "Christian" and "critical"; liberty was spotlighted as it emerged
between the age of Kant and that of Vatican I. Both Christian philosophy
and agnostic thought claimed independence, but each had its own espoused principles. "A positive Christian grasp of truth is the norm for the
believer's freedom.... The dogma of ecclesial faith offers something
individual faith does not have but which it seeks: a kind of negative
norm. This is reconcilable with freedom of scientific thought as much as

the inward dogmas of a private faith."[39] Braig's modest goals seemed to have been to indicate that everyone — not just Roman Catholics — had their own "dogma" and "worldview," but that the dogma brought only negative and flexible limits. For the anniversary of Leo XIII in 1903 an address pursued the topic (*Der Papst und die Freiheit*),[40] but this was largely a rhetorical defense of scholarly freedom amid the ecclesiastical presumption that disagreement with faith and church is an easily identified un-freedom.

In a talk to students in 1908 he observed that "the word 'modernism' is not a slogan for condemning the valuable discoveries and the progress of modern science but points to a cluster of errors."[41] The modernist critics of Catholicism, Braig continued, did not in fact deal carefully with historical research but set aside all that fell under church, dogma and sacraments by their wielding of a "law of evolution." Such an evolution raced forward, and when any form or idea appeared to have lost its strength, it was discarded like a dead leaf. But it is cultural, ecclesial, liturgical, and theological forms which sustain the perduring essence of religion! Braig concluded by mentioning his concern over situations where Catholic scholars asserted their Catholicity even as they promoted only the destructive modernist positions.[42]

Unlike many of his Catholic peers, Braig viewed the papal documents of 1907 and the oath prescribed in 1910 not as insults but as confirmations of his perception of contemporary theological turmoil. Everything objective in Christianity might be erased by those who reduced religion to anthropological and cultural processes, or to the unconscious — which he called "a feeling-monism."[43] *Der Modernismus und die Freiheit der Wissenschaft* of 1911 addressed the new situation of modernism under siege from papal proscriptions and worldwide investigations. Most of the pages treated the errors of modernism in terms of Christianity. Turning to freedom and the Vatican, the author noted that there was a difference between an ecclesiastical statement that this or that idea was a false expression of faith and a claim to offer the correct proposition about revelation.[44]

Braig's sympathy for the Vatican's warnings about the dictatorship of contemporary philosophies over revelation did not lead him to immature or hostile evaluations of his fellow theologians. While Braig was teaching, Schell's works were places on the Index, but Braig's reviews were warm and insightful in their praise of the Würzburg theologian. Schell's *Apologie des Christentums* (reviewed after the intervention of the Index) was marked by originality, universality, depth, and insight. "Its observations and responses to modern opponents of Christianity both in philosophy and the history of religion were numerous,

pages dedicated to the sacred causes of truth and of the church."[45] Braig
praised the work's objection to Christianity being absorbed by the history of religion school in either its epistemological or psychological form.
Schell had seen certain fundamental errors of contemporary philosophy:
the piling up of inflammatory expressions and new terms, pompous and
exaggerated slogans, a lack of logic, a tendency to replace persons with
things and concepts, a romance with the contradictory or the unconscious.
Still, "Schell's apologetics show that it is not enough to bemoan or ignore the 'genius' of modernity, but it must be met in a scientific and basic
way."[46] He understood the pressing, unavoidable challenge to Christianity
which commanded Schell's thought: "Without God, no world! Without a
concept of God no concept of the world!"[47] Nevertheless, particular criticisms of Schell were not lacking. The final work, *Christus* — like much
of the theology and exegesis inspired by idealism — sought the message
of Jesus too much in the abstract *paroles* of the Gospel according to
John. One needed a portrait of Christ drawn more from the Synoptics,
where historical concreteness inspires different cultural periods. To turn
from Schell to another controversial theological mind, Braig's eulogy of
F. X. Kraus praised that leader in reform movements for his theology,
politics, and priestly life. Kraus had not overwhelmed doctrinal theology
with historical research; he had shown through study after study the value
of disclosing the meaning of Christian faith within the forms of theology
and liturgy correctly described. After all, Braig concluded, the modern
battleground was history.[48]

VI. A Bridge into the Twentieth Century

Braig was born in Württemberg the year before Schelling died, 1853,
and he died in Freiburg in Breisgau in 1923 as Heidegger (in a rare time
away from Freiburg) was teaching at Marburg and writing *Sein und Zeit*.
Heidegger rarely revealed his personal life, but in a few autobiographical
lines he indicated his pathway back into the nineteenth century, back to a
figure who was an inspiration for a philosophy that for a while was viewed
as agnostic or nihilist. After 1911, in his first semesters as a student in
Freiburg (following a brief entry into the Jesuits), Heidegger attended
Braig's lectures on dogmatic theology. There, he said, the gifted teacher
imparted a positive impression of theology and spoke of a Roman Catholic
theology still in conversation with German culture and the great figures
of idealism. There too in the realms of faith and metaphysics problems
surfaced which would mold every theology drawn from a metaphysics.

Braig's *Vom Sein* gave him access to different scholasticisms, Aquinas but Suarez too.[49]

> After four semesters I set aside the study of theology and devoted my efforts solely to philosophy. One theological course I still attended in the years after 1911, that on dogmatics given by Carl Braig. That defined for me an interest in speculative theology; particularly impressive was the penetrating mode of thinking which the teacher in that lecture hour could summon forth. On the few walks when I had the opportunity to accompany him, I heard for the first time of the significance of Hegel and Schelling for speculative theology in contrast to the pedagogical systems of scholasticism. Thus the tension emerged, the tension between ontology and speculative theology as the constructive form of metaphysics in the historical circle of my quest.[50]

Braig's teaching, in light of Heidegger's recollection of inspiring lectures, would appear to have been more creative and vibrant than his monographs. The spoken word turned an obscure problem of metaphysics fashioning theology into a perduring impetus for original ideas. Was an independent but informed and meditative stance toward Hegel and Aquinas the gift of Braig? Caputo ranks his influence on Heidegger above that of Brentano.

A little before Heidegger arrived in Freiburg, another seminal figure of Catholic intellectual life in the coming century began to study there: Romano Guardini. As a student in 1906, he heard Braig and also enjoyed the open speculative theological atmosphere. After some time in Tübingen, Guardini returned to Freiburg for doctoral studies in 1912 to 1915. Professor Braig had suggested for a dissertation topic a comparison of Thomas Aquinas and the modern psychologist Wilhelm Wundt. This unnerved Guardini, who went to a younger, more traditional Engelbert Krebs to work on the topic of Bonaventure's theology of redemption.[51]

In 1881 at the age of twenty-nine Braig wrote that the goal of his work was "to contribute to an age of renewed speculative Christian knowledge in service of the faith through an unconstrained testing of everything given in spirit, nature, and history."[52] In the midst of the neoscholastic revival and the swirl of antimodernism he retained a mediating role. He was not willing to remove fully the rich nineteenth-century tradition of philosophy and theology in Germany and to replace it with an ideological and frequently superficial neoscholasticism. He could still introduce students to figures from the era of romantic idealism such as Staudenmaier and Schelling, who were already in 1900 rather neglected. He argued against historicism but not against history, against psychologism but not against the experiential, against the dictatorship of the subjective forms of consciousness but not against the roles of divine and human subjectivity.

An apologetic theologian and a philosopher, relatively unknown, remembered by a few lines of gratitude from a famous philosopher or by the coining of a name for controversial theologies, Braig was a moderately independent thinker in a time of secular and ecclesiastical ideologies, a bridge reaching from the early nineteenth century to the early twentieth.[53] In his figure, teaching in the university and conversing with students in the parks of Freiburg, we glimpse momentarily a witness to the intellectual world which lay between Brentano and Husserl. It was a final time for nineteenth-century Catholicism, awaiting a new century but also increasingly isolated from German society. Like Paul Schanz, he too was a product of the Catholic Tübingen school. "His teaching radiated outwards. . . . He was critical of neoscholasticism, as were all who belonged to the Tübingen school. Certainly with Braig that stream of courageous inquiry and thinking had in Freiburg an honorable and worthy end. It is remarkable that the older direction lasted so long, and that neoscholasticism so powerful in the area of dogmatics came to Freiburg only in the 1920s."[54] A master of theological literature, Braig was gifted at synthesizing a range of views and at observing their excesses. His writings, however, rarely went beyond apologetics and synthesis to any theological creativity and depth. He stood out as a serious surveyor of theologies, as a deft apologete for traditional Christianity against the increasing number of claims to explain away revelation, but his lectures and books ended at the point where a personal and original theology would have begun.

PART THREE

The End of an Era

8

Reform for the Next Century
(1898–1906)

AS THE YEAR 1900 approached, the Catholic dialogue with modernity shifted away from the speculative toward the practical, toward the social and the political. German Catholicism had its own identity: It was not split by the anticlerical, monarchist factions set in motion by the French Revolution, and the German clergy received a more thorough training than the clergy in Latin or Anglo-Saxon countries. Germany was less touched by modernist slogans and excesses, even as German industrial expansion raised new issues for the working class. Many Catholic intellectuals in Germany were priests who viewed the agitated, well-reported dialogues between Christianity and culture to be part of their world. In 1890 Paul Schanz contrasted the old worldviews (Greek and medieval) with the new structures of positive science. The followers of the old view, he said, could not fashion for their faith a vital and coherent framework in the modern world and wanted to dismiss every doubt and challenge. The new, of course, could be arrogant in their ridicule of anything outside of precise research.[1]

During the decades leading to 1914 Germany surpassed almost every country in economic and technological power. The middle class benefited greatly while the working class found its life changed: urban populations had work but not adequate housing or social stability. The representatives of idealist philosophy were viewed as purveyors of abstraction, and a "realistic" philosophy inevitably meant materialism. Such widespread instability led to division and prejudice within the increasingly urban Reich, for often political and social movements were supported by clergy or church movements. Germany sped toward a social crises which had multiple dimensions and could be overcome only by some kind of rebirth. Christianity lost its dominance over many areas of German culture, even as the idealist theories of self and society lost their power. At the same time further measures of secularization and centralization forced the Catholic church to struggle for its freedom. The national culture of the late nineteenth and early twentieth centuries in Germany was largely

Protestant-liberal and very much influenced by industrialization. Catholics were frequently viewed as provincial, rural, conservative, as enemies of progress.

Since 1885, however, German Catholics had been seeking to be participants in the Reich. They also sought their own stance toward modernity, a modernity which ranged from clinic to factory, a modernity increasingly attacked by an aggressive Vatican. Christianity did not ignore the natural and psychological sciences into which philosophical idealism had evolved, but, as attention shifted away from speculation to social life, not Catholic Kantians but Catholic parliamentarians gathered to discuss church reform in movements similar to those involving John Ireland and Isaac Hecker in the United States, the Sillonists in France, Baron von Hügel in England, and the followers of Rosmini in Italy. In the conflict between modernism and Catholicism a long and fixed tradition stood before a present age which found elsewhere new sources for its life and inspiration. The Kulturkampf had rallied Catholic diocesan life but it had also produced an isolation, a condition of social minority and of clerical dominance. For Bismarck the Center Party was "*reichsfeindlich,*" and so Catholics (for whom cooperation with Marxists and socialists was not a possibility) seemed caught between patriotism and religious conviction. From 1880 to 1914 a constant concern of German Catholics (18 million in comparison to 31 million Protestants) was full acceptance in society, the removal of their "rental status" in the Reich as it had existed under Bismarck.

After 1890 publications armed with statistics argued that Catholics were marginalized in education and the professions.[2] Illustrating the difference in incomes, the Protestant 35 percent of the population in Cologne (the "German Rome") paid 50 percent of the taxes while in Baden Protestants paid twice the amount Catholics did. In 1869 in Prussian territories there were seven million Catholics and ten million Protestants, but out of 556 university professors only a tenth were Catholic and in the sciences perhaps a twentieth, and the percentage declined in the following years.[3] Funds for universities and schools almost doubled in the years after 1890 (hundreds of new primary schools were built), but the percentage of Catholics in professorships or school administration fell yearly.

Nonetheless, by supporting the objectives of Wilhelminian politics, Catholics and the Center Party attained more influence in the 1880s, but they never reached beyond the outer courts of power; in Berlin and Prussia there could be no question of significant positions, but even in Catholic Rhineland and Westphalia the ministries were filled by East-Prussians, and in Bavaria by agnostic liberals.

The excesses of ultramontanism and the cultural repression of Catholics brought the dual struggle of Catholicism to its climax in the years from 1900 to 1914. On the one hand, it wanted to "leave the ghetto," to be a participant in modern liberalism; on the other hand, it sought to modify clerical and curial authoritarianism. Paradoxically, both the government's attacks and the Catholic engagement with the socially deprived helped the Catholic church resist the pressures of science, secularism, and religious liberalism. And yet Catholics were constrained by the ambitions not just of the state but of the church. The Kulturkampf had strengthened the authority of both episcopacy and Vatican. An ill-informed Rome saw most aspects of northern European life to be hostile to revelation and authority, while the ultramontane faction among journalists and theologians feared any further democratization in society. So the tension between a political and cultural inferiority and a militant ultramontanism grew in the first years of the twentieth century. Caught between Berlin and Rome, Catholics sought in a surge of addresses, books, and journals a new—even a reformed—identity.

I. *"Reformkatholizismus"*

"Reform Catholicism" was a name given to various movements and figures who advocated change and renewal in the church. Their interests ranged from an acceptance of developments in natural science to an advocacy of pastoral changes that were displeasing to the Vatican. Georg Schwaiger describes the reformers as "loyal to revelation and the church even though they dealt with the problems of the time more decisively and sometimes more obstreperously than their contemporaries."[4] Also called "Contemporary Catholicism" or "Critical Catholicism," *Reformkatholizismus* was not a single organization but a term including various programs for change. The most diverse issues came together in their causes: late-idealist philosophy and the question of clerical celibacy; natural science and religious art; social reform and the role of the laity.[5] All shared a certain anti-Roman and anti-Jesuit stance. There was even an animosity to the political Catholicism of the past as exemplified in the Center Party. If a few of these reformers eventually left the church, at the beginning they sustained loyalty to Catholicism and, in contrast to modernists according to Rome's description, they intended to respect the basic structures of the faith and the church.

"*Reformkatholizismus*," the collective name for diverse reformist groups, was coined by a priest of Bamberg, Joseph Müller, in his book *Reform Catholicism, the Religion of the Future for the Educated of All*

Confessions, published in 1899.[6] Author of undistinguished philosophical textbooks, Müller's aggressive but unsubstantial book gave a name and slogan—"*Reform*"—to the liberal directions within Catholicism at the turn of the century, even if most advocates of change disliked that name and preferred "progressive Catholicism."

Müller began by observing Catholics and Protestants engaged in multiple types of social competition; he too used statistics to argue that Catholics were behind. Protestants, although a small minority, had a considerable role in Catholic *Länder*, but the opposite was not true. Catholics were converting to Protestantism for social advancement. The seminary education of the clergy and the dominance of religious orders through their cloistered isolation from the universities kept Catholics from public life, and thus Catholics were not adequately represented in the sciences and arts. What were Catholics to do before a campaign asserting that to be German was to be Lutheran?[7] Müller made several suggestions for overcoming this worsening situation: contrast the richness and fullness of the Catholic past with the few principles of Protestantism; acknowledge the neoscholastic monopoly as a hindrance; present church authority in a more positive light; encourage vernacular in the liturgy, an end to celibacy, a focused role for bishops, and a part for the laity in ministry and decision making. Catholicism too could support "progress," the motto of the times. There should be a rapprochement with Protestantism by means of a positive interpretation of theologies of inspiration and justification, complemented by a legitimate critique of the Vatican and the Jesuits. Müller did not call for reform in the speculative areas of exegesis or philosophy but in the relationship of Catholicism to the current life of the German Reich. The church had lost its influence upon the educated classes, and Vatican authority and neoscholastic logic could not reverse that trend; he saw the condemnations of Frohschammer and Schell as serious mistakes. "What is most characteristic of our age is that no one will subject oneself to an *imperium*."[8]

"*Reformkatholizismus*" meant for many simply renewal and reformation in the thinking and structures of Roman Catholicism. It was critical of liberal Protestantism and atheism but also of frozen neoscholasticisms. In the spring of 1906 a group of laymen, including prominent members of the Central Party, founded a Society for Christian Culture, which advocated a change in the procedures of the Congregation of the Index.[9] As the neoscholastics had romanticized the Middle Ages, Reform Catholicism idealized the romantic restoration in the early nineteenth century. Without questioning the revealed content of Christianity, it accepted the rapid succession of scientific discoveries in the natural and the social sciences.

In September 1900 the fifth international Congress of Catholic Scholars met in Munich (their title recalled the assembly of Döllinger in 1863). The addresses protested exaggerated conservatism, and Jesuit historian Hartmann Grisar argued against the model of two theologies, one for scholars and one for the common people. On October 20, 1902, a meeting of Catholic intellectuals (including members of the Bavarian royal family) interested in reform was held near Munich. Herman Schell gave the main address, in which he urged a restoration of Catholic intellectual life as well as a greater role for the laity. He was not in favor of ending clerical celibacy or of carping at Vatican authority.

Schell was not only not a modernist but kept his distance from reform movements even as he approved of their general direction.[10] Nevertheless, German reform movements cannot be understood apart from the figure of Schell and his Roman condemnation. His stature as a speculative theologian was unequaled, and his lectures on Catholic dialogue with science and religious culture as well as his writings on a progressive church for the coming century had enormous influence. His censure (unaccompanied by charges of clear doctrinal divergency) was a disciplinary action without German support and brought a loss of credibility for Rome; further petty attempts to silence him during his lifetime and to ignore him after his death only made Catholics of a non-ultramontane bent determined upon change.

Franz Xaver Klasen, the editor of *Das 20. Jahrhundert*, convinced the Bavarian group to set up an organization and a newsletter. This meeting alarmed some German Catholics, for it gave political form to the swirling movement begun by theologians, formed by polemical academics, and then amplified by journalists. The rabid neoscholastic Michael Glossner attacked Müller's "brochure" and saw that the slogan "*Reformkatholizismus*" could lead to dangerous misunderstandings. Glossner recognized that Müller did not want to remove church authority—but were not the sources of this "platform Protestantism of *Wissenschaft*" already separated from church authority? How could scholasticism be the source of Catholic inferiority? There could be no easy harmony between church and modern education just as there could be none between Christ and Belial. "The division reaches to logic itself, to the simplest laws of thinking."[11]

This period of meetings and pamphlets increased Rome's anxiety in the years just prior to the anti-modernist measures of 1907. The Vatican urged German bishops to denounce lay organizations for church reform and to combat plans for remembering the dead Schell. Bishop P. W. Keppler supported the reform movements through 1902. Keppler, former professor in Freiburg and bishop of Rottenburg (the diocese for

Tübingen) had approved (with reservations) the publication of Albert Ehrhard's books on the future of Catholicism, but then, in a lecture "On True and False Reform," he displayed a surprising hostility to theologians and journalists whom a few years earlier he had praised as friends. Keppler had become frightened over the ensemble of criticisms of the church's institutions: he granted that areas in the church needed improvement (as a university professor he had taught that the church's moral theology was outdated) but the church also had to criticize the times. "False reformers in all ages can be recognized because in their plans the religious, supernatural power plays no role. Recently they were speaking of a 'religious Catholicism' and so you would think they prize most the religious powers of reform—but they do not!"[12] One particular reformer, he continued with an implicit reference to Franz Xaver Kraus, by urging a shift from "political" reform to "religious" reform, had injured the church. Above all, the emotion generated by so many suggested reforms would lead to chaos.

The reform movements gained prominence in the press. Cardinal Rampolla communicated to Bishop Keppler Leo XIII's praise for his address. The suggestions of ecclesiastical reform soon yielded to social and political issues. Activists, not modernists, represented liberal German Catholicism, and only after the Roman anti-modernist decrees did a very few Catholics like Joseph Schnitzer espouse a theological modernism. The appointment of the former Dominican Master General Andreas Frühwirth as nuncio in Munich in 1907 aimed at securing a theological outpost which would observe any shift of Catholic intellectuals toward reform.[13] At the time of the papal sanctions against modernism in 1907 the "Reform-Catholic" tendencies in Germany, with their different goals and activities, had hardly anything in common with the doctrinal mind-sets censured by the Encyclical *Pascendi*.[14]

II. Theologians of Reform

The goal of the German Catholic reform movements was to overcome the ghetto mentality in which Catholicism had been isolated since the Kulturkampf. Encounters with modern politics and literature and reconciliation with modern science were needed, while the exclusiveness of neoscholasticism as well as the authoritarianism of the central church administration were rejected. Herman Schell, Albert Ehrhard, and F. X. Kraus[15] were theologians associated with *Reformkatholizismus*, although all were too committed to theological scholarship to be identified with any one cause. Lesser figures were Sebastian Merkle and Philipp Funk.[16]

A third group might include more volatile and radical advocates like Otto Sickenberger, Thaddäus Engert, and Joseph Schnitzer, who came to prefer the movement to the Roman church.[17] The arrival of the twentieth century was greeted by a number of publications, large and small, outlining each author's program for Catholicism in the coming century.[18] To portray this general movement of reform within German Catholicism at the intersection of centuries we will look at three figures who wrote programs for the twentieth century. The first is a historian, Albert Ehrhard (an earlier chapter has summarized Schell's program). The second is Georg von Hertling, a centrist politician with a background in university philosophy and a commitment to Catholic renewal and identity. Finally, we will sketch Joseph Schnitzer as an example of *Reformkatholizismus* becoming *Modernismus*.

Albert Ehrhard

From J. A. Möhler and J. J. I. von Döllinger on, the century had produced Catholic church historians who held critical and reformist views about the interpretation and direction of Roman Catholicism. Albert Ehrhard, historian and professor at universities like Vienna and Strassburg, became an advocate of a more open attitude in the church. Born in Alsatia, he studied theology in the Strassburg seminary, was ordained in Münster in 1885 and pursued doctoral studies in Munich and Würzburg from 1885 to 1887. The great historian Joseph Hergenröther (1824–1890) at the Vatican Archives provided Ehrhard—in Rome for specialized studies—with a model for the scholarship which would produce his church history and three-volume study on Photius. There was also the influence of F. S. Hettinger (1819–1890), a leading apologete, who treated Ehrhard as a younger colleague and entrusted the editing of certain works to him. This acquaintanceship drew him out of historical research into contemporary theological debate. Würzburg also brought friendship with Herman Schell, the epicenter of conflict and creativity. Ehrhard was a more composed and peaceful personality than the enthusiastic Schell, and they disagreed over the degree of critique and reform necessary for the new century. Nevertheless, the Munich cultural philosopher Alois Dempf believed that it was the Würzburg atmosphere which led Ehrhard to his theory that the church, like culture, lived in historical cultural epochs. "Church history is the middle point of world history in the sense that it has to do with the highest and most important factor of development for humanity, the Christian religion. The cultural ideas of Ehrhard temper his view of history; religion ought not be separated from culture in a stance of denouncing the world. But too, religion is not historically determined, a mere cultural appearance on the same level as state, science, and art."[19]

As a professor in Vienna, Ehrhard experienced radical movements which advocated separation from Rome, for a few Austrian Catholics wished to be free of the civil and ecclesiastical repressions they identified with the distant Counter-Reformation. With money from Protestant churches and ideas from liberal philosophies of religion, they influenced a very small percentage of the population, but journalistic conflicts and publicized conversions to Protestantism kept them in the public eye. Amid the turmoil of Vienna, Ehrhard studied closely two significant publications of 1900: Adolf von Harnack's *Das Wesen des Christentums* and then H. S. Chamberlain's *Grundlagen des 19. Jahrhundert.* For Harnack, Catholicism was a pagan residue which the Christian ethic had not removed, while Chamberlain saw the church, precisely as international, to be inimical to German nationalism. Both implied that a liberal German Christianity would replace the mediterranean superstition of Catholicism. Vienna also brought to Ehrhard the motif of "culture" as a framework for the understanding of religion in history.

Not completely at home in Vienna, he accepted a professorship in Freiburg in 1902 to replace Kraus, but soon moved on to Strassburg and ended his career teaching from 1920 to 1927 in Bonn, where he died in 1940. Ehrhard achieved lasting recognition for his employment of secular history in a multivolume history of the church and for studies in Greek patristics and Byzantine theology. He had friends among the hierarchy, for Cardinal Kopp of Breslau favored his reform plans for seminary education and convinced Rome to make Ehrhard a monsignor in 1901.

The Twentieth Century

By the end of the year 1900 Ehrhard had completed *Catholicism and the Twentieth Century in Light of the Church's Development in Modernity* (to which Bishop Keppler gave ecclesiastical approval), a book which the debates around him drew from his pen. Although it mirrored in form and content the interests of a church historian, it went through twelve printings in little over a year.[20] Ehrhard had found Schell's similar book on Catholicism and progress in the future too bold and so it is ironic that the historian was plunged into bitter controversy after publishing the same kind of work.

The situation of the church, he wrote, did not come from a particular heresy but from a multitude of questions, indeed from the issues of how Roman Catholicism would be a "vital factor in culture," and of how it would escape the predictions of those, like Chamberlain, who asserted that without fundamental changes the church would lose two-thirds of its members in the coming century. The current situation in the Catholic church was externally a state of siege by elements in society and internally one lacking clarity and courage.

A new century can enter into world history quietly and harmlessly. But this first year of the twentieth century according to the Christian measure of time is certainly well suited to explore the heritage of the century just laid to rest, and further, to uncover the tasks of the new century. . . . For Catholics there is nothing more important than to look at the destiny of Catholicism and of the Catholic church in the new century.[21]

The present world in which Catholicism finds itself was determined "by three great phenomena":[22] (a) the church seen as an opponent of modern culture; (b) the growing alienation of educated and cultural circles from the Catholic church, even in countries where the Church predominated; (c) the critique of theologies, church politics, and liturgy.

Solutions to clusters of problems lay first in the historical knowledge of why they emerged. One must discern the areas in which the Catholic church and the modern world seem to be, or are, opposed, and then work in the twentieth century to overcome these conflicts. As a remote background for the church's difficulty with modernity Ehrhard singled out five "groups of factors." First was the decline of a strong influence of the church upon the life of Christian people. Beyond this was the factor of the rebirth of pagan-classical cultural ideals, and, thirdly, the emergence of new approaches to natural science and to history. These involved philosophically the end of scholasticism and politically the delineation of the nation, hence a rejection of the universalism of the Middle Ages. Finally "the most powerful factor of the modern age proceeds from the alterations in the life of the mind: subjectivism and individualism."[23] A lack of a universal perspective, individualism and subjectivism, laicism, humanism, positivism in history, science, art and psychology—these marked the birth of the present epoch at the juncture between two centuries.

Before Ehrhard offered remedies for this condition, he sketched its background from the Renaissance and Reformation to the end of the nineteenth century. Protestantism would be "an authentic source of *religious life*," while the Enlightenment with its hostility to revelation and faith was more questionable. Catholicism renewed itself in the age of romanticism. "In France and Germany for an entire human generation from 1815 to 1848 [there was] a unified character which brought together church restoration, religious romanticism, and Catholic liberalism."[24]

The second half of the nineteenth century began with a time of transition whose changes were so severe that it "can be designated *a new age.*"[25] The starting point was easy to find, the accession of Gregory XVI to the papacy. This time of upheaval witnessed struggles for both freedom and tradition, a turbulent era which appeared in all the European countries and in North America. Two aspects dominated the church's further conversation with modernity: an emphasis upon confessionalism and an intensive ecclesiastical central authority. Spiritually this centrism was ultramontane, while theologically it found a narrow unity in neoscholasticism.[26] After the 1870s the central period of modernity began "in which we now live and move and whose depiction therefore offers particular difficulties."[27] The evaluation among Catholics of the century now concluding was quite disputed: Was it a time of ceaseless revolution or one of restoration? Was it a time of hostility to religion or of "spiritual secularization"?

The Meeting with Modernity

At the turn of the century, the spirit of the modern world appeared to some Catholic thinkers as hostile or alien to the church. Ehrhard stated:

> Such an opposition reveals itself in a *threefold struggle* which modernity has imposed upon the Catholic church: first, the struggle over its divine character as the sole commissioned bearer of the Christian religion . . . ; second, the struggle concerning the absolute truth of its religious teachings and moral prescriptions vis-à-vis modern philosophy and liberal Protestant theology; . . . and third, the struggle for efficacy in espousing a theistic worldview and a moral-religious ideal of life vis-à-vis the anti-theistic and anti-religious movements of today.[28]

But the idea that the individualism or subjectivity of modernity was *a priori* opposed to Catholicism was to be rejected as was any insistence that Catholicism eschewed progress or that authority excluded freedom. "So again and again we reach the insight that behind these subtle assertions of an essential opposition between the Catholic church and the modern world, particularly the German world, no authentically scientific spirit stands."[29] A "law of progress" was always at work: faith and religion had their individual and collective movements. Society should recall that it owed much of its culture to Christianity, while Catholicism should understand that its life, in theory and practice, was intertwined with the succession of cultural periods.

> From these insights comes the important result that the educated Catholic cannot be forced to give up the Catholic church in the name of modern culture . . . but also the more important consequence that the efficacy of the Catholic church does not consist in an eternal

fight with the modern world but in the reconciliation of the modern spirit with Catholicism and through this reconciliation the salvation of modern society.[30]

Interestingly, Ehrhard saw one area where Catholicism was carrying on a dialogue with the "modern worldview": philosophy. When modern philosophy was not frozen, it contained metaphysics and was capable of theology. "The position of modern thinking is not unchanging. I view the entire development of modern philosophy not as the end but, in its perduring stimuli, as the beginning of a new effort in serving to explain the world and moral life theoretically—its term, however, lies far, far in the future. . . . More than before, [Catholicism] must cultivate an inner relationship to modern philosophy; it should not be content with always opposing it with earlier philosophies but must understand and critique modern philosophers in order to conquer the new intellectual problems which touch the contemporary world. . . ."[31] Ehrhard concluded his book with a survey of concrete issues that he arranged around theology, philosophy and history: the role of Catholics in politics and universities, the authority structure of the church, religious education in schools, seminaries, literature, and art.[32]

Resonance and Controversy

In comparison with the decades of shallow ecclesiastical understanding which would follow, Ehrhard's views were a mature appreciation of modernity and held a strong confidence in Catholic history. Catholicism had to understand and work within the issues of the age: it could not influence this age while trying to live in another. Ehrhard's first book attracted considerable attention in Germany and Austria; read in France and Great Britain, it drew congratulatory letters from Adolf von Harnack, Sebastian Merkle, and Joseph Sauer, while both university students and imperial Kaiser were enthusiastic.[33] Curiously much of the popular press found this dry and careful study to be radical. Von Hügel wrote from Rome of how the book had its admirers and "unjust opponents"; he was considering an English translation with a detailed commentary.[34]

Initially the sharpest criticism was voiced in Austria, where Ehrhard (then in his late thirties) had recently been made a member of the Austrian Academy of Sciences and a monsignor. Representing Vienna and its archbishop, Cardinal Gruscha, A. Rösler called the work anti-Catholic.[35] There were bishops and cardinals who defended him (Bishop Keppler had received painful letters from Rome over the bestowed *imprimatur*), but rumors spread through Rome that, even if the *Osservatore Romano* mentioned the book positively, the Index was studying it for censure. Ehrhard traveled to Rome to remove the cloud of suspicion and was received by Leo XIII and Cardinal Rampolla, who mentioned a few desirable modifications for the new edition of the book.[36]

Opposition to Ehrhard intensified. Keppler, who through this period chose a middle course, was strongly influenced by conservatives in the composition of his address, "True and False Reform" in 1902. While not mentioning the historian by name, he was clearly combating his book as he described critical reformers as dilettantes ("*Margarinekatholizismus*") picking and choosing among the practices and beliefs of Catholicism. Though he did not use the term "modernism," Keppler spoke of "modernized Christianity" and concluded that this desire for dialogue between education and faith, culture and Catholicism would end only in "Americanism." In January, Rampolla wrote to Keppler congratulating him for his efforts against the "*temerarios pseudoreformatorum*" and their "*audaciam novatorum.*"[37] But the harmony hoped for by Rome between the Curia and Keppler was unrealistic; the bishop was no supporter of papal absolutism or of Vatican disdain for the government of Germany and would not go further in rejecting the considerations of intellectuals on German Catholics in the modern world.

In Ehrhard's intra-Catholic controversy (there was also a discussion of the book by non-Catholics) the battleground chosen by the ultramontanes was not "reform" or "philosophy" but "history" and particularly "liberalism." Ehrhard replied to his critics in 1902 with *Liberal Catholicism? A Word to My Critics.*[38] There he answered charges of being a liberal urging schism or an irresponsible diluter of dogma. Later he turned into an article a lecture he had been giving to Catholic circles in Berlin defending his view of the church in the twentieth century; "The International Situation of Catholic Theology" depicted *Pascendi* not as a defense of faith but as a danger to theological scholarship.[39] Distancing himself from both the directions of a Loisy and the constrained cultural politics of the Curia, he published in 1908 "The New Situation of Catholic Theology." There would never have been, he observed, a rediscovery of Aristotle or a theology of Aquinas if the present curial controls had been operative in the thirteenth century.[40] Suspected of "*Reformkatholizismus*" and modernism, he had his honorary prelature withdrawn in 1908 (it was returned in 1922), although some German bishops continued to defend him. He wrote: "Modernism was quite unsuited to try to separate me from the Mother church I love deeply. Modernism is not specifically anti-Catholic but is directed against Christian religion in general by undermining its foundations and presuppositions."[41] Chosen rector of Strassburg University in 1911, he fought against the imposition of anti-modernist oath. Alois Dempf concluded that he lived as a historian drawn into being a prophet.

Because he worked at the highest level of research, he saw the false presuppositions which claimed to fashion a presuppositionless research, presuppositionless in insisting upon the removal of the miraculous, the description of all doctrine as hellenization, the indication that all church structure was Roman. . . . He created the hope that precisely the correct understanding of church history as the history of the highest achievements in culture would move the intelligence of his contemporaries—alienated from or hostile to the church—to appreciate anew tradition.[42]

Gifted as a lecturer and preacher and confident with the latest methods of historical research, Ehrhard was surprised at a fame which came not from scholarship but from a popular analysis of Catholicism amid the contributions and conflicts of modernity.

Georg von Hertling

Georg von Hertling began as a professor of medieval and social philosophy and ended as the head of the Bavarian state. He too published a study of German Catholicism at 1900, but his work is that of a distinguished statesman whose perspective differs from that of reformers and scholars.[43]

A Catholic in Hesse

To sketch Hertling's life is to voyage through the world of German Catholicism from the 1850s to World War I. He was born in Darmstadt in 1843 of the Palatine lesser nobility, his father was a judge of Hesse whose ancestors had followed the Palatine ruler Karl Theodor to Munich when he became elector of Bavaria in the late eighteenth century. Hertling's mother was related to Clemens and Bettina Brentano, artists and catalysts of Rhenish romanticism. His maternal grandfather was the first Catholic mayor of Frankfurt, and he grew up in an atmosphere where he was conscious of belonging to a minority, yet one in which he took pride. Visits along the Rhine, he said, left him with three great impressions: Gothic architecture, Joseph Görres' thought, and the personality of Bishop W. E. Ketteler.

His philosophical studies began in Münster, where he was introduced early to neoscholasticism by F. J. Clemens, Kuhn's first opponent. Considering briefly the priesthood, he thought of studying theology at Tübingen but then persued law and philosophy in Munich, where he heard Döllinger lecture on history. He chose Berlin, however, for his doctorate, drawn there by Adolf Trendelenburg's critique of Hegel and advocacy of Aristotle. After his habilitation in Bonn in 1867 he taught

the history of philosophy there. His memoirs give a fascinating account
of factions in the Catholic faculties and seminaries during the decade between the Munich assembly of 1864 and Vatican I. Hertling experienced
the alienation of his relative Franz Brentano, from the church, Döllinger's
exit, and the divisions in theological faculties after Vatican I. In 1876 he
founded the Görresgesellschaft, which gave him a forum for his ideas on
German Catholic life.[44] In 1875 he was elected to represent Coblenz in
the Reichstag, where he remained (with the exception of the three years
after 1900) until 1912. He influenced the legal framework of Germany
as a member of the Center Party. Active politically on the Rhine and an
adviser for the founding of the Catholic theological faculty in Strassburg,
in 1882 he accepted that university's newly erected chair for philosophy
agreed upon with the Vatican.

Hertling's concern with the life of Catholicism and with church-
state questions was all-pervasive. His involvement in theology, however,
was sparse, although he wrote a critique of *Der alte und der neue Glaube*
of D. F. Strauss and a response to Albrecht Ritschl. Hertling appeared
frequently at congresses to discuss the role of Catholics in universities,
the arts, and German cultural life. In 1892 he published a study on John
Locke and the next year a study on natural law and political theory. As
a philosopher and a statesman he advocated limiting the power of the
state and enumerating the rights of persons to be protected by the state.
His writings treated Aristotle, Augustine, Albertus Magnus, and Aquinas
as well as Darwin and Descartes. His university lectures were on the
history of philosophy complemented by social theory, and his stance in
philosophy and politics, while indebted to Greek and medieval thought,
was not neoscholastic. He urged a serious dialogue with contemporary
intellectual life and fashioned out the areas of law and political science
a Christian social theory and praxis rather than socialism.

After 1880 the philosopher devoted himself to politics but also to
social questions, e.g., workers' rights and the conditions of mothers. By
1909 he was leader of the Center Party in the Reich. In 1891 he was
made Reichsrat for the crown of Bavaria and in 1912 he was Bavarian
minister-president, a leadership both beneficial and popular. He was not
able to avoid a summons to be *Reichskanzler* from 1917 to 1918, although he foresaw the regime's brief duration and uncertain end in the
midst of the war.[45]

The Catholic Principle and Culture

Like Schell and Ehrhard, Hertling pondered the future of Catholicism at the turn of the century. Hertling's program for Catholicism had

been developed through addresses at the yearly meetings of the Görres-gesellschaft as he pondered the dialectic of "Catholic *Wissenschaft*" or the great motif of romantic idealism, "*Glauben und Wissen.*" Published in 1899, *Das Prinzip des Katholicismus und die Wissenschaft* offered a perspective from someone who was a philosopher, not a theologian; a statesman, not a bishop. "This book," Hertling wrote, "in a few weeks went through four editions, a sign of the degree of interest which existed then in these 'daily issues.' The non-Catholic press concerned itself with the work...but the conviction of the backwardness of Catholics was not so easily shaken and so my views were not really studied [by non-Catholics]."[46] There was a suspicion that Hertling's book might be censured by the Congregation of the Index, but the cardinals in Rome approved of the book, written as it was by a lay political theorist who held some of the highest positions in Bavaria and the Reich.

Hertling assessed the situation of German Catholics, acknowledging that they were poorly represented in political life, in parliament, in the civil bureaucracy, and in education. Even when Catholics qualified for positions, they were unlikely to receive a professorship in a prestigious institution aside from those in the Catholic south, for the potential colleagues, apart from qualifications, would dismiss the candidate with the remarks, "Who knows whether he's not ultramontane!"[47] In a strange ecumenism, Protestants and Jews were preferred to Catholics in Bavaria. What had begun the exclusion of Catholics? The secularization of the innumerable church institutions almost a century before. Catholicism was arranged around monastic institutions—abbey schools, orphanages, homes for the handicapped and aged—and, when they were seized by the state, Catholics were slow to build up new institutions.

The Catholic analyst of culture, he noted, should avoid two extremes: the claim that nothing valuable comes from an era marked by scientific agnosticism and the critique historical revelation; and the claim that the church alone was the matrix for culture. The world of 1900 viewed Catholicism as a religion of "the beyond," and indeed in this church the supernatural is not a myth but divine activity with historical objectivity.

> In Catholicism religion...has an objective, doctrinal content: a system of truths responds to the ultimate and highest questions about the origin and destiny of our poor earthly existence. Catholicism presupposes a faith in the facts of revelation and grounds the credibility of the individual truths precisely so that they form this revelation.[48]

The Catholic principle includes "the church founded by Christ in which humanity finds an effective institution of redemption, and the recognition of an ecclesial teaching authority to guard and proclaim revelation's truths."[49] Still, one has not grasped Catholicism at all if it appears like a cathedral or a distant empire; rather, it is a broad gathering of people, educated and simple, cultured and cloistered. The fact that Catholicism includes not just an intelligentsia but many classes and countries is an advantage—it is a true *"Volkskirche."*

Hertling addressed different questions. Could the "Catholic Principle" accept a contemporary understanding of science with its controversial characteristic of freedom? Do Christianity, religion, and Catholicism hold culture and education back? And he offered his responses. There is a difference between *Wissenschaft* at the beginning and at the end of the nineteenth century: now natural science is experimental, studying the conditions, limits, interaction of phenomena through applied not theoretical, mathematics. This move of knowledge and research toward measured objectivity became for some an argument that revelation is either a pure illusion or something objective which our minds can touch. Faith benefits by science, accepting both the limits and the freedom its own world offers without either faith or science immediately instructing the other. In life, faith and reason interact without diminishing the full rights of each sphere.

Modern Theology

Hertling's observations in theology are interesting, for unlike Schell and Ehrhard, professional theologians, the philosopher-statesman had an eye for concrete problems which he did not solve with a new theory but clarified practically. In one sense, he noted, faith in revelation is like natural science: both have their facts. Theology begins with faith, with facts and events as perceived by faith; in this, as was already recognized in the Middle Ages, it differs from other sciences. "Theology is in a strict and proper sense the systematic joining and complete unfolding of the truths of faith revealed by Christ and proffered by the church."[50] Faith is not a straitjacket but a realm for theology to explore. Dogma and the teaching authority of the church are markers for theology, but much of what they affirm was itself uncovered by theology at some point in history. So, to understand dogmatic statements we must understand the cultural and philosophical context of their words and ideas. Thomas Aquinas, "the greatest systematician known in history," is a historically fashioned figure even when he determines for subsequent centuries "form, expression, and mode of teaching."[51] If Christianity, Hertling observed, had hypothetically moved more toward Asia rather than toward Europe, theological form and expression (but not its content) would have been quite different from today's approach, marked by Greek thought-forms.

One can only conclude that future generations, like earlier ones, will have their own theologies.

Hertling was not positively inclined toward theologies drawn from Descartes, Kant, and Hegel: he did not object to the modern philosophical enterprise but thought that those philosophers (although their influence was widespread) were not in fact suitable to expressing Christian theology. Even if Catholicism was not sympathetic to the absorption of revelation into feeling and personality, nevertheless the role of the subject must be admitted. He approved of the work of the Tübingen school (where he once hoped to study theology) in historical and biblical research even as he criticized an exaggerated independence toward the New Testament.[52]

What is the relationship of church authority to theology? he asked. The church's role concerns the totality of the content of faith: a preservative service, and the magisterium is to be preferred to an individual's creative ideas. Controversy and conflict in theology should be avoided. Does this mean that a Catholic theologian faculty at a university is not possible? No, because Catholic theology clearly has a proper subject matter and principles; and besides these university faculties serve German Catholics as well as the wider public. The role of theology at the university is crucial and cannot be accomplished by seminaries or monasteries. "Not the historians but dogmatic theologians, apologetes, and moral theologians must use the questions and intellectual currents of the day."[53] For Hertling, the fundamental theological questions about faith and science were being used as excuses to end all Catholic theological faculties at universities. Hertling invoked the subject of one of his books, Albert the Great, as a defender of living theology: "What we should be investigating is how God, the highest architect, according to the measure of his free will serves the things created by him, not to work wonders, but to facilitate what can occur in the realm of nature, the natural causalities planted in things."[54] Difficulties arise whenever theologians decide that their views alone represent the entire population.

As 1900 approached, Catholics were less present in universities and chanceries and more active in church clubs, labor unions and congresses. Some of these organizations Hertling helped to fashion, many of them he vitalized. Never reactionary or ideological, ecumenical by being raised in a largely Protestant German culture, accepted by Prussia and Bavaria his leadership and ideas addressed labor movements, social questions, the nature of a Catholic intellectual, book publishing, and scholarship in science. Catholics were not so different from Protestants in theology or practice, and one might hope that Protestantism in the future would put away prejudice and discrimination. In 1925, Baden's

Kultusminister, a Protestant, began an address to the Görresgesellschaft in Heidelberg by describing this era: "Brave men like Hertling, Schell, Julius Bachem, and Carl Muth, shook the German Catholic world in order to lead it out of its fortress, to lead it again into the midst of the life and activity of the entire people, even when this seemed at first strange and uncomfortable. With an extraordinary expansion of all these activities Catholicism stands before us today, committed to engage and critique the scientific, artistic, social, political, and philosophical aspects of culture."[55]

Joseph Schnitzer

With Joseph Schnitzer the movement of reform became a volatile modernism, one ultimately rejecting dogma and papacy. Born in 1859 in Lauingen, he studied theology from 1881 to 1886 in Munich, completing during years of parish ministry a dissertation on the medieval theologian Berengarius of Tours. He taught in Dillingen for some years while writing a study on marriage in canon law. In 1902 he began teaching history of dogma at Munich. He published the first article of a life-long research project on Savonarola in 1898, disagreeing with Ludwig von Pastor's view of the Florentine Dominican. (In Rome the Dominicans worked to keep this article favoring their confrere off the Index.)[56]

Schnitzer's life was dramatically changed by the encyclical *Pascendi* and the year following it. The Munich professor wrote in his diary. "They [papal decrees] damn everything which I have thought, taught, and presented in print and lecture; to accept them would be moral suicide."[57] After corresponding with Schell and Ehrhard (but eschewing their prudence and moderation), Schnitzer published articles in 1908 which thoroughly criticized the Vatican's measures. Copies reached Rome with unusual rapidity, and their impact was such that within a week Pius X had suspended its author from his priestly ministry and even from the reception of the sacraments. This church historian's views about the central beliefs of Christianity went beyond suggestions for ecclesiastical change. Depicting the Vatican as ignorant and irresponsible, he wrote: "The Rome of the encyclical is the real Rome."[58] There, he commented, absolutism is forceably joined to scholasticism and antiquarianism, so that theology is reduced to something prelates know automatically (rendering theologians and researchers superfluous). Schnitzer's article ended in sarcasm: since the Holy Spirit only worked in the monopoly of prelates, the laity had no right to speak in the church. If the encyclical had missed any errors, there was no need for concern; the "Roman prelate-spirit" would continue to work and to bring under suspicion noble men whose only error was their research attained through hard work. The nuncio to Bavaria, Frühwirth, held back the publication of papal excommunication, trying to convince Schnitzer over some months to meet the Vatican's demands. Schnitzer was removed from lecturing in the theology faculty of Munich as his colleagues debated whether in fact his views were outside the Catholic interpretation of the supernatural character of Christianity, and then whether he could be moved to the faculty of philosophy.[59] Frühwirth informed the Munich university and government that Rome saw this as a test case for the world. In late 1908 (at the age of forty-nine) Schnitzer was forbidden any teaching position, excommunicated, and put on unlimited leave from the university. After acquiring a doctorate in Tübingen in philosophy, he worked on Philipp Funk's *Das Neue Jahrhundert* and published an overview of modernism.[60]

Schnitzer showed his interest in biblical-historical questions by publishing in 1910 *Did Jesus Found the Papacy?*[61] Texts in the Gospel according to Matthew were not historical, he concluded, and more important, Jesus could not have thought of leaving a solely hierarchical institution. Articles appeared advocating a mythological interpretation of Christian and Catholic traditions. Vatican and government officials (including von Hertling) worked at resolving Schnitzer's relationship to the university. Deliberations dragged on with the result that in 1914 he received a pension as honorary professor in philosophy. In 1923 he was listed as again holding lectures, this time in the area of the history of religions.

His interests had turned to the world religions: he lectured on their relationship to Christianity in Europe, traveled to Japan, and at fifty years of age studied Sanskrit, Pali, and Assyrian. Time was still spent working on research in Italy for the two-volume study, *Savonarola: Ein Kulturbild aus der Zeit der Renaissance*, which appeared in 1924.[62] At the age of seventy he published studies on original sin in human religion and in the Judaeo-Christian tradition.

As the twentieth century progressed, German bishops tried to reconcile Schnitzer to the church, but he would not take the anti-modernist oath. He lived in the hope that a *"papa angelicus"* would someday occupy the chair of St. Peter, full of renewal and reconciliation. He had shrewdly observed in 1911 in a lecture, "Catholicism and Modernism":

> Catholicism requires a religious pope. This is the shocking tragedy of the pontificate of Pius X, that he, the religious *human being*, had wanted to be a religious *pope* but became only an ultramontane pope because the situation and the conditions were stronger than he was. We live, however, in the unshakable confidence that a Pius XI

or Pius XII will follow Pius X and be a truly religious pope: even more, a *"papa angelicus,"* that angelic pope of the future who for many centuries has been the object of the ceaseless, never stifled longing of Christianity.[63]

Norbert Trippen sums up this strange career:

Without doubt Schnitzer changed in the course of his life, and he became a modernist in the sense of *Pascendi*. We would not be able to state this so firmly if his diaries and other writings did not support it. He saw himself as a modernist and expected to be so designated.[64]

He ended his career more perhaps as a liberal Protestant of his age than as a Roman Catholic caught up in facets of reform or modernism.

III. The Reform of the Future

Catholic intellectuals—some explicitly, like our analysts of the twentieth century, but many implicitly—perceived the changing age and their alienation from it. *Reformkatholizismus* was a network of movements espousing engagement with culture, advocating presence in society and culture, and modernity's intent upon reforming the church. One misses the similarity and differences among people and movements when one remains with concepts like *"Reformkatholizismus,"* "modernism," and "liberal Catholicism." There are ecclesiastical and theological differences between the true "modernists" like Joseph Schnitzer, Hugo Koch, and Franz Wieland, and those who temporarily admitted the title of "Reform Catholics" like Albert Ehrhard, or Sebastian Merkle; a third group, including F. X. Kraus, preferred to be called "liberal Catholics," while an "orthodox" ensemble would include Joseph Sauer, Heinrich Schrörs, F. X. Funk, and Georg von Hertling. And then there was a younger generation with figures like Martin Spahn and Carl Muth, about whom we will learn more in the next chapter.

The world changed markedly, cultural historians tell us, between 1900 and 1914. The theater became more daring, literature more psychological; painting found its way to abstraction while music offered both the emotional palette of late romanticism and multiple tonality. Epistemology flowed into psychology; *Wissenschaft* into applied technology. Geniuses as different as Freud and Kandinsky emerged. But creative and optimistic forces were not succeeding among the political and social conflicts in Germany on the eve of World War I. In many ways these upheavals intersected with the reformist controversies over the ecclesial, theological, and pastoral mission of Catholicism.[65] And yet, there was a freshness in the prognoses and programs of Schell, Hertling, and Ehrhard. In their writings lay the unity and variety of the century coming to a close, and the pages invariably offered a positive vision, a hopeful stance toward the arrival of a new century. H. Dachs observes:

> Although Pius X was convinced that Germany was a tumultuous assembly place of modernists, for all practical purposes there was neither in Austria nor Germany a significant modernist movement. From this, however, we should not conclude that harmony and peace dominated German Catholicism around 1900. . . . But one cannot call the reform movements of those years a variation of modernism, although all of them had their roots in the tension between church and world, revelation and science.[66]

The hostile Vatican reaction to German theologians, and then to the seldom discovered modernists, was a product of the methods of the leadership of the church; then, too, the press delighted in spotlighting the polemics which the Catholic church consistently stimulated. For Pius X, the word "modernism" named the cause of all the problems north of the Alps. Theological silence joined to social upheaval marked the turn of the century, and a future synthesis was difficult to imagine.

The reform movement never gained much support from the German bishops and it found only suspicion in Rome. In different ways both German bishops and curial cardinals were shaken by the situation the church had reached. Any weakening of the bishops' activity by Rome would bring not orthodoxy but a loss of independence and vigor in theology and social action. The spirit of reform, of newness, lived on in numerous social organizations, and this gave German Catholicism around 1900 a new public image. Unfortunately, at the same time that the practical concerns for a new ecclesial and social face for the church were being neglected, more measures from Rome impeded the meager reform movements and challenged creative Catholic theology. The next chapter describes the embattled conditions of Catholic life amid German culture in the last years of the nineteenth century.

9
Through and beyond Modernism (1907–1914)

THIS SURVEY of church and culture has moved from the conflicts between neoscholastic and idealist theologies to the instigation of reform movements and their conservative opponents. The history begun in the 1860s and now coming to a conclusion lacks comprehensiveness—it has only been an initial survey, one content with capturing briefly the contours of an age.

The lives of important theologians from 1860 to 1914 showed that scholasticism did not monopolize the German Catholic church in the second half of the nineteenth century. In Munich and Tübingen, Würzburg and Freiburg there were dedicated thinkers and tradition-minded schools where theology was carried on in dialogue with modern science and Protestant scholarship. Unfortunately, this narrative, which began as an explosion ignited by forces as disparate as the end of the Papal States and the emergence of scientific technologies, does not have a happy ending: that is postponed beyond a First and a Second World War.

This chapter describes the influential Vatican censures of 1907, the anti-modernist support of a theology which was neoscholastic but also curial. It not only traces the historical shift from theology to social action before the Great War but shows that the theologians arguing for an alternative to neoscholasticism and for theologies thought out of the modernity of their own century were not modernists in the eyes of their German colleagues or according to the Roman decrees. Only a very few, insignificant thinkers were heterodox. The important thinkers did not write in opposition to traditional Christian theologies or to the dogmas of the Catholic church. They did not live on the margin of the church or in alienation to it but were committed to working within German Catholicism. Even when their writings were condemned, few broke with the church. Historians note that the depth of theological life and education in Bavaria or Silesia made extremism among clergy and professors less likely. Precisely because of the high level of German academic theology (which Döllinger at the Munich assembly said was the mentor of the world) the community of educated professors and clergy was slow to accept the novel and the extreme. So we are led to end this history with the image of a theology which wanted to address and learn from the modern world but which was always challenged by elites fearful of modernity becoming modernism.

I. "Modernism"

In the decades following the brilliance of the Munich assembly and then the repressive Kulturkampf, German Catholicism sought to express its faith and tradition for and to the modern world. But by the first decade of the twentieth century, when networks of railroads and communications, electricity and medical laboratories were a reality, theology had not found a resolution and was still divided into its two directions. The more modernity spread through the panoply of culture, the more problematical was the Catholic response.

What was this "modernism" once viewed as modernity's climax and danger? It was initially a positive appreciation and appropriation of the characteristics, audience, and atmosphere of modern philosophy as it emerged after Kant. "Modernism" had multiple, slippery meanings, for modernism was initially just the expression of an open attitude to what is new and emerging. But this phenomenon has always been present, for younger generations see the world differently from older ones. To the extent that it became an "ism," it tended to replace Christian dogma and revelation with a metaphysical, historical, or psychological system. Roger Aubert wrote of its forms in Roman Catholicism:

> The term "modernism" was in use since the sixteenth century to characterize the tendency to esteem the modern age more highly than antiquity. In the nineteenth century it was used by some Protestants in a religious sense to designate the anti-Christian tendencies of the modern world and also the radicalism of liberal theology. When at the end of the century there was a movement in the Catholic Church urging reform of the Church and its doctrine in the sense of adapting them to modern needs, the term "modernism" was at once applied to it by opponents, first of all in Italy.[1]

We should recall that the last thesis condemned in the *Syllabus Errorum* of 1864 was: "The pope can and should reconcile himself with progress, liberty and modern culture."[2] Toward the end of the pontificate of Leo XIII a mélange of quite different groups espoused speculative or practical directives—ecclesiastical, political, or social—which their opponents (eventually including Pius X) summed up under the term "modernist." A modernist could be a thinker who tried to interpret Christianity and Catholic tradition in light of modern thought and culture: as such the term remains ambiguous, for it could mean simply the necessary task of relating Christian revelation to new generations or to different cultures. But as Carl Braig employed the term he fashioned, "modernism" meant the illegitimate dilution and ultimate replacement of revelation by cultural and philosophical terms and conceptualities.

Modernism was a spectrum with many tones. The Vatican's measures around 1907 identified modernism from an outside, largely German, viewpoint. Emile Poulat concluded: "Modernism never constituted that homogenous movement with systematicized thought corresponding to its reconstruction in the encyclical [*Pascendi*]."[3] Very few Germans held heterodox views or left the church over dogma. Some lived under a cloud of suspicion but escaped any action from the Congregation of the Index or the Holy Office; others, like Herman Schell, were condemned not because their creative theology held heresy but because their ideas were a potential source of confusion and scandal. German Catholic theology did not in intention or actuality develop or propound theologies which were "modernist," as the term has been understood pejoratively since the decrees of the Vatican and in subsequent uncritical histories. As Schell continued the theological direction of J. E. Kuhn, one receptive to subjectivity and history, so in an opposite vein, the decrees on modernism after 1907 continued the *Syllabus Errorum*.

The climate of repression surrounding the anti-modernist decrees was the church crisis which stands closest to us in time and thought. The years surrounding 1907 marked the end of Catholic theology in the nineteenth century. They concluded in a sad, constraining way the course of German Catholic theology from the middle of the past century to the First World War. In their anathemas and politique they brought a stifling end to the Catholic search for a vital intellectual and religious presence. These censures and an increasingly repressive atmosphere exercised for years an inhibiting influence on theologian and priest. Is theology to be only a re-reading of past ecclesiastical documents? Merely a honing of neoscholasticisms from the baroque? Is theology to be a catechism written in Rome once, for all the world, in a language and philosophy antiquated and hostile to everything modern? Ultimately condemnation, however, never supplants creativity. Theologies and ecclesiologies drawing on the forms if not the ideologies of European culture from 1750 to 1950 would appear repeatedly, and their traditional but creative inclusion in the expression of Christianity for the modern world was unavoidable.

II. The Instruments of the Holy See

The conflict between modernism and church authority reached its climax with the documents issued by the Vatican between 1907 and 1910: the list of errors, *Syllabus Errorum*; the encyclical *Pascendi*; the anti-modernist oath; the ill-fated encyclical on St. Charles Borromeo.[4] The German nunciatures were centers collecting information on suspicious German writings and the Index was the ordinary instrument used by Rome to discipline theologians after the assembly of scholars in 1863. In the cases of Jacob Frohschammer and Joseph Schnitzer pressure was brought upon the Munich university to remove them from their professorships, but this did not occur, because the school was administered by the state.

Leo XIII enjoyed friendly diplomatic relationships with the governments of Europe, and the urbane and educated pope did not intend to jeopardize this image by global condemnations of novel ideas. When Cardinal Giuseppe Sarto became pope in August 1903 he took the name Pius X, because earlier popes of the name Pius had courageously fought against error.[5] He soon initiated strong measures to direct narrowly the expression of church teaching and quickly moved to the censorship of scholars by approving the placing of five works of Loisy on the Index. In his first encyclical, *E Supremi Apostolatu*, he extended his motto, "to restore all things in Christ," to a practical program against "new, mistaken science not infused with Christ. . . , rationalism and semi-rationalism."[6] In his entire enterprise he was offering as a message for the age, not theology or education but piety and an abstract, scholastic theological vocabulary. Rome, of course, remained generally ignorant of the metaphysical and political forms whose Germanic representatives it condemned. It censored, not the abuses of neutral or good modes of thinking like history and democracy, but the forms themselves. The encyclicals *Ad Diem Illum* and *Iucunda Sane Accidit* in 1904 warned against innovators who would question through history the origins of Christianity, while *Il Fermo Proposito* of 1905 and *Pieni L'Animo* of 1906 insisted upon the regulation of Catholic Action and Italian political leagues by the church.

Schell's case was particularly prominent in Germany: his person and memory were unjustly linked to modernism. His writings had been placed on the Index without serious grounds. He was the most gifted speculative mind in German Catholicism and yet he was in life and death pursued by intrigues against him, actions unjustified by his theology and unwilled by the German bishops. Pius sent Ernst Commer a letter in June 1907 congratulating the theologian on his book critical of Schell's reconciliation of Catholicism with progress (Schell had died in 1906).[7] Those who wished to honor Schell's tomb with a monument (the bishops of Bamberg and Pasau, and Baron von Hügel were among them) were, according to the pope, "ignorant of Catholicism, rebels against the Holy See."[8] At an address to a consistory of cardinals the pope warned against the *"neo-reformismum religiosum"* which was spreading.[9] These inflammatory phrases in the Vatican were symptomatic of the documents issued to describe and condemn modernism; by 1908 Laberthonnière, Tyrrell, Schnitzer, and Loisy were under one form or another of ecclesiastical censure. Aubert notes: "The systematic repression of any remnants of the modernist movement was, above all, the work of the Holy See itself, which for some years had lived in an atmosphere of panic."[10]

In July the Holy Office issued the decree *Lamentabili Sane Exitu*, which after a brief preface condemned sixty-five propositions, an ensemble drawn largely from Loisy.[11] Pius X issued the encyclical *Pascendi Dominici Gregis* in September. Not a list of condemned authors but a Vatican summary of the totality of modernism, it opened by speaking of "the traditional deposit of faith" encountering "profane novelties of language as the expansions of false science." A new philosophical movement and foundation (deduced after research to be pieced together from writings by Loisy, Tyrrell, and two Italians, R. Murri and E. Buonaiuti) had appeared—that of "modernists"—whose errors were reduced to two: (1) an agnosticism of reason which questioned the argumentation of theodicy; (2) an immanentism of the mind which derived the data and truths of revelation and faith from the activities of consciousness. These errors, according to the pope, were both moral and intellectual; they flowed from pride, illegitimate curiosity, and ignorance of scholastic philosophy. The encyclical advocated a full return to scholastic thought as the basis for all philosophy and theology. What made modernists "the most pernicious of all the adversaries of the church" was that they operated within the church, attacking Scripture and authority. This "synthesis of all heresies" meant "the destruction not of the Catholic religion alone, but of all religion." The final lines of *Pascendi*, however, tried to avoid the impression of a complete withdrawal from contemporary thought:

> The adversaries of the church are wrong without doubt to take up again the old calumny that the church represents the enemy of science and of humanity's progress. The pope plans to found an institute which will draw together illustrious scholars from all areas to further, under the light of Catholic truth, all true progress in science and scholarship.[12]

It was difficult to see much relationship of *Lamentabili* to Germany, while *Pascendi* recalled approaches and fears more from the time of Anton Günther than from that of Herman Schell.

III. Reaction in Germany

The reaction in France and Italy was intense: the Vatican documents were seen not as a picture but as a caricature of modernism; *Pascendi*'s reconstruction of the modernist doctrines was "almost a fantasy of theological imagination and none of the theologians implicated could recognize their thought therein."[13] The younger clergy and laity, active in church politics more than in scholarship, were given no direction as to how they should resolve their dissatisfaction with the frozen state of theology and the absence of church renewal.

In Germany the reception was hostile, although it was not clear that modernism existed there. As we saw, some members of the Catholic royal family of Bavaria, the Wittelsbachs, were sympathetic to reformist ideas, but the Lutheran and Prussian Kaiser was pleased with the encyclical; he liked a pope defending the traditional principles of Christianity. (Could not modern ideas in church reform lead to modern ideas in politics in the Rhineland and Silesia?) Figures close to the imperial court suggested that Protestants and Catholics send the pope a word of their appreciation of the papal letter. Albert Ehrhard was one of the few important Catholics who did so, while among the Protestants Adolph Harnack, Friedrich Paulsen, Albert Hauck, and Ernst Troeltsch followed this directive.[14] Of course most Protestant intellectuals were appalled at the measures. Karl Holl exemplified them, designating the encyclical as producing the greatest Catholic crisis since the Reformation. Since Protestants and Catholics lived together in Germany, this response of one church to modernity and science was a problem for all Christians. Holl noted the central issue of history: neoscholasticism was blind to history, and it seemed that historical knowledge and historical theology were inimical to Catholic life. If the doctrine in *Pascendi* had infected the Catholic church, then the pope would have an obligation to speak. But, if the Vatican's stance was exaggerated, as seemed the case, claiming that not only dogma but philosophy were postulates of the church, did this not announce "the death of Catholic science?"[15]

Leading Catholics like Georg von Hertling, L. Erzberger, and F. X. Kiefl agreed that the letter had no application in Germany. Ehrhard in an article on the "new situation of theology" presented the German position. True, modernism as presented in the encyclical was irreconcilable with Catholicism—but did it exist in Germany? The suggested practical measures would make scholarly work impossible and threaten the existence of Catholic professors at universities. Did not the Roman measures imply that all historical-critical work was injurious? Modernism was rampant in France and Italy, Ehrhard continued, precisely because they had lost a philosophical mooring which was both solid and contemporary. Their centers of scholasticism stood in sad contrast to the great traditions of Tübingen and Munich. How miserable was the state of Catholic theology and how small was its influence on the cultural life of both countries.[16] Ehrhard concluded by declaring his Catholic loyalty, but subsequently he was obliged to indicate to the bishop of Strassburg and to Cardinal Merry del Val that he had not intended to compromise papal power.

For several reasons the modernism condemned in Roman decrees was not recognized as applying to Germany. First, there had been for almost a century speculative theologies constructed along the lines of romantic idealism; the thought forms of subject and process, of freedom and history. The consideration of Trinity and church in light of the transcendental activity of the self had then led to some historical-critical approach to doctrine and Bible, and most of this had occurred without harm to the church. Second, a one-sided or subjectivist role of Kant as developed by French thinkers[17] was not present in Germany, where a more sophisticated understanding of the entire idealist tradition existed. Third, respectable German theologians had not made modern motifs into a dogmatist replacement of revelation by epistemology but had included with criticism new directions, for instance, immanentist apologetics. Peter Neuner reviews the result in this way:

> The authors of the encyclical and the pope saw in modernism a closed system, an international conspiracy which has emerged for only one purpose: to shake and to destroy the church in its foundations. Although at times they could see both parallels and differences between freemasonry and modernism, they also asserted their identity. But while the masons were outside the church, the modernists were inside the church, and were consequently much more dangerous. These terrifying, apocalyptic views of the pope may be enough to explain how the measures against modernism came into existence. But the encyclical gave the bishops the odd obligation of constructing a veritable system of supervision and censure. The return to neoscholasticism (which a modest acceptance of biblical criticism hardly challenged) turned out not to be sufficient to heal and calm down the modernist shadows. This politics had its own inner dynamics, creating under Umberto Benigni an international system for supervising theologians, bishops, and cardinals according to a standard where extremely conservative views were identified with the true doctrine of revelation. In the final years of Pius X the number of books on the Index, the variety of positions condemned, and

[the number of] excommunications resembled that in the time of the Jansenists.[18]

Certain incidents followed upon these defenses of German theology. The Vatican withdrew Ehrhard's ecclesiastical honorary title of monsignor. Joseph Müller, director of *Die Renaissance*, was suspended from the priesthood by the archbishop of Munich, while in Cologne, Cardinal Anton Fischer forbade seminarians' attending a course by Heinrich Schrörs at the theological faculty of Bonn, because the theologian was known to have advocated reforms. (Riots and press attention forced the cardinal to modify his stance.) The bishops of Prussia and the Rhineland had assembled in Cologne in early December 1907 to consider the difficulties *Pascendi* might raise. The prince-bishop of Breslau, Cardinal Georg Kopp, had not waited for the meeting to protest in strong terms to Rome the inadvisability of issuing such a document filled with repercussions for Germany without consultations with the country's bishops.[19]

The Vatican remained immovable in its view of Germany as dangerous. Was it not the very place of origin of both Protestantism and idealism (as Kleutgen had observed fifty years before)? Were not these two movements the sources of all modernisms? Theological faculties at the state universities and proliferating lay movements gave rise to concern, as did a new range of journals which mounted a thorough critique of the Roman anti-modernist steps. (*Osservatore Romano* criticized German Catholic journals for publishing such pieces.)

IV. The Second Act in Rome: The Oath against Modernism and the Encyclical on Charles Borromeo

Loisy said in 1909 that the impact of the documents of 1907 had caused French modernist movements to be in "full collapse."[20] For Germany, however, the Vatican continued to collect reports of any movements of reform and to advocate the removal of professors and the censorship of books. The pope took a further step: in a *motu proprio* of September 1, 1909, *Sacrorum Antistitum*, he demanded from all clergy a particular public and verbal oath which came to be known as the "Oath against Modernism."[21] This was a kind of creed (supplementing the sixteenth-century *Professio Fidei Tridentina* of Pius IV) with articles countering modernist principles. At first the oath was to be taken by all clergy with pastoral or educational ministries. Subsequently it was required of clerics both orally and in writing before key events like ordinations to major orders or final religious vows. It was also taken before assuming a theological teaching position, and by pastors and religious and ecclesiastical superiors upon entering their offices. Its purpose was to unmask crypto-modernists.

In terms of the church throughout the world the clergy as a whole submitted without much outward resistance. German Catholics with their tradition of and debate over freedom and *Wissenschaft* were horrified at this primitive measure. Would it not insure that Catholics were excluded not only from their own research but also from academic life? Typical of the academic protest throughout the Reich was an article by Karl Adam, then a young professor in Munich. The issue, he wrote, was not Catholic professors secretly propagating modernist errors or rejecting papal disciplinary action. "What makes the oath for professors a burning issue in the life of higher education is *the issue of the right of the historical-critical method in the area of Catholic theology*." A Catholic scholar did not wish a "freedom-without-presuppositions," but some freedom was required. What was at stake was not just the result of research but the process of acquiring scientific knowledge. Moreover, the language of the oath was haughty in its Latin imperial tone and simplistic in its theology. The non-Catholic would be shocked by the text and could hardly find in it any encouragement for an intellectual life. The public and the press viewed it "as the official death sentence over the totality of Catholic science." Adam feared the worst: "the complete exclusion of Catholic theological faculties from the organism of the universities."[22] Rome had to respond to a German request for an interpretation of the oath with modifications and exemptions.

The literature in Germany prompted by the projected oath, arguing both sides of the issue, was large and ranged from pamphlets to systematic expositions.[23] Theologians made it clear that they were not in schism from the propositions of the oath, but that its phraseology and ideology were inept; the Tübingen faculty spoke of their agreement with the "ground" of the oath and their capability of taking it, but of their professional decision not to do so.[24] The protests of so many professors and bishops resulted in the exemption of teachers of theology at the university level from taking the oath.

In the few months before the *motu proprio* of 1910 with the oath against modernism, a strange document was being readied by the Vatican, one more anti-German and anti-Protestant than anti-modernist. This curial composition had a singular history and was to be little known. It was an encyclical, *Editae Saepe*, issued formally on May 29, 1910, to commemorate the three-hundredth anniversary of the death of St. Charles Borromeo. The exaltation of this Milanese church leader of the Counter-Reformation was meant to be a lesson for Germany at the turn of the twentieth century. It implied that once again the German church created a dangerous, extraecclesial movement: this time, not Protestantism but modernism. Even more than the other measures, this text illustrated an absence at the Vatican of accurate knowledge about theology and church north of the Alps and an ignorance of German culture and ethos. In late May 1910 the encyclical appeared in Italian on the pages of *Osservatore Romano*. (It was published in *Acta Apostolicae Sedis* in early June.) Still imagining communications as they had existed in a feudal past, the Curia was astonished to learn that two days after appearing in *Osservatore* Catholic and non-Catholics periodicals in Germany had published translations. The pope joined the modernists to Protestant Reformers and viewed both according to Philippians as "enemies of the cross of Christ . . . whose god is their stomach" (3:19).[25] The success of the Reformation was due to corrupt princes and peoples, and the Protestant church continued to distort faith and morals. Naturally, the encyclical caused an uproar in Prussia; Wilhelm II found it annoying, while Adolf von Harnack responded to its view of the Reformation. Communications and delegations on the letter reached the Vatican quickly, even though the document had not yet been formally issued in Germany, the country of its destiny. If bishops belonging to the conservative Berlin-Breslau direction stayed out of the battle, since these resided in areas most affected by the encyclical's attack on Protestantism, other heads of dioceses urged modifications. In Berlin six thousand people assembled to protest the letter, and politicians suggested a new Kulturkampf, one realizable in more subtle steps like freezing the salaries of Catholic priests. Several *Länder* forbade the publication and public reading of the encyclical.

Curial officials worked on revisions of the text, but by mid-June the Vatican had decided to withdraw the document and Cardinal Kopp of Breslau could report to the Prussian government on June 15 that each German bishop had received a letter forbidding any publication or circulation of the document. *Osservatore Romano* reported that although the encyclical had been published in the *Acta*, the Holy Father, because of certain consequences of this publication, had "on his own initiative and on the grounds of prudence" withdrawn its presence in Germany.[26] The Vatican had been surprised by the intensity of the German reaction, for the letter had not been judged to be provocative. The views on Germany coming from curial advisors and ultramontane sources were inaccurate, while balanced sources like many German bishops or the nuncio in Munich, Frühwirth, were not appreciated. The goal of the encyclical had been simple: as the Reformation had been halted, so would modernism be ended; in this Pius X would resemble Charles Borromeo.

V. The Aftermath of the Anti-Modernist Measures

Pascendi could be used not only to critique modern philosophy and theology but to advance neoscholasticism. The conservative professor in Munich, L. Atzberger, in *Was ist der Modernismus?* divided Catholic intellectuals into Thomists and Kantians; Kant stood for modernity and all varieties of idealism and immanentism. The "providential meaning" of the encyclical was to clarify the existence of modernism in the Catholic church.

> The modernists are striving for nothing less than the introduction of a new philosophy, a new idea of faith, a new science of faith, a new view of history and criticism, a new apologetic. They want to alter formally the entire religious and ecclesiastical thought within Catholicism, and in connection with that approach they would reform church life. All this flows from three bases . . . agnosticism, immanentism and religious evolutionism.[27]

The Vatican documents found many usages, not only the control of seminary personnel but the redirection of religious education. Jean-Baptiste Lemius's *Catechism on Modernism according to the Encyclical "Pascendi,"* printed at the Vatican, sold tens of thousands of copies in Germany. But when Benedict XV succeeded Pius X in 1914, the exaggerations and negative effects of the long campaign against modernism were sufficiently apparent and disturbing, even sometimes clearly unjust, that the new pope's first encyclical was directed against the repressions and suspicions of the rigidly integralist movement.

There were three basic flaws in the content and approach of the anti-modernist documents. First, the difficulties of introducing the critical-historical method into the study of Scripture were confused with any new conceptuality or theology. Second, modern philosophy was described in global and abstract axioms apart from its historical and systematic context; for instance, the Vatican's finding of a radical solipsism in the turn to the subject, even though this was already well accomplished. (The Vatican seemed to find its sources for modernism only in the past, in Schelling rather than in Eduard von Hartmann, in Descartes rather than in Marx, Feuerbach, or Freud.) Finally, the campaign preferred any neoscholastic product to theological conversations concerning the relationship of an objective historical revelation to a world-creating consciousness. Since the 1790s German Catholics had been discussing such topics as the theological and apologetical implications of human subjectivity (not limited to Aristotelian reason), biblical criticism, and the history of dogma, the distinct identity and power of the supernatural but its intimate relationship to the nature and destiny of humanity. Why should they be ignored or discarded?

Schools of modernism did not exist in Germany, and the curial descriptions of modernism did not represent the theological correlation of revelation and modernity. The German tradition of dialogue with modernity was not the same as the condemned movement. Norbert Trippen writes: "The system of heresies implied with the word 'modernism' was almost unknown in Germany; certainly without significance and influence. Liberal Protestant theology exercised only a small fascination upon German Catholic theologians. Neoscholasticism never had in Germany the exclusive dominance it had in Spain or Italy."[28] Few qualified theologians had contributed to the documents of 1907.

The vigor of the German response, however, confirmed in the Roman eyes that modernism did exist. Ehrhard and Schnitzer were embroiled in controversy, while exegetes and theologians like Sebastian Merkle, Franz Xaver Kiefl, and Fritz Tillmann had to withdraw from public debate. Curiously, the effect in Germany was that exegetical studies were weakened for some decades, while dogmatic and fundamental theology were neglected for historical studies. There was a general demoralization of the clergy, who saw innocent theologians deprived of their positions and who argued emotionally over the value of the imposed oath. The Vatican's war on "modernism" in Germany was a theological enterprise which aimed at and obtained considerable ecclesiastical-political control. Its presence and form were confused; for instance it was possible to find German and Roman conservatives who acknowledged that Schell, the admitted leading theologian of the time, was not heretical in his writings nor agnostic (Kantian) in his philosophy, and yet the committee planning a monument to him could be viewed as a potentially dangerous cell of revolt.[29]

The anti-modernist measures of Rome were not an isolated uproar in the history of modern Catholic theology. The years around 1900 did not present a rare meeting of modernity with Roman Catholicism (although this has often been the historian's opinion). Rather they were a violent and unpredictable climax to unresolved tensions occurring at the end of a century. Certainly it was necessary for the Vatican to take some stance against the hasty metamorphoses of revelation into mere mental forms. In the long run, a church declines when it ceases to defend historical revelation and the autonomy of the transcendent. But the question of how the Catholic church would live in the modern epoch remained unresolved. (Was not its ground the theology of nature and grace?) Was modernity itself—whether that of Hegel or of positive science—to be condemned as corrupt? Was grace to be found only in the terminologies of curial officials? Erich Przywara looked back at modernism from the 1930s and described it as "a religious-theological agnostic irrationalism whose consequences were pantheism and atheism." He distinguished three types of modernism: (1) that of the doctrines condemned in Vatican documents, (2) that contained in movements toward reform, and (3) simply the intention to express Christian revelation in terms of a particular age; the second two types were not always included in the first, and only a very few figures in the German church and theology around 1900 were legitimately included under the first, ecclesiastical form.[30]

In Germany not all extra-scholastic theology and philosophy was modernist and not every new theological approach was Kantian. Around the world during the first half of the twentieth century generations of clergy and teachers were taught that all philosophical theology conversant with subjectivity and process was modernist. Many, such as Reginald Garrigou-Lagrange in the thirty years before Vatican II, as neoscholasticism was reaching an ever greater dominance, linked the French "*nouvelle théologie*" (new in its method and pastoral praxis) with modernism. "Where is this new theology leading? It is returning to modernism. Because it has accepted the proposition made to it, to substitute for the traditional definition of truth *adaequatio rei et intellectus*, as if it were chimerical, the subjective definition *adaequatio realis mentis et vitae*."[31] Emile Poulat wrote:

> Subtle games and abstract clerical quarrels, reformers' armchair illusions, heresies quickly mastered, *modernism* would seem to be in the church only a brief episode on a road already quite long and eventful. This ecclesiastical conflict lives within a more vast conflict and is explained by it. It sends us back to the phenomenon of global civilization, the transformations of society over whose value Catholics were profoundly divided. . . . Since the faithful absorbed (without even being conscious of it) new forms of thought and a new type of culture, their faith could not be held captive by a dead language and an antique imagery. What good was it to go to people if one had only the old catechism to serve them?[32]

The papal condemnations of an ill-defined modernism postponed but did not block Roman Catholics' expression of Christianity in modern thought-forms.[33]

VI. From Speculative Theology to Social Issues

As the First World War approached, Catholic interests moved from theology and philosophy to society. This shift had been developing in the latter nineteenth century. Already in 1849 Wilhelm Emmanuel Ketteler of Mainz, "the social bishop," addressed in his sermons "the great social questions of today." The church, he proclaimed to his thousands of hearers, must help the working class against the tyranny of unbridled capitalism. Unions and cooperatives were to be founded; legislation against child labor and for factory inspection was needed. He sought in the 1860s an alternative to liberalism and socialism. Some see in his thought traces of the romantic, organic view of the church (and state) sketched out by Drey and Möhler of the Tübingen school. This social theory was meant to counter the static, absolutist government of Bismarck.[34] By the 1890s, bishops, theologians and journalists were establishing a tradition of social Catholicism, observing and criticizing the latest shifts in society. They fashioned not a philosophical system but the church's social encounter with modernity. Industrial patterns of work and production led to a shift from an emphasis upon charity to social engagement through new institutions empowered by the church. Movements and unions at first supported and then offered an alternative to the political Catholicism of the Center Party. The new German issues and ideas influenced Leo XIII and *Rerum Novarum*. The battle in German countries concerned a *practical* rather than a *theological* modernism. Certainly the social issues were significantly rooted in the values of the Enlightenment and in the developmental systems of Schelling and Hegel. But Rome's attention had come to be focused upon the more active currents in German Catholicism, which were social, cultural and political; that vague but disturbing "Reform-Catholicism" was suspected of furthering a practical modernism. Rome wanted no national individuality in culture, politics, and social views; indeed, it preferred a paternalistic, quasi-medieval universalism for all areas and for all Catholics.[35] As Catholics after 1900 were deterred by Rome from pursuing philosophy and theology, they turned to practical areas of politics, social life, and art. If the intersection of church and German life from 1825 to 1865 had been the university, after 1885 it became the labor union.

Bismarck's successors had no inclination to wage war with Catholicism but wished to use Catholic political movements to their own advantage. In 1890 seminarians were again exempted from military service and dioceses received the monies that had been seized from them. The creation in 1902 of a new Catholic theological faculty at Strassburg was a Prussian gesture toward reconciliation. But some remnants of the laws of the Kulturkampf remained: the Catholic church was administered in some lands by Protestants and only in 1917 were the anti-Jesuit laws fully removed. R. Lill writes: "Both Wilhelm II and Pius X furthered the progress of normalization. During his thirty year rule the Kaiser frequently emphasized — sometimes thoughtlessly — the Protestant character of his dynasty and rule, but he also found sympathetic words for Catholics and Catholic institutions."[36] In Rome, however, Pius X found much to admire in the stability of Germany and Austria: their's was an order seemingly untouched by European political upheaval and potential revolution.

If by supporting national and military objectives of Wilhelminian politics, Catholics and the Center Party attained more power,[37] still the custodians of power admitted a Georg von Hertling only rarely. Meanwhile, among the lower classes Catholic movements and assemblies, *Tagungen* and *Vereine*, multiplied in the 1880s (often appealing to a papal document to support their new beginnings) and the large charitable enterprises like the venerable and successful Caritasverband expanded. In 1890 the Volksverein für das katholische Deutschland was founded; by 1914 it had 767,000 members. This was a particularly forceful entry of the church into the concrete life of the age. The Volksverein's center in Mönchengladbach held a thousand meetings throughout Germany and distributed over four million brochures. It then began to offer "practical social courses" in 1892 to which hundreds came from all over Europe and even from North America.[38] An article in *Hochland* observed in 1914: "The controversy over journalism, the conflict over the unions, the crisis of the Center Party—these are three phases of one cultural struggle which realizes in different areas the same basic tension and opposition."[39]

Labor Unions

Some would trace the strong involvement of the German Catholic church in labor issues back to the pastoral renewal of J. M. Sailer and to J. B. Hircher's application of Tübingen theology to morality. Others would note that Jesuit and other neoscholastic moralists played important roles in supporting this area, which was far from ultramontane.[40] Perhaps the exemplary conflict where the Center Party, the church and the Volksverein all met was the labor unions. As early as 1869 Bishop Ketteler and others had urged the founding of unions. Trade unions could build upon the Catholic workers' associations which were already in place by 1889 (there were 168 of these as well as 100 more for youth and women). The popular formation of these groups led the younger clergy to serve as chaplains in factories, particularly in the Ruhr. In 1890 Lorenz Huber—priest and labor leader, the son of a Munich family of lawyers— founded an advanced form of Catholic workers' union for the center of Munich. Karl-Egon Lönne writes: "The ultramontanes forced (at this time) the Center Party into defensive positions. There it declined in a certain isolation. But even reactionaries supported the Christian unions because their emergence mirrored the increased religious formation of political and social powers in Catholicism, ideas furthered by the Curia and Pius X."[41]

Catholic unions were strongly ecclesial and confessional, and yet it became clear in the 1890s that cooperation with the new Protestant unions, even if it resulted in an interdenominational entity, would better confront the militant atheism of the social-democratic unions. Rhenish and Bavarian bishops were sympathetic to the Center Party and to the numerous Catholic regional movements and clubs, and, perhaps motivated by a hostility to the government which still limited their ministry, they supported the labor unions. Naturally not a few labor leaders were agnostic and anti-clerical, viewing the church, like state and business, as opposed to social humanitarianism. Bishops like the liberal Archbishop Franz von Bettinger placed social issues above ecclesiastical ones and viewed the unions (and the Volksverein) as associations through which Christian ideas could work for social improvement. The integralist episcopacy and laity, however—led by the Prince Bishop of Breslau, Georg Cardinal Kopp, and by Bishop Michael Korum of Trier—wanted full church control through priests. Thus a new conflict over modern life appeared, dividing not only theologians and laity but bishops. The existence of Protestant unions led Catholics to favor (or tolerate) interdenominational unions which would oppose the secular or socialist cells. Priests who had previously led the Catholic workers' clubs continued their ministry in the interdenominational ones. But when these unions began to employ strikes and to urge an evolutionary (even revolutionary) reformation of the existing system, they caused concern to church and state.

Rome, like Berlin, considered the unions to be dangerous—but for opposite reasons: they were liberal and unconfessional. Lill writes: "The result of the conflict [over the nature of the Catholic labor movement] would not have been in doubt if it had been played out only in Germany. The great majority of politically active Catholics, particularly in the west and south, rejected the integralist position. Conservative bishops supported by theologians like Franz Hettinger, Georg Ratzinger, and Albert Weiss, however, could not convince all their colleagues, and in 1910 Cardinal Fischer got the Fulda conference to approve membership in the unions."[42] In 1912 the controversy over the interdenominational unions reached a crisis: the pope bemoaned the Germans yielding to views of the press while Merry del Val blamed Cardinal Fischer and the German bishops. Pius X, however, interfered directly in these events only once. In an essay, "Zentrum and kirchliche Autorität," Theodor Wacker (1845–1921), a priest from Baden, analyzed conflicts between party and church in exaggerated terms and was placed on the Index.[43]

The issue of the unions was widely discussed by moral theologians as it came to attract more Vatican involvement than the political issues of the Center Party. Jesuit Tilmann Pesch, a neoscholastic who, despite his chosen field of social ethics, looked with fear on the rapidity and extent of change in Germany, wrote to the Dominican Nuncio Frühwirth: "A secularization is taking place which is much worse than that which robbed the church of its material goods."[44] After a trip to Rome, Cardinal Fisher believed that the Vatican would be neutral, but it 1912 the pope spoke against the bishops' approval of Christian unions. The Prussian bishops almost reached their goal, a formal condemnation of the Christian unions. This would have been a disaster for the efforts of Catholicism to mediate between Gospel and culture and would have fanned the antipathy toward Christianity which was gaining influence in labor and socialist movements. But Cardinal Fischer orchestrated a compromise which appeared in *Singulari Quadam* in autumn, 1912. The pope praised Catholic labor unions and noted that social problems could not be solved without recourse to revelation and moral law. If "interdenominationalism" was a danger, Catholics could work with non-Catholics as long as the unions did not interfere in the teachings of the church; moreover, Catholics should hold a second membership in Catholic workers' associations. Since some of the aspects of the interconfessional unions could only "be tolerated,"[45] conservative bishops continued their opposition for the next few years, and the secular press used these critiques to discredit the structure and goals of the unions. The Christian unions began to suffer a constant loss of membership, for they no more enjoyed much activity free of the church and to some extent a successful competition with the free unions was hindered. Little by little Catholic workers lost contact with the church. In the years just before World War I the ecclesial dispute over the unions was seen as the most important crisis and greatest loss for the Catholic movements in Germany since their emergence.

The Press

When the Kulturkampf began there were 126 Catholic periodicals, but by 1885 there were 248 and by 1913, 450 with two and a half million subscribers. Catholic dailys in Cologne, Augsburg, and Munich were among the most important newspapers. This press campaign had been initiated early in the nineteenth century by Joseph Görres and continued by J. E. Jörg in the *Historisch-politische Blätter*, whose pages advocated a Catholic engagement—sometimes liberal, sometimes conservative —with modernity.[46] In the last years of the century the power and the organs of the Catholic press multiplied and their articles were the means by which church and art, culture and theology met and by which faith both critiqued and drew from modern culture. In 1901 an Eichstätt chancery official founded a *Pressverein*, an association of journalists and publishers.

Julius Bachem (1845–1918) was the editor of a prominent Cologne paper. He saw in Pius X's *Politik* of pursuing Catholic identity through isolation a great danger for the times. In 1900 he published in the *Historisch-politische Blätter* the instantly famous essay, "We Must Get out of the Tower." He ridiculed anachronistic hopes and models of a Christian state, whether Protestant or Catholic, and argued that cooperation between Protestants and Catholics was inevitable in social and political issues. The church's teachers had the right to present the general norms of morality, but their concrete application in politics and society should be left to Catholics who knew something about the precise area. This program became known as the "Cologne Direction."

Influenced by the addresses and articles of Schell exploring contacts between modern culture and the church, Carl Muth called for a positive Catholic understanding of the society which was unfolding in Europe. His anonymous pamphlet on Catholic literature in 1898 began what came to be called "the literature controversy" and a series of Muth's brochures and articles culminated in his book *Steht die katholische Belletristik auf der Höhe der Zeit?*[47] In 1903 he founded the significant *Hochland*, "a journal for all areas of knowledge, literature and art" containing short stories, serialized novels, and poems. A typical year's issues might look at religion in Louvain neoscholasticism or in the writings of the "poet-philosopher," Ralph Waldo Emerson. The liberal Herman Schell discussed in an issue "The Divine Powers in Christianity," and then the conservative Max Ettlinger surveyed borderline questions between natural science and philosophy. The paintings of Dürer and Rembrandt were discussed as well as the operas (*Salome*, *Elektra*) of Richard Strauss. The journal was a "platform and mirror" for a Catholicism which was mature, renewed, but also loyal to the Reich.[48] A colorful narrative of church and culture in this period could be drawn from the issues of *Hochland*.

Two years after his book on reform-Catholicism Josef Müller began a journal, *Renaissance* (1901–1907). Another liberal periodical was *Das Zwanzigstes Jahrhundert* (1902–1909) with its motto, "Religion, Deutschtum, Kultur." The editor, a Westphalian priest named Franz Xaver Klasen, published there in 1904 his program for church independence and renewal under the title, "What We Want." The issues were the freedom of the individual, the right of dissent and criticism, the damage done to publications placed on the Index, an end to the church's indiscriminate hostility to culture, modern forms of government, the vernacular in the Mass and sacraments and an ecumenical attitude toward Protestants. This popular paper was renamed in 1909 *Das neue Jahrhundert* and given the dubious subtitle "Organ der deutschen Modernisten." Its tone could be inflammatory but this was moderated by the next editor, Philipp Funk, who argued in its pages that German Catholicism was not moving in the direction of French modernism or of the Austrian "Away-from Rome" movement. The church's reform was a matter to be disputed within the confines of the church.

Other Catholics, however, took pen in hand to oppose the reformers: a war of journals debated the issues. Some founded the literary quarterly *Über den Wassern*, while in Vienna a traditionalist "Catholic Cultural Program" under Richard von Kralik developed its own periodical, *Gral*.[49] These widely read publications produced a not always harmonious choir of ideas and voices which unnerved Rome concerning the future of German Catholicism. But what was not grasped by the Vatican was that this flood of print had mainly to do with practical church life, with literature or social upheaval, and not with the authorship of Genesis or the history of Greek dogma.

The supervisor of the Pope's anti-modernist campaign, Umberto Benigni, saw the expansion of journalistic influence as a direct attack upon church doctrinal authority and yet another example and confirmation of German reformism. Pius X and Merry del Val disapproved of the Cologne Direction. Rhenish periodicals had tended to defend Ehrhard and Schell. To counter these liberal directions, an Italian curial cardinal addressed the Katholikentag in Essen in 1906 and in unrealistic rhetoric proclaimed the necessity for Catholics to obey the pope in everything. The protests against this exaggeration of authority were so numerous that a papal letter was sent to Cardinal Fischer to confirm the freedom of German Catholics in nonreligious fields.

The influence of Bachem's essay and program illustrated the new power of the press. Not system, whether neo-Kantian or neoscholastic, but journal was forming Catholic identity and Catholic literature was more and more free of an anti-world stance, particularly through the leadership of Carl Muth and *Hochland*. The ultramontanes, however, argued that the Catholic press in its dialogue with the modernity was abandoning the Counter-Reformation, melding Catholicism into Prussian Protestantism, and furthering Gallicanism. Curial, ultramontane, and neoscholastic minds saw the journals' discussion of literature, theater, politics, and social conditions as a capitulation to secular society. Should not a real Catholic press simply repeat the church's dogmas and report on papal discourses? A few reactionary bishops and seminary professors described the situation in Germany as one where the labor unions were de-Catholicizing the lower classes, as journals were accomplishing the same for the upper classes.[50] Once again conversation with modernity equalled advocating heresy. It was one thing, however, for Rome to condemn exegetes, priests and theologians; it was something else to condemn a journal or a writer.

The Vatican received (and encouraged) hysterical reports; it did not study the data sent to it, and exaggeratedly identified every gesture toward being part of a modern state with capitulation to the Reformation or the Enlightenment. German Catholics could only feel confused, abandoned by cardinals and popes and left to their own survival. As we saw previously, the former master general of the Dominican Order, the Austrian Andreas Frühwirth, was appointed nuncio to Bavaria (a position established in 1784 for that distinct political entity and retained in the new Reich), because Frühwirth was German-speaking and a theologian—a sign of Pius's desire for some good relations during these troubled times. The nuncio proved himself generous and competent toward the Munich press and in an opening interview stated that he had no commission to attack "modernism" in Germany and that he understood that the role of Catholic theology at German universities could not be dismissed.[51] Frühwirth avoided conflict, sent balanced reports on German theologians to Rome, and sought to delay severe Vatican measures. His mediation was crucial in the exemption from the anti-modernist oath and in the repression of the Borromeo letter. Issues of politics and labor unions brought him to Rome in 1910, where it was presumed he represented a balanced viewpoint on issues which were disturbing the pope and the cardinals.[52] Upon his return to Munich, however, he found himself attacked by Benigni's circle and by reactionary publications as unfaithful to the pope for covering up the virulence of German modernism and error.[53] Nevertheless, he did not lose the Vatican's confidence and at the beginning of his final year of service at the nunciature, 1915, he was named cardinal.

While the Sunday Mass attendance of workers declined and theology and the philosophy of religion found less and less expression, popular piety increased. Pilgrimages and parish missions, parish societies and devotional publications reached record levels.[54] And yet, there was an atmosphere of division in the German church polarizing theologians and bishops, unions and journals. The integralists saw everywhere attempts to modernize the church, to break free of Roman authority; they blamed a de-Catholicization of the masses not on new urban and industrial situations but upon a failure to restore medieval life. In the last analysis the conflict was over whether Catholics would remain in a ghetto, whether their traditions (less urban, less enthusiastic about industrialization and capitalism) could find a convincing voice addressing all of Germany. The weakening of German Catholicism, from within and from without, was, according to Thomas Nipperdey, a tragedy with enormous consequences.

"Great changes, the result of the tension between tradition and modernity, enveloped the church and its opponents. The entire fabric of the time was still penetrated by religion, but without a unified program, without a stance towards the changing politics and social structures of modern urban life which was positive as well as critical, the church was not able to offer its prophetic traditions to the violent upheavals which could not be held back from European history after 1914."[55]

VII. Embattled on a Dual Front

Some would say that after the measures begun in 1907—measures which were effective in France, Italy and England—Rome gave special attention to German developments. Were not the procedures of the Cologne faction as dangerous as speculative theological innovations? Was not the Center Party pursuing the declericalization of public life and the separation of the spiritual and the temporal? Catholics still had the problem of their minority status in the higher realms of culture. Leadership in assisting the working class did not remove the threat of exclusion from university life. The Vatican offered little encouragement or practical programs on how to live within the intellectual and social structures of the age. On the contrary, it viewed new cultural movements as dangerous; theology was suspended between the proliferation of neoscholastic texts and the threat of censure; democracy and modern art were seen as threats to revelation.[56]

The dispute with Rome over labor unions including non-Catholics and the expansion of the Catholic press offered ways of influencing society, and Catholics in government were active in social and political issues in a new, more direct way. The older theoreticians in the declining Central Party with their styles from the years of the Kulturkampf were replaced by younger activists such as Matthias Erzberger (1875–1921) and Martin Spahn (1875–1945). They represented a new kind of leadership that was acquainted with the working class and interested in urban issues as much as in political philosophy, preferring parliament to professorship.[57] The historian Spahn, who also worked as a political organizer and social journalist, criticized the pontificate of Leo XIII for being uninformed about Protestantism and German Catholicism. He claimed the repressive mentality of Bismarck was still active in Prussia and noted "the psychological distance" of the Rhine and Westphalia from Berlin, and Karl Bachem in 1911 evaluated retrospectively the actions of the 1870s—"the most perfect system ever devised"—for suppressing church freedom.[58]

With almost a million and a half Catholics in the labor movement and a network of charitable help for the socially needy, the German church appeared to have channeled its repressed theological and philosophical energies into society's structures. At the Katholikentag in 1903 the archbishop of Milan, Cardinal Ferrari proclaimed that Germany was teaching the world—but less in theology and history (the fields which had led Döllinger to make a similar proclamation in 1863) than in social theology.[59] And yet, it was precisely the political and social forms of the imperial Reich which were most important before and after the Great War, while the spectrum of worlds from *Tondichtung* to *Verein* only multiplied the questions over what it meant to be German and Catholic.

In the years around 1907 Germany had produced a practical dialogue with modernity, a religious exploration in press and industry. *Pascendi* had scattered talent and imagination, but theologians and bishops, priests and laity found other roads for their energy. New directions for philosophical theology were to appear only after 1919. The conclusion will summarize the long history we have been pursuing, noting the triumph of a kind of curial theology, the vast influence of neoscholasticism, the unfinished encounter with the forms of life and society in the modern era, and the uncertain future of Catholicism during and beyond world wars.

Conclusion

THE PRECEDING CHAPTERS, neither a detailed history of this complex period nor a catalogue of Roman Catholic theologians, have given an overview of Catholic theology between 1860 and 1914. Modernity has a history, and its points of contact with Roman Catholicism are not only hesitant but multiple. The nineteenth century had different epochs, historical variations on its themes of subjectivity and science, freedom and history. Drey's employment of Schelling is not the same as Braig's critique of von Hartmann, and modern thought-forms expressed and challenged revelation not only in abstract philosophies of religion but in social movements and literature. After 1860 the great systems of *Natur* and *Geist* yielded to the positivisms and technologies of science and state. The nineteenth century ended not in 1900 but with World War I, in an atmosphere which rendered the future of both culture and religion uncertain. These chapters leave the impression that Catholicism has not yet completed its conversation with modernity and that this dialogue occurs in different degrees from decade to decade.

I. Out of the Nineteenth Century

Just as the years 1798, 1810, 1830, and 1848 delineated different realizations of idealism and romanticism in the Catholic restoration, so the second half of the nineteenth century had several segments. The 1850s were a time of transition from idealist currents to neoscholasticism; the 1870s and 1880s recorded the Kulturkampf and the Catholics' struggle to overcome being marginalized citizens in the Reich. The twenty years before the First World War found a Catholic vitality in theology and in the press; the anti-modernist campaign saw a shift of attention from transcendental philosophy to social issues.

Neoscholasticism achieved a rapid success within Catholicism and, ultimately, almost a monopoly. Neoscholasticism is not the perfect preservation of Aquinas nor are the texts of Vatican I much concerned with their own or later times except to set up broad danger signs. But we should not undervalue scholasticism's appeal and contribution; its critique of modernity was needed. A defense of objective revelation tried to correct powerful philosophies of mind and text headed for the dictatorship of form and the de-emphasis of content. As the church struggled to realize itself in the modern world, Catholic clergy and laity became anxious that emphasis on subjectivity and freedom would suppress faith; that, for instance, democracy and socialism could change the forms of the church. Not a few bishops feared that after political democracy would come ecclesiastical democracy.

An understanding of Catholic intellectual life requires a view of the history of the neoscholastic revival. Both idealist and scholastic approaches formed Catholic theology at this time. Clearly a culturally engaged Catholic theology did not first appear in 1945 or 1965. Surprisingly, in the midst of the neoscholastic conquest, the expansion of ultramontane initiatives and the increase of Roman control over local churches and theological problems, there were Catholic schools and theologians who were knowledgeable of past and present modern philosophers and Protestant theologians. From 1870 to 1910 a few not-ungifted thinkers composed theologies in dialogue with idealism and new cultural movements. They drew into their practical and theoretical writings and approaches and motifs of the end of the century. Pointing out the existence of these theologies in dialogue with philosophy and science expands our understanding of Catholic theology from Trent to Vatican II. This orientation to theologians who labored amid late idealism and neoscholasticism will, it is hoped, lead others to write more detailed studies of these fields and scholars.

Some cultural currents of the nineteenth century were blocked for Catholics. The papal documents of 1907 and the movement they climaxed brought contemporary theology almost to a halt. It was not the speculations of a Catholic Nietzsche which summoned forth Pius X's anti-modernist measures but the popular books by Schell and Ehrhard on German culture and Catholicism. Rome's offensive was in favor of one scholastic approach, and this seemed to question the legitimacy of theology itself. Change and reform in Catholic life were risky and unnecessary. Culturally engaged theology was not needed: did not the magisterium already know the principles and the applications of revelation? Certainly, apart from the pages of the Tübingen *Theologische Quartalschrift* or the addresses of Schell and Hertling, Catholic intellectual life did not converse extensively with Hartmann, Ritschl, Troeltsch, Hermann, Cohen, and with the neoidealist or neo-Kantian schools. Richard Schaeffler has written:

The effect of the crisis of modernism in the history of thought can be described in a few sentences. Only scholastic philosophy, then understood as the path of reason for the knowledge of eternal truths transcending historical change, was normative. The dialogue between Catholic theologians and Kantian and post-Kantian philosophy slowly faded away. This was particularly unfortunate because the problematics of history and truth unleashed by modernism was handled with some intensity in certain Kantians schools, and theology could have profited from discussion, but conversation with Kant would remain for some decades simply not an option.[1]

II. A Theological Style

Eras produce styles. Catholic theology unfolded from 1860 to 1914 in two theological languages, one looking to Aristotle, one to Schelling. The first language, of neoscholasticism, came to dominate, and this way of conceptualizing Christianity reached through a century from the First Vatican Council to the Second. In spite of and mostly counter to the work of the theologians we have sketched, an ecclesiastically inspired approach (in a general, theological sense) gained ascendancy. What were its essential characteristics?

What was most striking was how under Pius IX, instead of condemning propositions from individual books or authors, the bureaucracy of the Vatican challenged the basic movements of the age and condemned globally entire approaches not just in exegesis but in metaphysics and politics. Moreover, these condemnations were not simply the exercise of jurisdiction but the articulation of a theology. The theology of the Pian era was, first, written in a dead language, an artificial Latin imitating either medieval or baroque writers (curial Latin was an artificial melange of both periods). Second, this theology expressed itself in the terms and concepts of a scholasticism, even if no single medieval doctor was restored and even if Jesuit neoscholasticism was different from Dominican philosophy and theology. A definite theological style, one with little suppleness, emerged out of a mixture of curial, conciliar, and neoscholastic languages. The documents of Vatican I were its model and judge. Their theological expression was an austere linking of clear, abstract terms in Latin propositions, and it avoided coming too close to Scripture or to any particular theologian. Was not this mix timeless? It certainly succeeded at being a-modern, but its ability to inspire Christian life or to address concrete moral issues was limited.

Theology was commanded to have the same rigid standards as dogma and to avoid development and pluralism. Christian teaching was a timeless metaphysics, and so philosophy should be as tightly controlled by the church as revelation. When theology errs it is because an erroneous philosophy has been admitted. Even if modernist principles were not found in Schell or Schanz, Roman documents aimed at a purer, all-encompassing, timeless product. There was a kind of system in this theology: every facet of ecclesiastical thinking and life had its place, and Roman theology, like the administration of the church, was monist: degrees of certitude, hierarchy of revealed truths, distinctions between canon law and dogma were neglected; in this static religious machine oiled by the motto, "bonum ex integra causa, malum ex quocumque defectu" (something is good when every aspect is sound; bad from any defect whatsoever), every piece had an eternal and divinely constituted location in the one religious machine.

In the conflicts with supposed German modernism, *Pascendi* attacked the need for any approach to the divine beyond Aristotelian logic. In the act of faith, in the reception of the sacraments, in ecclesiology and in the being of Christ, objective aspects were stressed, and the introduction of individuality and process in human life was avoided as uncontrollable. What was dangerous—history, life, modern society—lay outside reason, where erring modernists propagated two errors: a metaphysics of process and the search for truth in life as well as in logic. The historical context framing Christian doctrines and practices was avoided. Indeed, to speak another language, to approach the issue of divine activity or soteriology with different words and thought-forms was to render one suspect. The magisterium's treatment of revealed truth shifted attention away from the great themes of Christianity to logic and metaphysics, to curious employments of Aristotelian hylomorphism.

Appearing like a subtle but manipulating Renaissance curian official, this theological style was Roman not only in language but in control. An increasingly assertive papacy refereed theological positions and formulated the correct ones in sparse ecclesiastical propositions, arranging concepts already stated somewhere in the many documents issued by the Vatican. Yves Congar describes how Leo XIII composed dogma, ecclesiology, social ethics, and education into "a synthesis of the doctrines of the Roman school of Vatican I (including documents not promulgated) and a sociology inspired by Thomism." Because the regime of Rome occupied "center and summit," an era of juridicism opened up. "In the last analysis an orthodoxy—not only of faith but of theology—is fixed by a kind of canonization of the conceptual system and of the verbal inheritance of scholasticism. This up to our own times is identified with Catholicism."[2]

With its sponsorship of a theological style and its fear of theological diversity or creativity, the Vatican became a university. Previously, the Curia had drawn on European schools and their theologians for advice and solutions, but universities were no longer trustworthy. In the second half of the nineteenth century, with the mistrust of theologians (which began with the Munich assembly) and of bishops and national episcopal conferences (who viewed the pastoral needs of their dioceses differently than did Rome), the members of the Curia included permanent but not always well-educated theological advisers. This shift to the Vatican as a substitute university theology faculty also involved, for the century after 1860, the extensive employment of more or less competent theologians drawn exclusively from the Roman schools. Other universities and theological traditions were more and more viewed as adversaries or even heretics. This theological style discouraged speculation and public expression of Christianity. Applied ethical issues were pondered apart from history and the gospel, while speculative doctrinal studies were touched through the safer area of textual research.[3]

Paradoxically, Roman, Latin theology displayed its own "modern" stance. There was a definite turn toward the subject, a fascination with the mental, and a curial system. Revelation became propositions of dogma more than historical events. Latin definitions were compared. Within apologetics the epistemological was highlighted to establish levels of certitude in faith and argumentation. Thomism was defined as a realism, but a realism of accurate concept and timeless existence over against the vagaries of modern philosophies. The result of this was that Aristotelian categories and causes distracted from the gospel of grace and overemphasized theodicy. Theology became an extrinsically arranged aggregate of Latin concepts without organic unity and supported by church authority. Rome had produced its own modern system, which distracted people from faith's questions to philosophy's language and offered a mélange of philosophy, theology, and law. Even within this limited theology, the quality of thinking and teaching declined —even as the appreciation and knowledge of Aquinas increased. As Gerald McCool has pointed out:

> Unfortunately, however, the quality of the new professors at the Gregorian and at other Roman institutions fell far below the quality of the professors whom they had replaced. . . . The Roman professors who introduced the philosophy and theology of St. Thomas to their students in the Roman institutions in the last two decades of the nineteenth century were seminary professors rather than creative philosophers and theologians. Their published works were basically

school manuals whose purpose was the clear exposition of safe "received" Thomistic doctrine rather than the stimulation of original thought.[4]

In the conflict over scholastic and idealistic approaches, two ways of thinking, two families of language confronted each other. Skeptical of modern benefits, the church espoused a terminology from the past which could only lead to the condemnation of anyone who would draw, out of the nineteenth century or for the twentieth, a new life and meaning from traditional dogmas.

III. Perduring Themes

The motif of understanding and faith which occupied Hegel and Görres in 1805 emerged during these decades as a new form in the balance of nature and grace, and it found consequent applications in church and modernity, faith and university or labor union. While there was less interest in Jesus and the sacraments, issues like the Scriptures' witness to a historical revelation, faith, certitude, and church authority were widely treated. As the decades passed, the dialogue between faith and modern science increased, and moral theology was drawn into the concrete issues of an industrial age. What was a divergence of theological systems in the 1860s became disputes over social issues in the 1890s.

In the early works of Scheeben and Schell, both inspired by Kuhn, the Trinity was brought forth as the central doctrine that defined what was essentially Christian. The Trinity must be expressed in modern ideas but in ways clearly opposed to pantheism. This topic faded as speculative theology faded. Dogmatic theology became either historical research or apologetics.

We have seen in the figure of Alois Schmid the entrance of apologetics into the university curriculum. The different directions of apologetics are endlessly debated. Should apologetics follow only the logic of neo-Aristotelianism or should it employ the newer immanentist approaches? Apologetics treats the logic of theodicy's proofs, the compatibility of faith and revelation with active consciousness, and the prerogatives of the church. An "age of apologetics" says a great deal about how the church viewed culture in the last years of the century. Apologetics describes a Catholicism suspicious not just of the initiatives but of the entire life of modernity, but it also encouraged culture to see the church as antiquarian.

In the latter nineteenth century, ecclesiology was removed from dogmatic theology and inserted into apologetics, canon law or theological gnoseology. The church was presented not as the sacrament of the

Kingdom of God or the extension of the mystery of Christ but as a pyramidical, hierarchical organization with apologetic claims and a universal, immediate jurisdiction centered in the office and person of the pope. Church membership and office became facets of an individual juridically validated, while any lack of acceptance of the church was seen as bordering on willful infidelity. By 1900 the church's relationship to Trinity, Christ, and grace (still stressed in Scheeben and restored in Schell) was widely absent in the ecclesiological texts.[5]

J. E. Kuhn was a more imaginative and profound thinker than Herman Schell, and Schell was more gifted than Karl Adam. There is no doubt that Catholic speculative theology ranging from history to social ethics did not show a high level of creativity in dealing with the long history of Christianity or with the variety of modernity. Why? The answer may lie in the considerable appeal of a neoscholastic alternative to agnostic idealism and Protestant liberalism as well as in the militant centers of the "new" philosophy and theology like Mainz and Münster. Secondly, the string of condemnations over half a century from Günther and Frohschammer to *Pascendi*, joined to the policing of all publications by nunciatures and the Curia, had their effect. By the end of our period serious investigation of historical issues or speculative approaches had almost ceased.

So the history of theology does not always proceed under the laws of progress, and the Roman Catholic conversation with modernity follows its own history, different from decade to decade.

The century's course raced ahead into our century, forming philosophers and historians of dogma, scientists and painters, proceeding through different stages of romanticism and idealism to moods as diverse as psychologism and impressionism. Geniuses emerged as different as Kandinsky and Freud. Schaeffler sees two phases bridging the nineteenth and twentieth centuries. After Vatican I theology placed its efforts not in revealed areas like Christ and the Eucharist but in the metaphysics of proving God's existence and of knowing the divine nature. Inquiry's preference for certitude and credibility over personality and spirit mark theology and philosophy about 1900. Perhaps Schell was unappreciated because his thought was too properly theological: Trinity and human sin were not the issues of the day for Rome. A second phase appeared in the first years of the twentieth century. Ontology declined in influence as the issue of history expanded. Could the historical and incarnational nature of Christianity survive the power of social history? But attention to history was a dubious gift; a potential source of relativity, it would summon forth numerous unimaginative defenses of revelation as ideas accepted by the will impelled by supernatural faith.

IV. *Kirche* and *Reich*

During this period German Catholics were embattled on two sides: politically from Prussian and Protestant Berlin, and theologically and ecclesiastically from Italian and scholastic Rome. Ernst Hanisch notes:

> The conflicts into which German Catholicism entered in the twentieth century were in many ways an inheritance from the previous century. . . . The nineteenth century destroyed many values of conservative Christianity. Other values which history had suppressed were not readily accepted. These new values were political freedom, equality and political democracy. German Catholicism stood in a particularly acute tension between authority and freedom—most of the time authority conquered to the loss of freedom.[6]

An increasingly contentless Christianity composed from 1840 to 1914 by Protestant university faculties keenly attentive to philosophical currents never interested many Catholics. Progressive Catholics had little inclination to become liberal Protestants, although the shock of Vatican I in 1870 and the authoritarianism of the anti-modernist measures of 1907 suggested that step to a few. Catholics received stimuli, insights, and challenges from Protestant thought, but with Ernst Troeltsch and other Protestant heirs to the idealist tradition idealism seemed to have become secular, mental and static. These systems easily absorbed God and religion into the collective self of culture. This was quite different from the dynamic unfolding of a transcendental history whose theory fifty years earlier in Schelling had explained culture. Moreover, by the 1890s Protestantism had generally adopted a skeptical stance toward the "spirituality" of Catholicism (devotions, sacraments, and papacy).[7] Catholics moved away from liberalism in general because liberals in government after the 1840s had exchanged Catholic interests for anti-religious positions. And so, neither liberalism nor modernism achieved in Germany a solid position among Catholic clergy or intelligentsia.

In Döllinger's address in 1863 the future of Catholic theological expression lay in German *Wissenschaft*, because of German dominance in history and philosophy. By 1893 history, process, and freedom seemed dangerous and impious in the eyes of Rome. Certainly Rome's defense of church authority, of tradition and revelation, of epistemology, and of a faith not absorbed in the history of subjectivity enabled a church to exist without either sectarian disintegration or a public liberalism.

In fact, something new had occurred with modern philosophy. Creators of *Wissenschaft* were claiming to replace Christianity, not just to interpret it. Some great figures were too close to revelation (Schelling,

Kierkegaard), while others (Nietzsche, Eduard von Hartmann) were hostile to it. Pius X was viewed by many in Rome during his lifetime as a saint: his restoration of music, liturgy, and sacraments and his positive organization of aspects of Catholic ministry in the foreign missions were distinguished. But Vatican defense could have been accomplished with a greater degree of theological maturity, intellectual understanding, honesty, and charity. The Curia's lack of information, as well as its moods of oscillation or haste, weakened its positions. A misunderstanding of the German situation was often accompanied by extreme measures. Rome seemed incapable of leading without angrily condemning and punishing. From the Munich assembly to the struggle over interconfessional labor unions, the German bishops were increasingly ignored by Rome. Thus the best sources for comprehending the pastoral situation, for easing political tensions, and for improving ecclesial morale were dismissed condescendingly.

V. Toward the Twentieth Century

The Catholic reformers of the early 1900s asked: Did orthodoxy and authority involve isolation and immaturity? The wounds of Döllinger's excommunication and of Schell's condemnation were reopened by the anti-modernist campaign. If this attack did not effect the German theology and church as much as that in other parts of Europe, it did weaken the intellectual life and independence of Catholics. German Catholics lost much of their potential for leadership in their society and their church. The anti-modernist oath divided the clergy and embarrassed intellectuals, while at the same time these measures inclined the bishops, clergy, and laity to accept direction, even the protection, of the state. Alternatives to "Roman allegiance" or "state-Catholicism" were not easily found. As Heinrich Lutz observed:

> The climate in the late-Wilhelminian era was in some areas not unfavorable to Catholicism. The self-criticism of liberalism and a new acceptance of religion in life were positive values. But was there a way out from the self-isolation of the Catholic population beyond aesthetic and philosophical approaches? The answer came at the end of the Wilhelminian period. With the outbreak of war the entire problem of integrating Catholics into German society was completely changed. German destiny—and with it the destiny of Catholicism—rearranged itself in a new way through the crucible of the war. German Catholics unanimously accepted the war, hoping

that from this bloody sacrifice they would finally be fully rehabilitated by the state.[8]

German Catholics had received a feeling of inferiority which had grave political consequences in regard to their enthusiasm for entering both the First and Second World Wars. Ernst Hanisch writes: "The bracketing of political and constitutional questions would lead in 1914 and 1918 to short-sighted stances with drastic consequences: in 1914 to a cheering patriotism for the 'Holy War'; and then in 1918, as Catholics assembled in a democratic republic, to mushrooming hostility and ambition."[9]

The gifted theologians who knew both the old and the new theologies died at the end of this era: Kuhn and Scheeban in 1887 and 1888, Schanz in 1905, Schell in 1906, Schmid in 1910. Only Carl Braig lived beyond the World War. They were not immediately succeeded by equally gifted thinkers.

VI. The Unfinished Agenda

As was the case in 1848, 1863, 1907, and 1950, modernity is an unfinished period. For a church whose forms are frequently drawn from baroque theology and polity and from romantic piety, the Catholic dialogue with modernity remains incomplete. The thought-forms and insights of modernity were silenced but the role of history and transcendental activity (not totally absent from Augustine or Aquinas) were never fully evaluated, answered, or integrated. The theologies which would synthesize patristic and medieval theologies with modern stances were repressed. After World War I modern philosophy assumed new forms: phenomenology, existentialism, transcendental thought. Although the renaissance of interest in Hegel and Schelling around 1900 was short-lived, schools of neo-Kantians flourished, eventually influencing Catholic theology. Phenomenology reached disciples intent upon renewing intrinsically church and worship. The historical study of the Middle Ages contains in itself the critique of every ideological neoscholasticism. All of this is exemplified in Heidegger's reminiscences in his own *Lehrjahre*: His pastor gave him, in the gift of Franz Brentano's book, access to an Aristotelianism deeper than that used by the neoscholastics, while at Freiburg his professor, Carl Braig, introduced him to past idealisms, some with Catholic theological branches.[10]

It can accurately be said that the conquest of an austere curial neoscholasticism, with all its enemies vanquished, reached its greatest extent not in 1950 with *Humani Generis* but during the years before 1919, following the anti-modernist campaign. Beyond World War I there lay a restoration, more linked to life than logic, to sacrament than to textbooks. The historical sacramentality of grace erupted in a multiple renaissance of patristic theology, liturgy, and spirituality, while theology began to explore post-Kantian philosophy. The creative Christian theologies which determine the Catholic church today did not begin just before Vatican II but had their origins in this time between world wars. In the life of Roman Catholicism before, during, and after Vatican II motifs from the nineteenth century were significant. The early Tübingen school influenced the understanding of tradition and the historical life of the church; the centrality of Christ as Word of God was reconsidered within the history of religions; the levels of symbol and sacramentality corresponded to an acceptance of the subjectivity of the human person and the collective personality of the one human race.[11] It is no coincidence, then, that the issue which opened the wounds of intra-Catholic conflict over modernity—nature and grace with its numerous practical and theoretical modalities—is the theme taken up again by the *Nouvelle théologie* and grounds so much in the writings of Teilhard de Chardin and Rahner, the conciliar texts, ecumenical studies, the social encyclicals, and old and new spiritualities. The conciliar theologies of Vatican II replaced the curial-scholastic style by using ideas from Möhler and Schell. Based more upon a sacramentality of culture than in an arrangement of terms, Catholicism today, after Vatican II, occupies a middle ground between the absorption of revelation in language or psyche and papalist or biblical fundamentalisms.

The history sketched in the previous chapters teaches how some issues currently discussed vigorously in the Catholic Church are not brand new, e.g., inculturation, local churches, social issues, Catholics and universities, church and state, the authority and responsibility of national bishops conferences, the problem of exaggerated papal authority, the identification of any "modern theology" with atheism, pantheism, and liberal Protestantism. Scholars strove to do justice to subjectivity and grace, to history and revelation; in short, to work within a middle position between secular modernism and neoscholasticism. To live within a culture and age, even while pursuing a critique of some of its bases and forms, is unavoidable for an incarnational faith. Anti-modernist Catholicism rejected the structures of modernity as false, while in fact these structures were often neutral. Bernhard Welte writes of religion at the end of the nineteenth century:

> What two issues remain to challenge this next century, the twentieth? They are precisely those which emerged to an almost mythical prominence at the beginning of the nineteenth: the activity of consciousness and the history of self, culture, and society. This problem

of the historical in theology vis-à-vis positivist, historical research, before the growing historical consciousness and the philosophical tools at hand, now showed itself to be much greater and more disturbing than it was in the 1820s for the Tübingen theologians. It became clear that for its solution dogmatic theology needed categories of understanding which were carefully prepared in philosophical and fundamental-theological work.[12]

The world-altering shifts of the late nineteenth century were never fully critiqued and employed by Roman Catholicism, and idealism and romanticism lived on in different metamorphoses for a century and a half after Hegel's death. We cannot help but observe Catholics' ignorance of their theological history. When the *kairos* of theology and church stays unrecognized, its process cannot be understood. Major theologians remain unknown; suspicions of heresy are hasty and unjust. What is old appears as new. Thus Vatican II, for many outside of France and Germany, appeared suddenly, seemingly without preparation or ancenstors. The rapid and significant changes brought by Vatican II to worldwide Catholicism shocked many because they had no idea that a century and a half of thinkers and movements were preparing and debating them. In fact, the council took up critically the issues of Schelling and Engels and learned anew from theological heirs to Drey and Staudenmaier. The theologians studied in this volume anticipated Vatican II more than they reflected Vatican I. They did not reject the conclusions of the council of 1870, but they found in those texts only sparse guidelines for articulating revelation with their own times. Thus Döllinger's assembly in Munich points, remotely, toward the next century, even to the years leading to Vatican II, and Schell's theology has more in common with Henri de Lubac and Karl Rahner than it has with Michael Glossner or Christian Pesch.[13]

VII. *Envoi*

In Thomas Mann's *Magic Mountain*, figures meet and discuss their destinies at a Swiss sanitorium. Hans Castorp and his cousin, Joachim, Settembrini, Clawdia Chauchat, and *Hofrat* Behrens personify the conflicts of Europe at the turn of the century. The mysterious east of Russia, the agnostic liberalism of northern Europe, the Spanish neoscholastic veneration of past religion, the boisterous claims of communism and capitalism—all meet in the hospital high amid the Alps. Their conversations amid the snowy peaks present a drama-in-ideas of the period in which this history of theology comes to an end. In Mann's novel, as the First World War was nearing, Leo Naphta—the Jesuit who was also a Communist—would restore a past world and avoid the dangerous and ugly freedoms of modernity. "A vindication, in this respect, of scholasticism is on the way, even well under way, unless all signs fail. Copernicus will go down before Ptolemy. The heliocentric thesis is meeting by degrees with an intellectual opposition which will ultimately succeed. Science will see itself philosophically forced to put the earth back in the position of supremacy in which it was installed by the dogma of the Church."[14] For Mann's characters one could substitute Catholicism's own figures: journalists and reformers, conservative politicians and liberal labor leaders, clerical philosophers and papal nuncios, university professors and bishops, curial officials in Rome and cultural commentators in Munich. All groups would share an awareness of an approaching apocalypse, an uncertainty about their solutions to great problems, and a feeling of being caught in the plans of great powers with which they had little contact.

Future studies will show the relationship of Catholic theology and ecclesiology to the political violence in cities like Munich and Vienna from 1919 up to the end of Hitler. The paradoxical effect of Roman control over piety and polity was to weaken German Catholicism so that its advocacy of life over death was not as strong as it might have been.

Our narrative of theologians has pondered a time of many discoveries; of breakthroughs from electric lighting to atonal music. Great thinkers and artists of the *fin de siècle* noticed that they were living in a time not only of discovery but also of fragmentation. Their's was an age lacking synthesis and harmony. In 1907 Hugo von Hofmannsthal looked anxiously at his times in a lecture whose published form quickly became widely known (Rilke read it to friends on Capri).

> This is the mystery of our age, one of the mysteries out of which the form of our age is composed: in it everything is simultaneously there and not there. . . . This era is, to the point of illness, full of unrealized possibilities and yet, at the same time, full of things which only appear to exist for the sake of their life and do not really bear life in themselves. It is the essence of this era that nothing which really has power over human beings expresses itself metaphorically, externally; but everything is assumed into an inner world. . . .
>
> Our times flee the splintered condition of this world only to uncover yet more fragmentation. They find all the elements of human existence exposed: mechanism of the spirit, bodily conditions, ambiguous relationships in existence. They all lie there like material for constructing a house. . . .

The century we are leaving fashioned for us phenomena too strong; its larvae of mute appearances have been stimulated into too wild a dance. . . . Then came the age which was searching for synthesis, but in a thousand dark hours the deep sources which had sprung forth failed the individual.[15]

For Catholicism the nineteenth century ended with uncertainty and fragmentation. The controversies over dogma and authority extinguished originality, while Catholics felt social and political isolation. Neoscholasticism reached a negative termination in its hostility to both the world's hopes and faith's speculation. The conflicts over labor unions concluded with a solution alienating as well as assisting the working class but ultimately furthered the European pastoral disaster of losing classes to the church. "There emerged," Welte noted,

a theology of the *disassociation of the multiple* . . . corresponding to the isolation typical of thought, feeling, and existence in the modern period in general. . . . More and more theology tended to be an aggregate, externally posited, of individual sentences without unity. In faith, sacraments, and church the external and objective moments are sharply emphasized but then separated from the subjective, the personal, the inner. The disassociation of church and society, of theology and world, of Catholics and Protestants corresponds to the split mode of thinking in theology itself.[16]

After World War I Catholicism would find a renaissance, a resurrection of its resources in symbol and mysticism, in church and movement. If anti-modernism briefly silenced theological originality, the shock of the war arranged the stimuli differently. The role of history in medieval thought, the new philosophies attempting to draw subjectivity and objectivity together, the Bible's centrality and vitality, modern literature and art all were found to disclose the dimension of the holy. The tragedy of defeat in Germany eased the confessional tensions even as it permitted Catholics some ecclesiastical freedom. Distinctions between the ideologies of modernity—of secularism or Marxism—and its legitimate thought-forms were now recognized; there was a new acceptance of living in one's own age and rejection of a nostalgia for the medieval and the baroque. Today modern thought-forms are neither ideologically embraced nor fundamentalistically rejected by Catholics, who have benefited by not being overwhelmed by the earlier liberal absorption of revelation and tradition. What is today called "postmodern" is so far either a premodern conservativism or the verbal methodologies of modernity carried to an austere emptiness. Catholicism, as an interpretation of revelation and as a vital church, however, has not yet fully understood, much less realized, its life within a cultural epoch reaching from the American Revolution to the end of Marxism in Eastern Europe.

Both papacy and imperial government would change after 1919. Liturgy and spirituality came to balance the austerity of an apologetics obsessed with past miracles and prophecies. The possibility of fashioning a pastoral and reflective theology within the later segments of modernity would exist. Welte concluded: "History has taught us that major, luminary figures of theology for a particular age cannot be fashioned by force: they need the grace of their hour bestowed by the mystery of history. But their appearance can certainly be prepared."[17] From 1920 to 1960 liberating historians and gifted theoreticians of the dialogue between neoscholastic and idealist worldviews were preparing metaphorically the Petrine basilica's hall for a gathering of theologians and church leaders intent upon revivifying the beliefs, sacraments, and theologies—the very world—of Western Christianity. How that would happen is the further history of Catholic thought, from 1919 to the surprising summons of Vatican II in 1959, and beyond to the vital postconciliar period.

Synchronology

1850

Philosophy	Roman Catholic Theology	Culture
A. Comte, *Système de politique positive* (1854)	Pius IX (1846–1878)	R. Wagner, *Lohengrin* (1850)
F. Schelling (d. 1854)	J. Kleutgen, *Die Theologie der Vorzeit* (1853–1874)	E. Delacroix, *The Lion Hunt* (1854)
J. Frohschammer, *Über den Ursprung der menschlichen Seele* (1854)	Dogma of the Immaculate Conception (1854)	Lincoln and Douglas debates (1858)
J. Sengler, *Erkenntnislehre* (1858)	F. de Lamennais (d. 1854)	J. A. Ingres, *The Turkish Bath* (1859)
C. Darwin, *Origin of the Species* (1859)	A. Rosmini (d. 1855)	C. Dickens, *A Tale of Two Cities* (1859)
J. S. Mill, *On Liberty* (1859)	Apparitions at Lourdes (1858)	

1860

Philosophy	Roman Catholic Theology	Culture
K. Marx, *Das Kapital* (1867)	F. Pilgram, *Physiologie der Kirche* (1860)	J. Burckhardt, *Civilization of the Renaissance in Italy* (1860)
E. von Hartmann, *Philosophie des Unbewusstseins* (1869)	Munich assembly of theologians and papal letter *Tuas Libenter* (1863)	E. Manet, *Olympia* (1863)
J. Kleutgen, *Die Philosophie der Vorzeit* (Münster, 1860–1863)	A. Schmid, *Wissenschaftliche Richtungen auf dem Gebiete des Katholizismus in neuester und gegenwärtiger Zeit* (1862)	E. Renan, *La Vie de Jésus* (1863)
F. Brentano, *Von der mannigfachen Bedeutung des Seienden nach Aristoteles* (1862)	*Syllabus Errorum* (1864)	R. Wagner, *Tristan und Isolde* (1865)
	M. J. Scheeben, *Die Mysterien des Christentums* (1865)	Dynamite invented by A. Nobel (1866)
	J. J. I. von Döllinger, *Der Papst und das Concil von Janus* (1869)	

1

1870

L. A. Feuerbach (d. 1872)
W. Wundt, *Physiological Psychology* (1873)
E. von Hartmann, *Phänomenologie des sittlichen Bewusstseins: Prolegomena zu jeder künftigen Ethik* (1879)

Vatican I and the Dogma of Infallibility (1870)
J. H. Newman, *Essay in Aid of a Grammar of Assent* (1870)
Kulturkampf begins (1871)
J. J. I. von Döllinger excommunicated (1871)
M. J. Scheeben, *Handbuch der katholischen Dogmatik* (1873)
P. Guéranger (d. 1875)
Leo XIII, *Aeterni Patris* (1879)

Franco-German War (1870)
First Impressionist Exhibit in Paris (1871)
G. Verdi, *Aida* (1871)
J. Brahms, First and Second Symphonies (1877)
H. Ibsen, *A Doll's House* (1879)

1880

C. Braig, *Die Zukunftsreligion des Unbewussten* (1882)
F. Nietzsche, *Thus Spoke Zarathustra* (1883)
W. Dilthey, *Einleitung in die Geisteswissenschaften* (1883)
H. Cohen, *Kants Begründung der Ästhetik* (1889)
H. Bergson, *Essai sur les donnés immédiates . . . .* (1889)

H. Denzinger (d. 1883)
J. B. Franzelin (d. 1886)
P. Schanz, *Apologie des Christentums* (1887)
C. Werner (d. 1888)
M. J. Scheeben (d. 1888)
C. Werner, *Der heilige Thomas von Aquino* (1889)
H. Schell, *Katholische Dogmatik* (1889)

F. Dostoevsky, *The Brothers Karamazov* (1880)
R. Wagner, *Parsifal* (1882)
C. Debussy, *The Afternoon of a Faun* (1882)
Oxford Movement (1883)
G. Mahler, Symphony no. 2 (1888)
Eiffel Tower (1889)

Philosophy	Roman Catholic Theology	Culture
	1890	
J. Royce, *The Spirit of Modern Philosophy* (1892)	J. H. Newman (d. 1890)	C. Monet, studies of Rouen Cathedral (1892)
F. Brentano, *Über die Zukunft der Philosophie* (1893)	École Biblique founded (1890)	E. Munch, *The Scream* (1893)
M. Blondel, *Action* (1893)	J. J. I. von Döllinger (d. 1890)	O. Wilde, *Salome* (1893)
P. Natorp, *Religion innerhalb der Grenzen der Humanität* (1894)	Leo XIII, *Rerum Novarum* (1891)	P. I. Tchaikowsky, Symphony no. 6 (1894)
H. Rickert, *Kulturwissenschaft und Naturwissenschaft* (1899)	J. Frohschammer (d. 1893)	Y. B. Yeats, *Poems* (1895)
	Lord Halifax begins the Anglo-Catholic movement (1894)	G. Puccini, *La Bohème* (1896)
	H. Schell, *Der Katholicismus als Prinzip des Fortschritts* (1897)	
	1900	
B. Croce, *Aesthetics* (1902)	A. Schmid, *Apologetik* (1900)	A. von Harnack, *Das Wesen des Christentums* (1900)
W. James, *Varieties of Religious Experience* (1902)	E. Troeltsch, *Die Absoluheit des Christentums und die Religionsgeschichte* (1901)	J. Conrad, *Lord Jim* (1900)
H. Cohen, *System der Philosophie* (1902–1912)	A. Loisy, *L'Evangile et l'Eglise* (1902)	T. Mann, *Buddenbrooks* (1901)
G. E. Moore, *Principia ethica* (1903)	A. Ehrhard, *Der Katholizismus und das 20. Jahrhundert* (1902)	J. B. Shaw, *Man and Superman* (1903)
B. Russell, *Principles of Mathematics* (1903)	Religious orders dissolved in France (1903)	H. von Hofmannsthal, *Electra* (1903)
E. Cassirer, *Das Erkenntnisproblem* (1906)	Pius X (1903–1914)	R. M. Rilke, *Book of Hours* (1905)
H. Bergson, *L'Evolution créatrice* (1907)	P. Schanz (d. 1905)	Die Brücke painters group (1905)
O. Braun, *Hinauf zum Idealismus!* (1908)	H. Schell (d. 1906)	Cubism with Picasso and Braque (1908)
W. Dilthey, *Der Aufbau der geschichtlichen Welt in den Geisteswissenschaften* (1910)	*Pascendi Dominici Gregis* (1907)	A. Schoenberg, *Five Pieces for Orchestra* (1909)
	C. Braig, *Modernstes Christentum und moderne Religionspsychologie* (1907)	
	F. von Hügel, *The Mystical Element of Religion* (1908)	

1910

P. Rousselot, *L'Être et l'esprit* (1910)
P. Tillich's dissertations on Schelling (1910, 1912)
E. Husserl, *Ideen zu einer reinen Phänomenologie und phänomenologischen Philosophie* (1913)
M. Scheler, *Vom Umsturz der Werte* (1919)
M. Heidegger's dissertation on Scotist philosophy (1916)
E. Stein's dissertation on phenomenological psychology (1916)

A. Schmid (d. 1910)
Statement of the 24 Thomistic theses (1910)
H. Grisar, *Luther* (1911)
C. Braig, *Der Modernismus* (1911)
M. Grabmann, *Geschichte der scholastischen Methode* (1911)
Benedict XIV (1914–1922)
R. Guardini, *Vom Geist der Liturgie* (1918)

S. Freud, *Psychoanalysis* (1910)
R. Strauss, *Der Rosenkavalier* (1911)
A. Schoenberg, *Pierrot Lunaire* (1912)
V. Kandinsky, *On the Spiritual in Art* (1912)
A. Einstein, *General Theory of Relativity* (1913)
New York Armory Show of Modern Art (1913)
I. Stravinsky, *Le Sacre du Printemps* (1913)

4

Abbreviations

C	Yves Congar, *L'Eglise de Saint Augustin à l'époque moderne* (Paris: Cerf, 1970)
CP	*Christliche Philosophie im katholischen Denken des 19. und 20. Jahrhunderts*, ed. E. Coreth, 2 vols. (Graz, 1987, 1988)
DHS	V. Berning, *Das Denken Herman Schells* (Essen, 1964)
EThL	*Ephemerides Theologicae Lovanienses*
H	*Hochland*
Hgn	A. Haugen, *Der Reformkatholizismus in der Diözese Rottenburg (1902–1920)* (Stuttgart, 1962)
Hn	H. Hürten, *Kurze Geschichte des deutschen Katholizismus 1800–1960* (Mainz, 1860)
Hoc	E. Hocedez, *Histoire de la théologie au XIXe siècle*, 3 vols. (Brussels, 1947–1952)
HPBl	*Historisch-politische Blätter*
J	H. Jedin et al., eds., *Handbuch der Kirchengeschichte* (Freiburg, 1963–1972)
JPsT	*Jahrbuch für Philosophie und spekulative Theologie*
K	*Der Katholik*
KD	H. Schell, *Katholische Dogmatik* (Munich, 1968–)
KL	H. Schell, *Kleinere Schriften* (Paderborn, 1908)
KThD	*Katholische Theologen Deutschlands im 19. Jahrhundert*, H. Fries and G. Schwaiger, eds. (Munich, 1977), 3 vols.
LThK	*Lexikon für Theologie und Kirche*, 2nd ed. (1957–1967)
MThZ	*Münchener theologische Zeitschrift*
NCE	*New Catholic Encyclopedia* (1967–1979)
PhJ	*Philosophisches Jahrbuch*
R	A. Rauscher, *Der soziale und politische Katholizismus* (Munich, 1981), 2 vols.
Sch	K. Schatz, *Zwischen Säkularisation und Zweitem Vatikanum: Der Weg des deutschen Katholizismus im 19. und 20. Jahrhundert* (Frankfurt, 1986)
Sp	W. Spael, *Das katholische Deutschland im 20. Jahrhundert. Seine Pionier—und Krisensituation, 1890–1945* (Würzburg, 1964)
ThO	(Tübingen) *Theologische Quartalschrift*

Tr   N. Trippen, *Theologie und Lehramt im Konflikt: Die kirchlichen Mass-nahmen gegen den Modernismus im Jahre 1907 und ihre Auswir-kungen in Deutschland* (Freiburg, 1977)

W   B. Welte, "Zum Strukturwandel der katholischen Theologie im 19. Jahrhundert," *Auf der Spur des Ewigen* (Freiburg, 1965), pp. 350ff.

Notes

Introduction

1. T. O'Meara, *Romantic Idealism and Roman Catholicism* (Notre Dame, Ind.: University of Notre Dame Press, 1982).

2. H. Hürten, *Kurze Geschichte des deutschen Katholizismus 1800–1960* (Mainz, 1860); A. Kolping, *Katholische Theologie Gestern und Heute* (Bremen, 1964); A. Rauscher, *Der soziale und politische Katholizismus* (Munich, 1981), 2 vols.; W. Spael *Das katholische Deutschland im 20. Jahrhundert, 1890–1945* (Würzburg, 1964); K. Schatz, *Zwischen Säkularisation und Zweitem Vatikanum* (Frankfurt, 1986).

3. See H. Brück, *The History of the Catholic Church* (New York, 1885), 2: 407ff.

4. Hermann Broch observed: "It has frequently been remarked that the distinctive cultural phases of modern European history have always lasted for about three generations. The nineteenth century is no different: it lasted not from 1800 to 1900 but approximately from 1848 to the First World War" (*Hugo von Hofmannsthal and His Time: The European Imagination, 1860–1920* [Chicago, 1984], p. 143).

5. "If one accepts the usual division of recent Catholic theology into periods, that from 1760 to 1830 is the epic of decline, 1830 to 1860 a time when German speculative theology was flourishing, and from 1860 until now we have the more or less complete return to scholastic theology. The year 1870 can serve as a marker since the Vatican Council and its constitution on faith expressed the principles upon which Catholic theology and the truth should be construed . . . , an enterprise which is thoroughly ecclesiastical and apologetic" (Paul Schanz, "Die Katholische Tübingen Schule," *ThQ* 80 [1898]: 1ff.).

1. The Second Half of a Century (1840–1914)

1. Ernst Bergmann, *Der Geist des XIX Jahrhunderts* (Breslau, 1927), p. 14; similarly K. Leese, *Philosophie und Theologie im Spätidealismus* (Berlin, 1925) who places dividing lines in 1830 and 1870; the period after 1870 is marked by both a critique of the modern philosophy being developed and by a total questioning of religion and Christianity.

2. See Peter Uwe Hohendahl, *Literarische Kultur im Zeitalter des Liberalismus* (Munich, 1985).

3. For this earlier time, see O'Meara, *Romantic Idealism and Roman Catholicism. Schelling and the Theologians.*

4. *Sch*, p. 95.

5. H. Schnädelbach, *Philosophy in Germany, 1831–1933* (Cambridge, 1984), p. 3. "The age around 1830 signifies a deep collapse. The novels of that period are particularly interesting for the historian in depicting the age, for instance Laube's *Das junge Europa* (1833)—free, enthusiastic, emancipated, social—and Gutzkow, inimical to religion, detached and uncertain, or Willkomm's, *Die Europeamüden: Modernes Lebensbild.* Europe is sick of and sated with civilization; the figures of the novel are alienated and disinterested and skeptical.... Here for the first time there are critical words for industrialization" (E. Fahrenhorst, *Das neunzehnte Jahrhundert: Beharrung und Auflosung* [Hildesheim, 1983], p. 14). See also W. Bauer, *Deutsche Kultur von 1830–1870* (Potsdam, 1937); G. Needham, *Nineteenth-Century Realist Art* (New York, 1988).

6. L. Trost, F. Leist, *König Maximilian II von Bayern und Schelling, Briefwechsel* (Stuttgart, 1890), p. 280; C. Hinrichs, "Schelling und 'der Konflikt der modernen Welt' in Ranke's 'Epoche der neueren Geschichte,' " in W. Berges, ed., *Zur Geschichte und Problematik der Demokratie* (Berlin, 1958), pp. 88ff.

7. *Histoire de la Philosophie* in the *Encyclopédie de la Pléiade* sees philosophy continuing in two lines. The first is the concluding aftermath of the great epoch of romanticism and includes Hartmann and Kierkegaard as well as Dilthey, Klages, and Keyserling reaching on up to Scheler and Jung. The second pursues a neocriticism becoming neo-Kantianism. Psychology (Fries, Beneke and Herbart) seeks a rapport between philosophy and science, while Vogt, Mach and experimental psychologists introduce an agnostic positivism hostile to metaphysics. Before the turn of the century a new search for metaphysics, whether in the past (neo-Hegelianism, H. Beckers) or on its own (A. Riehl) leads to a Kantian or even Fichtean theory of the self, to Carnap, Rickert, Natorp and Cohen. Nietzsche stands alone in the general current of life as modified by evolution, while neo-Thomism is initially tied to papal politics; *Histoire de la Philosophie* 3 (Paris, 1974).

8. Schnädelbach, *Philosophy in Germany*, p. 21.

9. Ibid., p. 34.

10. H. Plessner, "Zur Soziologie der modernen Forschung und ihrer Organisation in der deutschen Universität," *Diesseits der Utopie* (Frankfurt, 1974), pp. 130ff.

11. See M. Ettlinger, *Geschichte der Philosophie von der Romantik bis zur Gegenwart* (Munich, 1924); H. Noack, *Die Philosophie Westeuropas* (Basel, 1976).

12. E. Coreth, *Philosophie des 19. Jahrhunderts* (Stuttgart, 1984), pp. 125ff.

13. Kurt Leese names the period from 1830 to 1870 "*Spätidealismus*" but sees after that a further neoidealism; *Philosophie und Theologie im Spätidealismus* (Berlin, 1929), pp. 1ff. "In the philosophy of the university positivism never fully dominates. The impact of German idealism was too strong.... Soon there developed neo-Kantianism, defending the intellectual against each materialistic dilution"

(H. Stephan, M. Schmidt, *Geschichte der evangelischen Theologie in Deutschland seit dem Idealismus* [New York, 1973], pp. 252f.).

14. *W*, p. 396.

15. K.-E. Lönne, *Politischer Katholizismus im 19. und 20. Jahrhundert* (Frankfurt, 1986), p. 11.

16. A. Kraus, "Der Kulturkampf in Bayern," *Geschichte Bayerns* (Munich, 1983), p. 563.

17. Ibid., p. 565.

18. *Hn*, p. 134.

19. W. Brandmüller, "Die Publikation des I. Vatikanischen Konzils in Bayern," *Zeitschrift für Bayerische Landesgeschichte* 31 (1968): 197ff., 576ff.

20. Cf. J. Bachem, *Preussen und die katholische Kirche* (Cologne, 1887); J. B. Kissling, *Geschichte des Kulturkampfes im Deutschen Reich*, 3 vols. (Freiburg, 1911–16); F. Vigener, *Ketteler* (Munich, 1924); K. Buchheim, *Ultramontanismus und Demokratie* (Munich, 1963); R. Morsey, "Bismarck und der Kulturkampf," *Archiv für Kulturgeschichte* 39 (1957): 232ff.

21. Cf. E. Soderini, *Leo XIII und der deutsche Kulturkampf* (Vienna, 1935); J. Heckel, "Die Beilegung des Kulturkampfes in Preussen," *Zeitschrift der Savigny-Stiftung für Rechtsgeschichte, Kanonistische Abteilung* 19 (1930): 215–353; R. Lill, *Die Wende im Kulturkampf* (Tübingen, 1973).

22. R. Lill, "Der Kulturkampf in Preussen und im Deutschen Reich," *J* 6 no. 2: 77. An *Evangelischer Bund* was founded in 1886 by Protestants who viewed the cessation of the Kulturkampf as capitulation to the Catholic church, and this carried on the confessional polemic; see M. Buchner, *Kaiser Wilhelm II, seine Weltanschauung und die deutschen Katholiken* (Leipzig, 1929); S. Merkel, *Die katholische Kirche: Deutschland unter Kaiser Wilhelm II* (Berlin, 1914).

23. A. Kraus, "Bayerns Weg in das Bismarckreich," *Geschichte Bayerns* (Munich, 1983), p. 551.

24. B. Hubensteiner, *Bayerische Geschichte. Staat und Volk, Kunst und Kultur* (Munich, 1985), p. 435. Representative of the Catholic criticism of Lutz's views are *Theologische Plaudereien des Ministers von Lutz* (Amberg, 1872); A. Kuhn, *Eine Ministerantwort im Lichte der Wahrheit* (Freiburg, 1871); *Christus oder—Lutz? Eintracht oder Trennung von Kirche und Staat?* (Regensburg, 1872); and Lutz's response, *Die ministerielle Antwort* (Regensburg, 1872).

25. D. Albrecht, "Von der Reichsgründung bis zum Ende des Ersten Weltkrieges (1871–1918)," in M. Spindler, ed. *Handbuch der bayerischen Geschichte* 4 (Munich, 1967): 324.

26. A. Kraus, "Der Kulturkampf in Bayern," *Geschichte Bayerns*, p. 573.

27. Alluding to the link between the *Kulturkampf* and the *Politik* of National Socialism, historians have seen the contra-constitutional treatment of the Jesuits, with expulsion rather than mass death, as a rehearsal for the Nazis' program for Jews: "Scandalous and deformed developments of recent German history were thereby given their foundation" (R. Lill, "Der Kulturkampf in Preussen . . . ," p. 41).

2. The Two Directions of German Catholic Theology (1864–1914)

1. "The Munich Nunciature assumed during this period a very important role. Although the nuncios were accredited by the king of Bavaria, their ecclesiastical area of influence from the time of Viale-Prela (1838–1845) had expanded beyond the borders of Bavaria" (R. Lill, "Die deutschen Theologieprofessoren vor dem Vatikanum I im Urteil des Münchener Nuntius," *Reformata Reformanda* 2 [Münster, 1965]: p. 483). For a detailed view of the Congregation of the Index vis-à-vis German theologians from 1850 to 1880 see F. Reusch, *Der Index der verbotenen Bücher* (Bonn, 1885), vol. 2.

2. For a detailed picture see John P. Boyle, "The Ordinary Magisterium: Towards a History of the Concept" (parts 1 and 2), *Heythrop Journal* 20 (1979): 380ff. and 21 (1980): 14ff.; P. Gams, *Die Verhandlungen der Versammlung katholischer Gelehrter in München* (Regensburg, 1863); J. Friedrich, *I. von Döllinger* 3 (Munich, 1901): 270ff. Haneberg (1816–1876) had been a member of Görres's circle in Munich. His field was Scripture (though he held a view of inspiration which Rome rejected). After refusing several dioceses, he became bishop of Speyer in 1872 but by then had separated himself from Döllinger and had worked on the preparations for Vatican I.

3. Gonella to Antonelli, August 21, 1863, cited in Boyle, part 1, p. 384f.

4. On the symbolic role of the Abbey of St. Bonifaz, see T. O'Meara, "The Origins of the Liturgical Movement and German Romanticism," *Worship* 59 (1985): 326ff.

5. Döllinger, "Die Vergangenheit und Gegenwart der katholischen Theologie," *Kleinere Schriften* (Stuttgart, 1890), p. 195; see also Gams, *Verhandlungen*, pp. 24–59.

6. Döllinger, "Die Vergangenheit . . . ," p. 186. The Munich congress adopted as a resolution: "Whoever adheres to the Catholic faith is bound in conscience by that fact to submit to the dogmatic decrees emanating from the infallible authority of the church in every scientific investigation. That subjection in no way removes or destroys that liberty which is natural and proper and at the same time necessary to science" (Gams, *Verhandlungen*, pp. 5ff.). In August 1863 Charles Montalambert addressed a similar congress in Malines on Catholic freedom.

7. H. Denzinger, A. Schönmentzer, *Enchiridion Symbolorum* (Herder, 1963), pp. 2775–2880. John Boyle argues that the source of this theology of ordinary magisterium lies with Joseph Kleutgen (*Theologie der Vorzeit* [Münster, 1853] 1: 47), the pioneer of the neoscholastic revival who, in turn, is arguing against the view of the leading Tübingen and Freiburg theologian, J. B. Hirscher (Boyle, part 2, 17ff.). Reaction to the congress fashioned *Tuas Libenter* and other documents drawn from the new approach of the Roman curia toward theologians, bishops, and the local church (Boyle, part 2, pp. 23ff.). The letter *Tuas libenter* would summon up—beyond dogma, Scripture, and theology—a global, ill-defined area expressed by the new term "ordinary magisterium."

8. *W.*, p. 395.

9. Lill, "Die deutschen Theologieprofessoren . . . ," p. 507. On the phases of Döllinger's scholarly struggle linked to the success of ultramontane forces, see *Sch*, pp. 112ff.

10. *J* 6, no. 1: 693f. and 772. A vivid picture of the Munich Assembly, its preparations and aftermath, can be gained from the literature of the time: e.g., F. Michelis, *Kirche oder Partei? Ein offenes und freies Wort an den deutschen Episkopat* (Münster, 1865) and the anonymous reply *Die Kirche und die Versammlung katholischer Gelehrter* (Mainz, 1864).

11. Karl Eschweiler wrote a book illustrating two directions exemplified by the figures of M. J. Scheeben and G. Hermes. Unfortunately these two examples were inaccurate and skewed. The representative of the scholastic direction, Scheeben, while a conservative, was a creative thinker who owed more to patristics than to scholasticism; Hermes's Kantianism kept him in the Enlightenment rather than idealist thought. See Eschweiler, *Die zwei Wege der neueren Theologie* (Augsburg, 1926).

12. *W*, p. 395. For histories that are frequently little more than lists of names and works, see M. Grabmann, *Die Geschichte der katholischen Theologie seit dem Ausgang der Väterzeit* (Freiburg, 1933); *Hoc*, vols. 2 and 3 (1952, 1955); J. Hergenröther, *Handbuch der allgemeinen Kirchengeschichte* vol. 4 (Freiburg, 1917): 659ff.

13. R. Aubert, "Scholastiker und Germaniker gegen die 'Deutsche Theologie,'" *J* 6, no. 1: 689ff.

14. On the relationships of Deutinger and Döllinger to Schelling, see O'Meara, *Romantic Idealism*, pp. 161ff.; L. Dotzler, "Über das Verhältnis M. Deutingers zu I. Döllinger," *Jahrbuch für altbayerische Kirchengeschichte* 23 (1963): 130ff.; L. Kastner, *Martin Deutingers Leben und Schriften* (Munich, 1875).

15. *Über die Stellung und Aufgabe der Philosophie in der Gegenwart* (Munich, 1847), pp. 4f., 10f.

16. (Munich, 1875). See also by Beckers, "Historisch-kritische Erläuterungen zu Schelling's Abhandlungen über die Quelle der ewigen Wahrheiten und Kant's Ideal der reinen Vernunft," *Abhandlungen der philosophischen-philologischen Classe der königlich Bayerischen Akademie der Wissenschaften* 8 (1858): 719ff.; *Die Unsterblichkeitslehre Schelling's im ganzen Zusammenhange ihrer Entwicklung dargestellt* (Munich, 1865); *Über die Bedeutung der Schellingschen Metaphysik* (Munich, 1861); *Über die wahre und bleibende Bedeutung der Naturphilosophie Schellings* (Munich, 1864); *Fr. Wilh. Joseph v. Schelling: Denkrede* (Munich, 1855); *Festrede zur Enthüllung des Standbildes Schellings* . . . (Munich, 1861); "Über die Vertretung der Schellingschen Philosophie an der Universität München," "Schellings Tod," and "Schelling's letzte Philosophie," in *Neue Münchener Zeitung, Beilage*, 1854 (nos. 67, 203, 245); "Schellings Nachlass," *Allgemeine Zeitung, Beilage* 1860 (nos. 172–175); "Schelling Theosoph?" *Allgemeine Zeitung*, 1865 (no. 365); "Jakob Böhme—Schelling—Darwin," *Allgemeine Zeitung, Beilage* 1883 (nos. 34–36).

17. A. Dryoff, "Martin Deutinger als Vorläufer der Wertphilosophie," *PhJ* 28 (1915): 458.

18. F. Kirchner, *Über das Grundprinzip des Weltprozesses mit besonderer Berücksichtigung J. Frohschammers* (Köthen, 1882), pp. 179ff. Other Catholic figures studied Schelling. J. N. Oischinger, who viewed medieval and recent scholasticisms as odd upstarts, wrote a *Speculative Entwicklung der Hauptsysteme der neueren Philosophie von Descartes bis Hegel* (Schaffhausen, 1854) devoting a hundred pages to Schelling. On Frohschammer and Oischinger, see T. O'Meara, "Thomas Aquinas and

the Idealist Tradition," *Gregorianum* 68 (1987): 719ff. Franz Brentano had considered the stages of Schelling's philosophy in his *Habilitation*, but he concluded that through their emphasis upon intuition post-Kantian thinkers were a degeneration from logic and scientific theory; see reminiscences by O. Kraus and E. Husserl in L. McAlister, *The Philosophy of Brentano* (London, 1976), pp. 3, 50.

19. Huber, *Der Jesuitenorden nach seiner Verfassung und Doktrin, Wirksamkeit und Geschichte* (Berlin, 1873).

20. Huber, *Professor Stöckl in Münster: Ein Beitrag zur Charakteristik neu-scholastischer Wissenschaftlichkeit* (Munich, 1864) answered by Stöckl, *Professor Huber in München: Ein Beitrag zur Charakteristik der gegenwärtigen Münchener Philosophie und philosophischen Polemik* (Mainz, 1865); Huber's *Die Philosophie der Kirchenväter* (Munich, 1859) appeared in the same year as Stöckl's *Geschichte der Philosophie der patristischen Zeit*.

21. See E. Zirngiebel *Johannes Huber* (Gotha, 1881); W. Ziegenfuss, "J. N. Huber," *Philosophen-Lexikon* 1 (1949): 438.

22. *Die Prinzipien der Theologie* (Munich, 1875), p. 186.

23. B. Casper, *Friedrich Pilgram* (Graz, 1970), p. 14; see also B. Casper, *Die Einheit aller Wirklichkeit: Friedrich Pilgram und seine theologische Philosophie* (Freiburg, 1961); Casper, "Friedrich Pilgram," *CP* 1: 319ff.; W. Becker, "Einführung," in F. Pilgram, *Physiologie der Kirche* (Mainz, 1931); H. Keller, "Zur Sociologie der Kirche," *Scholastik* 6 (1933): 243ff.; H. v. Mallinckrodt, "Sozialität und Verstehen" (Diss., Münster, 1970). F. J. Stegmann, *Von der ständischen Sozialreform zur staatlichen Sozialpolitik* (Munich, 1965); G. Zieler, *Die Wirklichkeit der Gemeinschaft: Der philosophische und theologische Beitrag Friedrich Pilgrams zur sozialen Problematik* (Mainz, 1965).

24. *Physiologie der Kirche: Forschungen über die geistigen Gesetze in denen die Kirche nach ihrer natürlichen Seite besteht* (Mainz, 1860), p. 202.

25. See F. X. Himmelstein in *Katholische Wochenschrift* 6 (1855): 441ff.

26. Yves Congar observes: "Pilgram said that he owed his major intuition to Möhler, the principle of community, inseparable from the principle of reality.... Pilgram developed all this in a remarkable way which often presented issues which occupy theology today" (*C*, pp. 423f.).

27. See Hergenröther, *Handbuch* 4: 668ff.; for the university lectures see *Verzeichnis der Vorlesungen an der königlichen Ludwig-Maximilians-Universitat zu München*, 1875–1910. Constantin Frantz was a Protestant whose thought into the 1880s drew on Schelling. His *Schelling's positive Philosophie* (Köthen, 1879), dedicated to Richard Wagner, worked at making "this rich treasure of ideas" relevant to the recent changes in philosophies drawn either to rationalism or to materialism-empiricism. His "Vorwort" gives a rare view of Schelling studies in the 1870s. Frantz suggested in conclusion that, like the Catholic Görres Society, a Schelling society should be founded which would contribute to the harmony of all Christians, forecast by the view of the churches at the end of Schelling's *Philosophie der Offenbarung* (pp. xvi, 302f.) See also F. Hoffman, "Die Gotteslehre Schellings," *Athenäum* 3 (1864): 1ff., 216ff., 349ff., 537ff. On the permanent heritage of Schelling for the University of

Munich, see Alois Dempf, "Schelling, Baader und Görres. Die Münchner Philosophen der Romantik," *Geistige Welt* 2 (1947): 10ff.

28. *Wissenschaftliche Richtungen auf dem Gebiete des Katholizismus* (Munich, 1862), p. 37.

29. "Uber Schelling, Baader und Görres," in Andreas Schmid, *Geheimrat Dr. Alois Schmid* . . . , (Regensburg, 1911), p. 233. "For all who ever heard his lectures or read his rich writings, the memory of Schelling will always remain in the highest honor. There is no one who has the least real acquaintance with the profound intellectual production of this man . . . who is not filled with extraordinary respect toward him. His spiritiual greatness called forth the astonishment of our century" (M. Deutinger, "Philosophische Briefe," *Abendblatt zur neuen Münchener Zeitung* 32 [1856]: 125). On the school of Munich, see *J*, pp. 311ff.

30. F. Strich, *Die Mythologie in der deutschen Literatur von Klopstock bis Wagner* (Munich, 1910), pp. 29ff., 107ff., 359ff.; A. Dryoff, *C. J. Windischmann und sein Kreis* (Cologne, 1916).

31. Recent exceptions are *Christliche Philosophie im katholischen Denken des 19. and 20. Jahrhunderts: Rückgriff auf scholastisches Erbe* (Graz, 1988) and the studies of G. McCool.

32. See G. McCool, *Catholic Theology in the Nineteenth Century* (New York, 1977); T. Schafer, *Die erkenntnistheoretische Kontroverse Kleutgen—Gunther: Ein Beitrag zur Entstehungsgeschichte der Neuscholastik* (Paderborn, 1961); *CP* 2: 145–175.

For nineteenth-century surveys, see M. Schneid, "Die neuere thomistische Literatur," *Literarischer Handweiser* 20 (1881) in five parts; T. Wehhöfer, "Die geistige Bewegung im Anschluss an die Thomistische Enzyklika Leo XIII," *Jahrbuch der Leo-Gesellschaft* (1897), pp. 109ff.; G. Feldnor, "Die Neu-Thomisten," *JPsT* 8, 9, (1894, 1895), five parts.

In this century, see G. La Piana, "Recent Tendencies in Roman Catholic Theology," *Harvard Theological Review* 15 (1922): 122ff.; M. Grabmann, "Einleitung," in M. J. Scheeben, *Natur und Gnade* (Munich, 1922), p. 1ff.; Grabmann, *Die Geschichte der katholischen Theologie seit dem Ausgang der Väterzeit* (Frieburg, 1933), pp. 218ff.; F. Ehrle and E. Pelster, *Die Scholastik und ihre Aufgaben in unserer Zeit* (Freiburg, 1933); "Il Tomismo dal 1870 a 1879," *Angelicum* 20 (1943), 300ff.; O. Pesch, "Thomismus," *LThK* 10: 160; G. Söhngen, "Neuscholastik," *LThK* 7: 923; O. Köhler, "Neuthomismus, Scholastik und die neuen Philosophen,'" *J* 6 no. 2: 320ff.; P. Dezza, *I neotomisti italiani del secolo XIX* (Milan, 1942/44), 2 vols.; J. L. Perrier, *The Revival of Scholastic Philosophy* (New York, 1948); G. F. Rossi, *Le origini del neotomismo* (Piacenza, 1957); J. P. Golinas, *La restauration du Thomisme sous Leon XIII et la philosophie nouvelle* (Washington, 1959); *Hoc* 3: 45ff., 110ff., 235ff., 351ff.; A. Walz, "Sguardo sul movimento tomista nel secolo XIX final all'enciclica Aet. Patris," *Aquinas* 8 (1965): 315ff.; R. Aubert, "Aspects divers du neo-thomisme sous le pontificat de Leon XIII," *Aspetti della cultura cattolica nell' eta die Leone XIII* (Rome, 1961), pp. 133–227.

More recently, see Thomas J. A. Hartley, *Thomistic Revival and the Modernist Era* (Toronto, 1971); F. van Steenberghen, "Die neu-scholastische Philosophie," in H. Vorgrimler, *Bilanz der Theologie* (Freiburg, 1969) 1: 352ff.; J. Weisheipl, "Thomism," *NCE* 14: 126–135; Weisheipl, "Scholasticism," *NCE* 12: 1167ff.; Marcel Regnier, "Le Thomisme depuis 1870," *Histoire de la Philosophie* 3 (Gallimard, 1974): 483ff.; L. Boyle, "A Remembrance of Pope Leo XIII: The Encyclical *Aeterni Patris*" in V. Brezik, ed., *One Hundred Years of Thomism* (Houston, 1981), pp. 7ff.; G. Mc-Cool, *Nineteenth-Century Scholasticism* (revision of *Catholic Theology in the Nineteenth Century*) (New York, 1989); "Neo-Thomism and the Tradition of St. Thomas," *Thought* 62 (1987): 131ff.; *From Unity to Pluralism: The Internal Evolution of Thomism* (New York, 1989); various bibliographies in *CP* 2; J. A. Gallagher, *Time Past, Time Future: An Historical Study of Catholic Moral Theology* (New York, 1990).

33. Paul Schanz referred to Aristotelian-scholastic theology as "concept-theology" or "modern-scholastic" while the older theology is called "naturalistic" or "realistic." "Zur Erinnerung an J. Ev. Kuhn," *ThO* 69 (1889): 532, 537; see also H. Schmidinger, " 'Scholastik,' und 'Neuscholastik'—Geschichte zweier Begriffe," *CP* 2: 48ff.

34. "Neuscholastik," *LThK* (1st ed.) 5: 522.

35. Hermesianism and Guntherianism continued in figures like J. B. Baltzer (1803–1871) and J. P. Elvenich (1796–1886); see L. Scheffczyk, "Einleitung: Der Weg der deutschen katholischen Theologie im 19. Jh.," *Theologie im Aufbruch und Widerstreit* (Bremen, 1965), pp. xxxf.

36. O. H. Pesch, "Thomismus," *LThK* 10: 161.

37. Surveying Franciscan, Augustinian, and other scholastic schools is *Hoc* 2: 362ff; on the Jesuits and scholasticism, *H* 2: 367ff. The subsequent chapters on Kuhn and Schmid illustrate the continuing discussion of scholastic theories of grace. Erich Przywara summed up the Jesuit approach of these decades in noting that "Molinism" in its frequent usage really refers to what would be better called "Suarezianism" and should be contrasted not with Thomism but with Bañezianism, for Molina and Suarez are "advocates" of Aquinas. "Die Problematik der Neuscholastik," *Kant-Studien* 33 (1928): 78.

38. G. Söhngen, "Neuscholastik," *LThK* 7: 924.

39. *Sch*, pp. 96ff.; *CP* 2: 132ff.

40. F. Vigener, "Die katholisch-theologische Fakultät in Giessen und ihr Ende," *Mitteilungen des oberhessischen Geschichtsvereins* 24 (1922): 28ff.

41. Among Haffner's writings are *Grundlinien der Philosophie* (Mainz, 1881), 2 vols. See H. Lenhart, *Die Phil.-Theol. Fakultät des Mainzer Priesterseminars* (Mainz, 1946); *Hoc* 2: 320.

42. Six volumes were published in Heinrich's lifetime and a final four were added by K. Gutberlet; *Dogmatische Theologie* (Mainz, 1873–1904) and see a review of this by Schanz in *ThQ* 82 (1902): 321. *Die Beweise für die Wahrheit und Nothwendigkeit des Christentums und der Kirche* (Mainz, 1863), and *Joseph von Görres* (Frankfurt, 1867) show how past liberals could become new conservatives. Heinrich at the Mainz *Katholikentag* had described the *Syllabus* in 1864 as the "greatest act of this century and perhaps many centuries" (*Sch*, p. 108). "The Catholic theological faculty at Tübingen, as is known, held in the first three years of its existence a quite unusual position in the Catholic church and Catholic science. True to Catholic

dogma to the extent it was expressly formulated, it delighted in every other religious and theological concern to pursue its own way; in points which did not have their formulation as formed dogma or belonged more in the area of discipline it pursued a meaning disparate from what had been valid to that point. It sought to be liberal, to give to Protestantism as much as seemed possible; and thereby in much it exaggerated even beyond what was legitimate. This was an original direction, one explicable and excusable from the sad situation of Catholic science in that age—but it was certainly not the right way" (*K* 1 [1863]: 546).

43. See H. Brück, *K* 70 (1890), part I: 481f.

44. See W. Baier, *Die Kirche als Fortsetzung des Wirkens Christi* (S. Ottilien, 1984); R. Baumer, "Berlage, A.," *LThK* 2: 231; K. A. Tillman, *Die Lehre vom Bösen im 19. Jahrhundert: J. H. Hirscher, F. A. Staudenmaier, A. Berlage* (Freiburg, 1982).

45. (Münster, 1839–1864).

46. *Die spekulative Theologie A. Günthers . . .* (Cologne, 1853); see also *Giordano Bruno und N. von Cusa* (Bonn, 1847); *CP* 2: 134ff.

47. Hasenfuss, "Commer, Ernst," *LThK* 3: 20.

48. *System der Philosophie* (Munich, 1883–1885).

49. *Die philosophische Wissenschaft: Ein apologetischer Versuch* (Berlin, 1882); *Immerwährende Philosophie* (Vienna, 1899).

50. *Die Kirche in ihrem Wesen und Wirken* (Vienna, 1904), pp. 71, 129, 237; see his *Die Katholicität nach dem heil: Augustinus* (Breslau, 1873).

51. *Hermann Schell und der fortschrittliche Katholizismus: Ein Wort zur Orientierung für gläubige Katholiken* (Vienna, 1907). To discredit Commer, C. Hennemann published the earlier friendly correspondence: *Ernst Commers Briefe an Herman Schell von 1885–1899* (Würzburg, 1907); Commer replied with *Die jüngste Phase des Schellstreites* (Vienna, 1909).

52. M. Glossner, *Lehrbuch der Katholischen Dogmatik nach den Grundsätzen des heiligen Thomas* (Regensburg, 1874), 2 vols. After a critique of Perrone (problem of form) and of Scheeben (not a textbook) and an assertion that this work will be based on *Summa theologiae*, he presents a supernatural theology in contrast to "the theosophical presentation of modern liberal theology" (p. xi). The introduction is neither an apologetics nor a theodicy but a "teaching on the church as principle of theological knowledge or source of faith," which occupies 150 pages. Then follows God as One, Triune, Creator (including the Fall). The ecclesiological introduction treats first the foundation by Christ and the Apostles; the passive constitution of the church is concerned with different kinds of members, while the active constitution is authority; this is followed by the four attributes. *Das objective Princip der aristotelische-scholastischen Philosophie . . . dem subjectiven Principe der neueren Philosophie* (Regensburg, 1880); *Der moderne Idealismus* (Münster, 1880); *Die moderne Philosophie* (Freiburg, 1889); *Katholizismus und Moderne Kultur* (Vienna, 1902). There are also studies on Cusa as a parent of modern philosophy and on the antimodernist measures of Pius X; see J. Hasenfuss in *LThK* 4: 972

53. *Der spekulative Gottesbegriff in der neueren und neuesten Philosophie* (Paderborn, 1894), p. 45.

54. "Apologetische Tendenzen und Richtungen," *JPsT* 4 (1890) to 9 (1895), six parts; *Die Lehre des hl. Thomas vom Wesen der göttlichen Gnaden gegenüber J. v. Kuhn* (Mainz, 1871). See also "Die Tübingen Katholische Schule . . .," *JPsT* 15 (1901): 166ff; 16 (1902): 1ff.; 17 (1903): 24ff.; P. Schanz, "Die katholische Tübingen Schule," *ThQ* 78 (1896): 27ff. Glossner's article advocated: (1) the human mind with only one, perennial philosophy which is Aristotelian; (2) the avoidance of history and the condemnation of culture after Luther and Descartes; (3) philosophy and theology dominated by a fundamentalism of terms and syllogisms; (4) support by ecclesiastical authority.

55. (Cologne, 1911–1913), 3 vols.; see Mausbach, *Catholic Moral Teaching and Its Antagonists* (New York, 1914) (translation of *Die Katholische Moral* [Cologne, 1901]). There was also *Katholische Moraltheologie* (Cologne, 1915–1918) in three volumes; *Altchristliche und moderne Gedanken über Frauenberufe* (Mönchen-Gladbach, 1910). *Religion, Christentum und Kirche* (Kempten, 1921) was written with G. Esser of Bonn. See also W. Weber, "J. Mausbach," *Zeitgeschichte in Lebensbildern* 3 (Mainz, 1979): 148ff.

56. E. Busch, *Karl Barth* (Philadelphia, 1976), p. 168. At Paderborn, Hermann Plassmann (1817–1864), professor of theology, composed a mediocre but influential summary of Aquinas, *Die Schule des hl. Thomas* in five volumes (Soest, 1858–61). Student under Franz von Baader, Jesuit novice, priest of Paderborn, he did doctoral studies at both the Dominican and Jesuit schools in Rome; see *CP* 2: 139ff.

57. A typical later study on the university issue in the years around 1900 is F. X. Heiner, *Theologische Fakultäten und Tridentinische Seminarien: Ein Wort zur Aufklärung und Verständigung* (Paderborn, 1900).

58. (Regensburg, 1907–1908), 2 vols.; (Regensburg, 1912).

59. Stöckl, *Lehrbuch der Philosophie*, 2 vols. (Mainz, 1870); *Geschichte der Philosophie des Mittelalters*, 3 vols. (Mainz, 1864–1866). See also Peter Walter, "Eichstätt," *CP* 2: 176ff., 191.; "Scholasticism," *NCE* 12: 1167. There were also Stöckl's apologetic writings which then found a certain climax in historical surveys: *Grundriss der Religionsphilosophie* (Mainz, 1872); *Der Materialismus . . .* (Mainz, 1877); *Das Christentum und die grossen Fragen der Gegenwart . . .*, 3 vols. (Mainz, 1879); *Geschichte der Philosophie . . . zur Zeit der Kirchenväter*, 3 vols. (Mainz [1859], 1891); *Professor Huber in München* (Mainz, 1865).

60. Morgott, *Der Spender der heiligen Sacramente und die Lehre des hl. Thomas von Aquin* (Freiburg, 1886); *Geist und Natur im Menschen nach der Lehre des heil. Thomas* (Eichstätt, 1860); *Die Theorie der Gefühle im System des hl. Thomas von Aquin* (Eichstätt, 1864); *Die Mariologie des heiligen Thomas von Aquin* (Freiburg, 1878). His reviews of Scheeben are reprinted in the new edition of the *Katholische Dogmatik, Gesammelte Schriften* 6; see Grabmann, "Franz von Paula Morgott als Thomist," *JPsT* 15 (1907): 46ff.; O. Willmann, *Aus der Werkstatt der Philosophia perennis* (Freiburg, 1912).

61. Gutberlet, *Lehrbuch der Philosophie* (Münster, 1878–84), 6 vols.; *Lehrbuch der Apologetik* (Münster, 1888–1894), 3 vols.; *Gott der Einige und Dreifaltige* (Regensburg, 1907); *Gott und die Schöpfung* (Regensburg, 1910); *Der Gottmensch Jesus Christus* (Regensburg, 1913). See also K. Gutberlet, *Philosophie der Gegenwart in*

Selbstdarstellungen (Leipzig, 1923); E. Hartmann, "Constantin Gutberlet," *PhJ* 41 (1928): 261ff.; P. Simon, "Konstantin Gutberlet," *H* 25 (1927): 437ff.; Kleineidam, *Die katholisch-theologische Fakultät . . . Fulda* (Cologne, 1961).

62. (Paderborn, 1903–07) 3 vols; American translation, St. Louis, 1911–1917. See also his *Natur und Übernatur* (Kempten, 1913).

63. See "Hundert Jahre, 'Stimmen der Zeit,'" *Theologie und Glaube* 61 (1971): 465ff. On the Jesuits at this tlme, see *CP* 2: 179ff.

64. T. Pesch, "Die Philosophie der Vorzeit in ihrer Bedeutung für die Zukunft," *Stimmen aus Maria Laach* 9 (1875): 153.; *Die moderne Wissenschaft* (Freiburg, 1876); *Institutiones philosophiae naturalis secundum principia S. Thomae Aquinatis ad usum scholasticum* 2 vols. (Freiburg, 1880); *Institutiones logicales . . .*, 3 vols. (Freiburg, 1888–1890); *Institutiones psychologicae . . .*, 3 vols. (Freiburg, 1896).

65. (Freiburg, 1899).

66. Jesuit A. Lehmkühl (1834–1918) was a respected moralist known for competence in sociology. He wrote on law in society and expounded a moral theology strictly constructed along the lines of a virtue theory. Wishing to synthesize Aquinas and Alphonsus Ligouri, as well as the theoretical and the practical, he issued a *Theologia Moralis*, 2 vols. (Freiburg, 1883–1884).

H. Pesch (1854–1926) specialized in economic questions of the Germany of his time and addressed the two potential foes of Catholicism: liberalism controlling the government and press and, secondly, socialism as a nonreligious mass movement of the working classes. He shows that amid the centers of a certain frozen scholasticism, independent theology was done, but this occurred in the areas of "practical moral" theology and was less possible in dogmatic theology. See his *Liberalismus, Socialismus und christliche Gesellschaftsordnung* (Freiburg, 1899–1901); *Lehrbuch der Nationaloekonomie*, 5 vols. (Freiburg, 1905–1923).

67. Sketching the controversy are the notes to the reprinted articles by Scheeben in *Gesammelte Aufsätze, Gesammelte Schriften* 8 (Freiburg, 1967).

68. (Freiburg, 1892). Two subsequent Jesuit philosophers at work against modern thought were J. Donat (1868–1946), whose *Summa philosophiae christianae* in nine volumes (Innsbrück, 1910—1921) enjoyed a considerable international success, and F. Klimke (1878–1924), who taught first at Innsbruck and then at the Gregorianum in Rome. Klimke saw monism as the root of all dangers and composed in two volumes an *Institutiones historiae philosophiae* (Rome, 1923). H. Lange (1878–1936) wrote a widely used dogmatics as well as *De Gratia Tractatus dogmaticus* (Freiburg, 1929). He helped to refound the Jesuits in Germany and began their periodical *Scholastik*. For further authors of textbook-systems in German-speaking realms, see Grabmann, *Die Geschichte . . .*, pp. 233ff.

69. For other theologians at Fribourg, see. A. Kerkvoorde and O. Rousseau, *Le Mouvement Théologique* (Paris, 1969), 1: 170ff. Less original but significant in extending neo-Thomism were T. Conconnier (1846–1908, a student of Zigliara) and J. J. Berthier (1847–1924), who taught in Rome after 1905.

70. *Apologie des Christentums* (Freiburg, 1878–1889); English trans. *The Christian Life* (St. Louis, 1956).

71. (Trier, 1914); (Basel, 1928).

72. A. Walz, "Weiss, A. M.," *LThK* 10: 1007; *Memoire Dominicaine* 42 (Freiburg, 1925): 545ff.; 47 (1930): 47ff. Against reform is Weiss, *Die religiöse Gefahr* (Freiburg, 1904). His autobiography gives a picture of his studies in Munich under W. Rosenkrantz and other figures of the Munich school whose thought he later dismissed as "a world of fog," "an acosmic subjectivism" leading to crises of faith; *Lebensweg und Lebenswerk* (Freiburg, 1925), pp. 196ff.

73. (Münster, 1895). See also his *Introductio in s. theologiam dogmaticam* (Ratisbon, 1882).

74. See A. Walz, *A. Kardinal Frühwirth* (Vienna, 1950), pp. 183ff.; "Esser, Thomas (Hermann Josef)," *LThK* 3: 1114. One should note the rise of neoscholastic journals: beyond *Der Katholik* and the *Historisch-politische Blätter* there came into existence E. Commer's *Jahrbuch für Philosophie und spekulative Theologie* (later *Divus Thomas*); C. Schneider's *St. Thomasblätter* (1888–1910); *Philosophisches Jahrbuch* (1888); a second *Divus Thomas* (Piacenza) (1880–). *Revue Thomiste* (1893–) was edited by the French Dominicans, *Ciencia Tomista* by the Spanish Dominicans (1910–), and *Scholastik* (1926–1965) by the Jesuits. In Louvain, *Revue neoscholastique de philosophie* (1894–) and in Italy, *Rivista Italiana di filosofia neoscholastica* (1909–).

75. E. Przywara, "Die Problematik der Neuscholastik," p. 79 (see n. 63 above).

76. O. Kohler, "Das Lehramt und die Theologie," *J* 6 no. 2: 323.

77. W. Kluxen, "Die Erforschung der mittelalterlichen Philosophie," in *CP* 2: 367ff.

78. See M. Grabmann, *H. S. Denifle* (Mainz, 1905); A. Walz, "Denifle, H. S.," *LThK* 3: 228; *Die katholische Kirche und das Ziel der Menschheit* (Graz, 1872; English translation in 1909).

79. See the essays in *M. Grabmann zum Gedächtnis* (Munich, 1949). Grabmann's study on Aquinas's ecclesiology is not theologically insightful and fits Aquinas into neoscholastic and Tridentine frameworks.

80. P. Schanz, "Zur Erinnerung an J. E. K.," *ThQ* 69 (1887): 531ff.; A. Hagen, *Gestalten aus dem Schwäbischen Katholizismus* (Stuttgart, 1950), 2: 418ff.; see also F. Wolfinger, "J. E. von Kuhn," *KThD* 2: 129ff.; L. Scheffczyk, "Die Tübinger Schule," *CP* 1: 86ff.

81. On how Catholic theologians of the older tradition viewed the arrival of Aquinas see T. O'Meara, "Thomas Aquinas and the German Intellectuals," *Gregorianum* 68 (1987): 719ff.

82. See S. Lösch, "Die katholisch-theologischen Fakultäten zu Tübingen und Giessen (1830–1850)," *ThQ* 108 (1927): 177ff. For a chronological arrangement of the writings of the controversy see Karl Jos. Mattes, *Die Kontroverse zwischen Johannes von Kuhn und Constantin von Schäzler über das Verhältnis von Natur und Gnade* (Freiburg, 1968), p. 43f. Clemens's "Unser Standpunkt in der Philosophie," *K* 39 (1859): 9ff., 129ff., presented the ideas of his Latin *Habilitationsschrift, De Scholasticorum sententia, philosophiam esse theologiae ancillam commentatio* (Münster, 1856); *Die Wahrheit in dem von Herrn Professor Dr. J. von Kuhn in Tübingen angeregten Streite über Philosophie und Theologie* (Münster, 1860). Kuhn responded in his *Einleitung in die katholische Dogmatik* (Tübingen, 1859) and *Philosophie und Theologie:*

Eine Streitschrift (Tübingen, 1860) as well as in "Glauben und Wissen nach Thomas von Aquin," *ThQ* 42 (1860): 273–340 and "Das Verhältnis der Philosophie zur Theologie nach modern-scholastischer Lehre," *ThQ* 44 (1862): 541. J. Kleutgen entered the argument at the time of Clemens's death (*K* 42 [1862]: 257ff.), and Alois Schmid examined the controversy in *Wissenschaftliche Richtungen* ... (Munich, 1862); see also the reviews in *K* and *ThQ* in 1863.

83. *Verhandlungen der vierzehnten Generalversammlung der katholischen Vereine Deutschlands*...(Aachen, 1862), pp, 276ff. For the background see Mattes, pp. 8ff.

84. Kuhn's *Bemerkungen* in *Offenes Sendschreiben an Herrn Dr. John v. Kuhn* (Frankfurt, 1863).

85. "Eine freie katholische Universität und die Freiheit der Wissenschaft," *ThQ* 51 (1963): 897ff.; "Die praktische Seite der Frage," 52 (1863): 30ff.

86. See K. Reinhardt, "Schäzler, Konstantin," *LThK* 10: 375. Apart from the works on grace, Schäzler published a study on the incarnation in Aquinas: *Das Dogma von der Menschwerdung Gottes im Geiste des hl. Thomas* (Freiburg, 1870); *Die päpstliche Unfehlbarkeit...* (Freiburg, 1870); *Divus Thomas...contra liberalismum* (Rome, 1874). Herman Schell wrote that Schäzler had made an important contribution to his education, teaching him to translate Latin scholastic terms into adequate German, as well as influencing his method of presentation and literary style. See J. Hasenfuss, "H. Schells Synthese von scholastischem und modernem Denken und Glauben im Sinne eines christlichen Personalismus," in J. Ratzinger and H. Fries, eds., *Einsicht und Glaube* (Freiburg, 1962), p. 389.

87. Schäzler, "Eine freie katholische Universität und die Freiheit der Wissenscahft," *HPBl* 52 (1863): 930.

88. Kuhn, "Die Wissenschaft und der Glaube mit besonderer Beziehung auf die Universitätsfrage," *ThQ* 46 (1864): 583ff.

89. Schäzler, *Natur und Übernatur: Das Dogma von der Gnade und die theologische Frage von der Gegenwart* (Mainz, 1865), pp. 15f. Kuhn agreed that grace is needed for a human destiny which is "properly God's union of the human being in a supernatural way with God" but that destiny should also be at work within active human nature. Far from accepting human nature and destiny as a discarded idea, a shell or a tube for higher realities, the supernatural, Kuhn preferred the word "grace" and implied that Schläzler's "*Übernatur*" is novel (a "popular modern expression"); "Das Natürliche und Übernatürliche," *ThQ* 46 (1864): 245. Grace is present in (not outside of) our lives, and Kuhn found Schäzler's language of human nature's expansion and completion ("*Ergänzung oder Vervollständigung*" to be the "fundamental statement upon which this theology stands or falls" (*Die christliche Lehre von der göttlichen Gnade* 1 [Tübingen, 1868]: 164). On language in the theology of grace, particularly the emergence of the word "supernature," See M. Bernards, "Zur konziliaren Diskussion über die Gnadenlehre im 19. Jahrhundert," *Mysterium der Gnade* (Regensburg, 1975), pp. 268ff. The author attributed to Schäzler a significant role in its spread, while it is absent in Hermes, Klee, Staudenmaier, and Kuhn. While Kuhn argued that Schäzler was Baius *redivivus*, Schäzler cried semipelagian and idealist. On Schäzler's

and other neoscholastics' critiques of receptivity, see F. Kreuter, *Person und Gnade* (New York, 1984), pp. 392ff.

90. Letter cited in G. Häfele, "Constantin von Schäzler," *Divus Thomas* 14 (1927): 440.

91. F. X. Kraus, *Tagebücher*, ed. H. Schiel (Cologne, 1957), p. 433. "Kuhn has absolutely nothing in common with Hermes: not the point of departure, the method nor the conclusions. . . . Between Kuhn and Günther the opposition is no less great and visible" (P. Godet, "J. Kuhn et l'école catholique de Tubingue," *Annales de Philosophie Chrétienne* 4 [1907]: 163, 165f.)

3. Matthias Joseph Scheeben: A Transcendent Synthesis

1. Eugen Paul, *Matthias Joseph Scheeben* (Graz, 1976), p. 10. For an extensive bibliography of works by and on Scheeben see Paul, *Denkweg und Denkform der Theologie von Matthias Joseph Scheeben* (Munich, 1970), pp. x–xxi; "Matthias Joseph Scheeben," *KThD* 3: 390ff.

2. A number of works deal with Scheeben's Roman formation: H. J. Brosch, "Das Werden des jungen M. J. Scheeben," *Stimmen der Zeit* 123 (1932): 395ff.; A. Kerkvoorde, "La formation théologique de M. J. Scheeben à Rome (1852–1859)," *EThL* 22 (1946): 174ff. On Möhler's influence, see Scheffczyk, "Der Weg der deutschen katholischen Theologie im 19. Jahrhundert," *ThQ* 145 (1965): 296; Kerkvoorde, "La formation . . . ," 180ff.; Paul, *Denkweg*, pp. 8ff.; H. Schauf, "Vorwort," to Scheeben, *Handbuch der katholischen Dogmatik* 6 (Freiburg, 1957): ix ff. Scheeben apparently used the lectures of Passaglia and Schrader throughout his life. He kept up a correspondence with Kleutgen as well as with the rector, A. de Lacroix, and with the spiritual director F. X. Huber; see Paul, *Denkweg*, p. 11. On this Roman school, see W. Kasper *Die Lehre von der Tradition in der Römischen Schule* (Freiburg, 1962).

3. *Theologicae Praelectiones* 4 (Prati, 1854), p. xlii gives references to Möhler.

4. See various letters cited in Paul, *Denkweg*, pp. 12f.

5. H. Schauf, A. Eröss, *M. J. Scheeben, Briefe nach Rom* (Freiburg, 1939), p. 132; see Paul, *Denkweg*, pp. 32f.

6. J. Kleutgen *Briefe aus Rom* (Münster, 1865), pp. 130f. (Sept. 4, 1892). "Kleutgen was not a teacher of Scheeben—he was never professor at the Gregorianum—but the *Theologie der Vorzeit* was a guide for the young Scheeben, and later the theologian used it as a resource" (Schauf, "Vorwort," to Scheeben, *Handbuch der katholischen Dogmatik* 6: xv). "Kleutgen was the first who twelve years ago undertook to rehabilitate scientifically the 'Theology and Philosophy of the Past' which had been neglected for a century. He did it with a vast and profound erudition, with clarity and peace. . . . No one will brand the author with the slogan "neoscholastic" as a member of a dark and closed direction, for Kleutgen showed that he stands on the height of our age and knows its ideas and performances well—he does not want a repristination but a regeneration" (Scheeben in *Literarischer Handweiser* 28 [1864]: 323).

7. Schauf, Eröss, *Briefe aus Rom*, pp. 89f. Of the Molinist and Thomistic controversies, Scheeben wrote: "A relative flattening of philosophical and theological insights occurred under the Jesuits after 1700. . . . The danger came partly from their

open attitudes to Aquinas, an easier accommodation to older or newer theologies and a more daring, sometimes (as with Molina and Vasquez) too bold and critical spirit. But twenty years ago they began to leave that enclosed situation and brought Thomistic speculation anew into public view... keeping the Thomistic doctrine alive, enriching it with treasures from other directions. In many ways they have achieved a contemporary extension of Aquinas, while the Dominican school, by a deplorable and exclusive clinging to the substance and form of the traditional teaching, have accomplished relatively less for the spread and continuance of science. In the past century... they could only save the dead form. At the same time, the Jesuits today and their scientific comrades can certainly heed the well-meaning warning of Schäzler that they should pay attention to the great Thomists of the first century after the Council of Trent, e.g., Bañez, John of St. Thomas, the Salmanticenses, giving them more attention than their traditional opposition did" (review of "C. v. Schäzlers 'Neue Untersuchungen,' " *K* 48 [1868] reprinted in *Gesammelte Aufsatze* 8 [Freiburg, 1967]: pp. 126f). See the review of Schrader's writings in *Literarischer Handweiser* (Münster) 8 (1869): 331f., and of Kleutgen's *Institutiones theologicae* in the same journal 21 (1882): 105f. and essays on Frohschammer and Kuhn in *K* 43 (1863); 51 (1871).

    8. On Scheeben and Aquinas see T. Pesch in M. Grabmann, "Scheebens theologisches Lebenswerk," in Scheeben, *Gesammelte Schriften* 1: xl ff.; G. Fritz "Scheeben, (M. J.)," *Dictionnaire de théologie catholique* 14: 1272. F. S. Pancheri's, *Il pensiero teologico di M. J. Scheeben e San Tommaso* (Padua, 1956) notes the Thomistic facets but develops his sources in the Augustinian and Franciscan school, while others have seen a Platonic thought-form in *Mysterien* (Paul, *Denkweg*, p. 15). Revived interest in Scheeben came from M. Grabmann, directed by his neoscholastic teacher in Eichstätt, F. Morgott. Strict Thomists have always had an ambiguous attitude toward Scheeben.

    9. Letter to the Eichstätt Thomist in 1882 cited in *Der Erneuerer der katholischen Wissenschaft* (Mainz, 1935), p. 104.

    10. *Handbuch der katholischen Dogmatik* 3: 1114; Paul, *Denkweg*, pp. 29ff.

    11. Paul, *Denkweg*, pp. 195, 319; cf. Scheeben in *Periodische Blätter* 10 (1881): 208.

    12. Kerkvoorde,"La formation," p. 191.

    13. Not only R. Vatter but H. J. Brosch, A. Burkhart and W. Kasper, as cited in Paul, "Scheeben und die Tübinger," *Denkweg*, pp. 315ff.

    14. M. Valkovic, *L'uomo, la donna... Scheeben* (Rome, 1965); Paul, *Denkweg*, pp. l2ff.

    15. "Geschichte der Theologie," *K* 47 (1867): 158.

    16. R. Vatter, *Das Verhältnis von Trinität und Vernunft nach Joh. Ev. Kuhn mit Berücksichtigung der Lehre M. J, Scheebens* (Speyer, 1940), p. 141; see Scheeben, *Handbuch der katholischen Dogmatik* 2: 820.

    17. See the articles in *Gesammelte Aufsätze*.

    18. *Handbuch der katholischen Dogmatik* 3: 702; see 276ff. Scheeben protested that he was not an idealist; Scheeben "Vorwort," to *Handbuch der katholischen Dogmatik* 3 and 4: xiii f. "Scheeben's theology shows the influence of the theology of the Roman Jesuits in the history of dogma and stands in contrast to the German theories involving dialectical history and active consciousness; the Roman move was

from the implicit to the explicit and leads *only* to new statements and not to new transcendental or past (but unseen) realities. This theory of *Dogmengeschichte* lasts through the first half of this century and significantly links the two Marian dogmas" (L. Scheffczyk, "Katholische Dogmengeschichtserforschung," *Dogmengeschichte und katholische Theologie* [Würzburg, 1985], pp. 125ff.).

19. (Mainz, 1861); (Freiburg, 1865); (Freiburg, 1873-1887).

20. "Das allgemeine Concilium und die Wissenschaft," *Das ökumenische Concil* 1 (1870): 100ff.

21. Paul, *Denkweg*, p. 103.

22. Cited in *Nature and Grace*, trans. C. Vollert (St. Louis, 1954), p. 8.

23. *Nature and Grace*, p. 12.

24. See Paul, *Denkweg*, pp, 158ff., 177. "The affirmation of the existence of uncreated grace is always underlying his notion of supernature" (B. Fraigneau-Julien, "Introduction" to *Nature et Grace* [Bruges, 1957], p. 29). On one human goal, on grace as a second soul, on natural desire see *Handbuch der katholischen Dogmatik* 3: 931–999.

25. Eugen Paul, "Matthias Joseph Scheeben," p. 387.

26. The three articles on the controversy are found in Scheeben, *Gesammelte Aufsätze*, pp. 70–168; see A. Schmid, "Die Controverse zwischen Kuhn und Schäzler," *Theologisches Literaturblatt* 1 (1866): 586ff. A second controversy on grace was with the Jesuit T. Granderath of Innsbruck: its area was even more refined—the nature of the created grace which makes one an adopted child of God in relationship to the Holy Spirit and particularly in light of the decrees of Trent. The four articles on this controversy with Granderath as well as detailed notes on the background are included in *Gesammelte Aufsätze*, pp. 169–302.

27. "C. v. Schäzlers 'Neue Untersuchungen' " (see n. 7 above), pp. 127ff.

28. The chapter on predestination at the end of the work is faithful to Aquinas, emphasizing first the divine wisdom and plan rather than the will, and second a basic universality of predestination. Scheeben criticizes an "ultramystical" view, falsely attributed to Augustine, which in arguing for divine power actually undermines God (pp. 712ff). *The Mysteries of Christianity*, trans. C. Vollert (St. Louis, 1946), pp. 738f. presents the progression of topics but without indicating their connections.

29. *The Mysteries*, p. 129.

30. Ibid., p. 142.

31. Ibid., p. 208.

32. See K. L. Klein, *Kreatürlichkeit als Gottebenbildlichkeit* (Bern, 1975).

33. Scheeben exaggerated: human nature is not "the lowest" in creation, and Incarnation is an alternative to pure mystery.

34. *The Mysteries*, p. 456. Interpretations of Aquinas on instrumental causality had considerable influence in Catholic circles during the nineteenth and twentieth centuries. With Scheeben we can number the important work of F. Morgott, *Der Spender der heiligen Sacramente* (Freiburg, 1886). This causal theology continues in Charles Journet's work, grounding his entire ecclesiology; see T. O'Meara, "The Teaching Office of Bishops in the Ecclesiology of Charles Journet," *The Jurist* 49 (1989): 23ff.

35. "When we speak of physical causality in connnection with Christ's humanity, we regard that humanity not as the principle but as the organ of the activity exercised by the divine Logos.... But I must confess that physical contact is not at all made clear in such theories. The spiritual contact in question is in itself a purely moral contact" (*The Mysteries*, pp. 458, 462).

36. *Handbuch der katholischen Dogmatik* 5, part 2: 1104f.

37. Ibid., pp. 128, 539. Scheeben criticized Melchior Cano (and thereby much of prior scholasticism) and Protestantism for a static view of theological and ecclesial sources (pp. 213, 245ff.). Paul presents a number of recent theologians evaluating positively Scheeben's theology of church and tradition (*Denkweg*, pp. 200–222). But the insightful M. D. Koster finds in this ecclesiology a prime example of a dualism separating the mystical and the juridical sides of the church. Koster, *Ekklesiologie im Werden* (Paderborn, 1940); Paul, *Denkweg*, pp. 214f. A positive view on Scheeben comes from E. Przywara, "Corpus Christi Mysticum—Eine Bilanz," *Zeitschrift für Aszese und Mystik* 15 (1940): 197ff. Scheeben wrote several meditative articles on the liturgy in the church year and the sacraments; both are sources and revelations of the life of grace. A. Eröss, "Dogma und Liturgie: Matthias Joseph Scheeben in der liturgischen Bewegung," *Liturgisches Leben* 2 (1935): 80ff.; see B. Fraigneau-Julien, *L'Eglise et le caractère sacramental selon M.-J. Scheeben* (Paris, 1958).

38. *Handbuch der katholischen Dogmatik* 1: 463.

39. "Päpstliche Unfehlbarkeit im Organismus der Kirche," *Das ökumenische Concil* 3 (1871): 84; the theology of the *Handbuch der katholischen Dogmatik* was even more focused on the papacy; 1: 493ff.

40. *Handbuch der katholischen Dogmatik* 1: 172. "There is a politico-clerical restoration as this church appears more and more like a state. Prolonged into the twentieth century, it has nourished an ever more powerful anticlericalism. But another restoration is pursued at the same time—theological in the strongest sense of the word. In the Roman College entrusted to the Jesuits by Leo XIII and reorganized in 1824... by G. Perrone, C. Passaglia and his students C. Schrader and Franzelin, theologians stressed the relationships of the church to the Trinity, Christ, and Holy Spirit. Perrone advised Scheeben to study Möhler" (*C*, p. 432). The pope's relationship to the church was like the prince's to the state; see *C*, pp. 488f.

41. It was published in a form completed by the Munich professor L. Atzberger; for a survey of its positive reception see M. Grabmann, "Scheebens" (note 8 above), in his edition of *Natur und Gnade* (Munich, 1922), pp. xxxiii ff.

42. *Die Encyklika Sr. Heiligkeit des Papstes Pius IX. vom 8. Dezember 1864: Nebst einer ausführlichen Einleitung* (Cologne, 1865). "Wissenschaft und Auktorität," *K* 48 (1868): 393ff.

43. Paul, *Matthias Joseph Scheeben*, p. 25; see L. Scheffczyk, "Die Lehranschauungen M. J. Scheebens über das ökumenische Konzil," *ThQ* 141 (1961): 129ff.

44. Scheeben, "Der Selbstmord der deutschen Wissenschaft im Angesicht des Concils," *Das ökumenische Concil* 1 (1870): 305ff.; "Die 'Bewegung gegen die päpstliche Unfehlbarkeit' in Deutschland," *Das ökumenische Concil* 2 (1870): 416ff.

45. In *Das ökumenische Concil* 2 (1870): 389.

46. "Christentum und Gesellschaft," *Periodische Blätter* 2 (1873): 304ff.

47. Weiss cited in C. Vollert, "Introduction," *The Mysteries*, pp. iv f.; *Theologisches Literaturblatt* 1 (1866): 381.

48. *The Mysteries*, p. v.

49. G. Philips, *La théologie catholique au XIXᵉ siècle* (Paris, 1904), p. 169.

50. On his links with "kerygmatic theology" see Paul, *Denkweg*, pp. 3, 12, 25, 27. Scheeben's reputation in America was as a theologian of the spiritual life; Alois Schmid in 1862 noticed that the goal of Scheeben's *Nature and Grace* was "to draw together insights of Scripture, pastristic theologians, and scholastics on the basic relationship of nature and grace and to vivify them with a mysticism contacting the person" ("Uber Natur und Gnade," *ThQ* [1862]: 17). Paul argues unconvincingly for existential aspects in Scheeben; *Denkweg*, pp. 171ff., 197. There are certain resemblances with Herman Schell; Scheeben lived only long enough to see Schell's dissertation on the Holy Spirit, which he called "a dogmatic work of exceptional significance" (*Kölner Pastoralblatt* 19 [1885]: 118 cited in *Handbuch der katholischen Dogmatik* 6: xx).

51. K. Eschweiler, *Die zwei Wege der neuren Theologie* (Augsburg, 1926), pp. 131ff., 164ff., 174f. For an interesting comparison, see P. Lengsfeld, *Adam und Christus . . . Scheeben und K. Barth* (Essen, 1965).

52. *W*, p. 403.

53. *C*, p. 465; "Scheeben was not able to write a tract on ecclesiology for his *Handbuch der katholischen Dogmatik*; he had little influence in this area before the 1930s. His vision of the church was linked to his theological synthesis and to certain personal positions. . . . These situated the church in the ensemble of supernatural mysteries: the Trinity, Incarnation, . . . economy of salvation . . . . The mystical body was composed of the visible and invisible by the *sacramentum et res*, which bestowed the character, and by sanctifying grace conferring divine adoption" (*C*, pp. 431ff.). Comparing him to Newman is G. Söhngen, "Neuscholastik," *LThK* 7: 924; H. Mühlen, *Una mystica persona* (Munich, 1967), p. 447.

4. Between Idealism and Scholasticism: The Fundamental and Apologetic Theology of Alois Schmid

1. Grabmann, *Geschichte der katholischen Theologie* (Freiburg, 1933), p. 231. J. Finkenzeller offers a bibliography of works on and by Schmid in "Alois von Schmid," *KThD* 3: 125ff. For a life, bibliography and a reprinting of a number of his articles see Andreas Schmid, *Geheimrat Dr. Alois Ritter v. Schmid: Sein Leben und seine Schriften* (Regensburg, 1911).

2. *Die Bisthumssynode* (Regensburg, 1850), 2 vols. The first volume, after surveying Protestant theologies and those of Catholic critics, moved on to the relationships of synods to councils and the distribution of votes in the church. The nature and function of the synod was drawn from centuries of documentations from such synods. The second volume is a history of diocesan synods through the Council of Trent.

3. See T. O'Meara, *Romantic Idealism and Roman Catholicism: Schelling and the Theologians* (Notre Dame, Ind.; 1983), pp. 161ff.

4. Schmid, *Entwicklungsgeschichte der Hegelschen Logik: Ein Hilfsbuch zu einem geschichtlichen Studium derselben* (Regensburg,1858), pp. 9, 262ff.

5. C. Schneider, "Alois v. Schmid," *Philosophisches Jahrbuch* 23 (1911): 111.

6. Schmid, "Über Schelling, Baader, Görres," *Jahresberichte der Görresgesellschaft* (1879) quoted in Andreas Schmid, pp. 232ff. Cf. "Die Lehre Schellings von der Quelle der ewigen Wahrheiten," *Philosophisches Jahrbuch* 13 (1901): 363ff.

7. "Über Schelling," pp. 236ff.

8. Ibid., p. 245. "The speculative dogmatics of Franz Baader never get beyond...a mystical naturalism of a high level" Schmid, "Baader, Franz v.," *Staatslexikon* [Freiburg, 1889] 1: 661).

9. "Über Schelling," p. 247.

10. Ibid., p. 233.

11. Schmid, "Der geistige Entwicklungsgang J. A. Möhlers," *Historisches Jahrbuch* 17 (1897): 322ff., 572ff. (text cited from Andreas Schmid, p. 296).

12. "Der geistige Entwicklungsgang," p. 355.

13. H. Schmidinger, "Scholastik und Neuscholastik," *CP* 2: 50.

14. Schmid, *Thomistische und Skotistische Gewissheitslehre* (Dillingen, 1859); idem, "Die Seinsweise Gottes nach dem hl. Thomas von Aquinas," *Compte rendu du H. Congrès*...(Fribourg, 1897), pp. 556ff.

15. Schimd, "Die Sprachweise des Theismus und die Sprachweise des Pantheismus," *Athenäum* 2 (1863); 189.

16. Schmid, *Wissenschaftliche Richtungen auf dem Gebiete des Katholicismus in neuester und in gegenwärtiger Zeit* Munich, 1862), pp. 67ff.

17. Schmid, "Die Controverse zwischen Kuhn und Schäzler," *Bonner Theologisches Literaturblatt* 18–21 (1866): 586f.; and see E. Paul, *Denkwege*, (see chap 3, n. 1), pp. 31ff.

18. "Die Controverse," p. 683.

19. Schmid, "Uber Natur und Gnade," *ThQ* 44 (1862), 3. For Schmid's writings on the practical side of theology—on liturgical issues and church organization—see Finkenzeller, "A. Schmid," pp. 130, 137f.

20. "Die Controverse," p. 714.

21. Schäzler, *Neue Untersuchungen über das Dogma von der Gnade und dem Wesen des christlichen Glaubens* (Mainz, 1867).

22. Schmid, *Wissenschaft und Auctorität* (Munich, 1868), pp. 238.

23. "Über Natur und Gnade," p. 46.

24. Ibid., p. 47.

25. This popular book was praised by quite diverse theological schools; for references to reviews by Frohschammer, Kuhn, Schäzler, Scheeben, and Kleutgen, see H. Lange, "Alois v. Schmid und die vatikanische Lehre vom Glaubensabfall," *Scholastik* 2 (1927): 344f. Similar is Schmid's "Die philosophischen Bewegungen der Gegenwart," *Österreichische Vierteljahresschrift für katholische Theologie* 2 (1863), 27ff.

26. *Wissenschaftliche Richtungen*, p. 37.

27. Ibid., pp. 176, 180.

28. Ibid,, pp. 73ff.

29. Ibid., p. 188. Lange argues that Schmid's views were included in the council's *Adnotationes*; "Alois v. Schmid," p. 379.

30. Vatican I, *De Fide Catholica*, c. 3 (Denzinger-Schönmetzer, 3014).

31. See G. Denzler, "Das I. Vatikanische Konzil und die Theologische Fakultät der Universität München," *Annuarium Historiae Conciliorum* 1 (1969): 412ff.

32. Treatments of the history of Roman Catholic apologetics in the modern period are few: L. Maisonneuve, "Apologétique (XIXe Siècle)," *Dictionnaire de theologie catholique* 1, part 2 (Paris, 1931), 1563ff.; E. Hocedez, "Apologétique: Controverses et Progrès," *Hoc* 3: 195ff.; A. Dulles, *A History of Apologetics* (Washington, D.C., 1971); H. Bouillard, "De l'apologétique à la théologie fondamentale," *Les Quatre Fleuves* 1 (1973): 57ff.; F. Fiorenza, "The Search for Proofs: Fundamental Theology and Apologetics," *Foundational Theology* (New York, 1984), pp. 256ff.; H. Fries, *Fundamentaltheologie* (Graz, 1985), p. 524; A. P. Kustermann, *Die Apologetik J. S. Dreys* (Tübingen, 1988), pp. 200ff.

33. Finkenzeller, "Alois von Schmid," p. 126.

34. In a two-part article, "Der apologetische Cirkel," Schmid argued that apologetic theology could be both a clear exposition of dogma and faith grounded upon revelation and a complex form of knowing embracing both faith and proof. The article ended by citing Thomas Aquinas on this proposed synthesis. *Österreichische Vierteljahresschrift für katholische Theologie* 11 (1872); 88ff.; 12 (1873): 67ff. A second preparation for the apologetical system is *Untersuchungen über den letzten Gewissheitsgrund des Offenbarungsglaubens* (Munich, 1879). Beyond different forms of apologetic skepticisms there are different grounds for faith: natural and supernatural, objective and subjective. Two hundred pages surveyed this topic from Raymund Lull to the Salmanticenses and then on to contemporary Protestants and Catholics like Kuhn, Scheeben, and Kleutgen. Schmid's critique of each group contained their views and his theories; consequently the historical and expository areas of the book do not fit well together.

35. P. Schanz, *Apologie des Christentums*, 3 vols. (Freiburg, 1888); for his surveys of the field (always mentioning Schmid), see "Apologetik und Dogmatik," *ThQ* 81 (1899): 32ff.; "Neue Tendenzen der philosophischen Apologetik," *ThQ* 78 (1896): 402ff. Schanz reviewed Schmid's work positively in *ThQ* 83 (1901): 615F. On Schanz see the next chapter.

36. *Apologie des Christenthums* (Freiburg, 1867; 1895).

37. Schmid, *Apologetik als spekulative Grundlegung der Theologie* (Freiburg, 1900), p. 6.

38. Ibid., p. 107; cf. p. 115.

39. Ibid., pp. 98f.

40. Ibid., pp. 103, 118, 155f.

41. Ibid., p. 82.

42. Ibid., pp. 105f.

43. *Wissenschaftliche Richtungen*, p. 87. "A. Schmid, who was first known as a speculative writer through a work on Hegel's logic, strives beyond the standpoint of scholastic speculation and seeks in a higher third way the mediation of the oppositions

he finds around him" (K. Werner, *Geschichte der katholischen Theologie seit dem Trienter Concil bis zur Gegenwart* [Munich, 1866], p. 628).

5. Addressing Science and History: Paul Schanz at Tübingen

1. Schanz, "Die katholische Tübinger Schule," *ThQ* 80 (1898): 7. The Catholic Tübingen school through Möhler influenced Vatican II (see T. O'Meara, "Revelation and History: Schelling, Möhler and Congar," *Irish Theological Quarterly* 53 [1987]: 17ff.) and continued on in this century through J. R. Geiselmann, H. Fries, W. Kasper, M. Seckler and H. Küng.

2. Schanz, "Die neue und alte Weltanschauung, *ThQ*, 72 (1890), 394f., 419, 437. "The natural sciences and a historical positivism in content and method determined the intellectual situation of the age in which Schanz lived. A Tübingen theologian working out of the spirit of the school must be in contact with those questions and with the demands of the age. It would be anachronistic to answer today's questions with answers from yesterday, even if these answers, as in the case of the first and second generation of the Tübingen school, still remained impressive" (H. Fries, "Paul Schanz," *KThd* 3: 191). See also Fries, "Theologie und Naturwissenschaft," *ThQ* 129 (1949): 129ff.

3. Printed in *ThQ* 58 (1876): 392. In 1880 Kuhn was lecturing on grace and Schanz on the New Testament; in 1895 Schanz lectured on dogma and sacraments—there were no courses in scholasticism. By 1900 Schanz was lecturing on dogmatic theology and apologetics and there was a special course on anthropology and theodicy in Thomas Aquinas. In 1905 both apologetics and ethics had doubled in the number of courses, and in 1910 Koch had taken over Schanz's courses and Ludwig Baur offered three courses in scholastic thought.

4. Josef Schmid cited in Fries, "Paul Schanz," p. 198.

5. Schanz, "Geschichte und Dogma," *ThQ* 87 (1905): 1.

6. Ibid., p. 2.

7. Ibid., p. 27.

8. Ibid., p. 36.

9. See Döllinger, *Die Lehre von den heiligen Sacramenten der katholischen Kirche* (Freiburg, 1893). Döllinger's remark is cited in Fries, "Paul Schanz," p. 194.

10. "Die katholische Tübinger Schule," p. 23.

11. See "Die katholische Tübinger Schule," p. 21; "Die scholastische Kosmologie," *ThQ* 67 (1885): 1.

12. On the controversies over nature and grace, see "Die katholische Tübinger Schule," p. 25ff.

13. See "Apologetik und Dogmatik," *ThQ* 81 (1899): 35; "Die katholische Tübinger Schule," p. 22f.; "Die scholastische Kosmologie," p. 55.

14. Schanz's review of J. B. Heinrich, *Lehrbuch der katholischen Dogmatik*, in *ThQ* 82 (1900): 147.

15. Review of W. P. Englert, *Von der Gnade Christi* in *ThQ* 79 (1897): 492ff.

16. "Die scholastische Kosmologie," p. 57.

17. Schanz "Der hl. Thomas und das Hexameron," *ThQ* 60 (1878): 21f.

18. Schanz "Zur Geschichte der neueren protestantischen Theologie in Deutschland," *ThQ* 17 (1893): 3ff., 226ff.

19. Ibid., p. 7.

20. Ibid., pp. 4, 17.

21. Ibid., p. 39.

22. Ibid., p. 65.

23. Ibid., p. 254.

24. "Apologetik und Dogmatik," p. 32.; cf. *Über neue Versuche der Apologetik gegenüber dem Naturalismus und Spiritualismus* (Regensburg, 1897); "Die neueste Apologetik und die Naturwissenschaften," *Literarische Rundschau*, 1881, pp. 16, 17; "Neue Tendenzen der philosophischen Apologetik," *ThQ* 78 (1896): 402ff. "Apologetische Zeitfragen," *ThQ* (1903): 333ff.

25. "Apologetik und Dogmatik," p. 33.

26. Ibid., p. 62.

27. Ibid.

28. Ibid.

29. Schanz, *Apologie des Christentums* (Freiburg, 1887/88); English translation of the 5th revised edition: *A Christian Apology* (New York, 1907), 3 vols.

30. Quoted in Fries, "Paul Schanz," p. 201.

31. *Theologischer Literaturbericht* (1904) cited in Fries, "Paul Schanz," p. 201.

32. Schanz, *Galileo Galilei und sein Process* (Würzburg, 1878).

33. Fries, "Paul Schanz," p. 207.

34. *A Christian Apology* 1: 257. In his early article on Schanz, Fries examines the two cases of Galileo and Darwin; "Theologie und Naturwissenschaft," pp. 142ff.

35. Schanz, *Über neue Versuche*, p. 12.

36. *A Christian Apology* 1: 331.

37. See texts from Schanz in Fries, "Theologie und Naturwissenschaft," pp. 155ff. "The Congregation for the Index too is not infallible" (*A Christian Apology* 1: 834).

38. *A Christian Apology* 1: 549.

39. *ThQ* 58 (1876): 400f; cf. *A Christian Apology* 1: 213.

40. Schanz, "Die alte und neue Weltanschauung," *ThQ* 72 (1890): 437.

41. *Über neue Versuche*, p. 66.

42. Schanz, "Die geistigen Strömungen der Gegenwart," *Die Kultur* 1 (1900): p. 3.

43. Fries, "Paul Schanz," p. 212.

6. Herman Schell: Idealism at the End of a Century

1. Wörter, *Die christliche Lehre über das Verhältnis von Gnade und Freiheit* (Freiburg, 1856–1866); *Der Pelagianismus* (Paderborn, 1868); *Beiträge zur Dogmengeschichte des Semi-Pelagianismus* (Paderborn, 1898).

2. Sengler, *Über das Wesen und die Bedeutung der speculativen Philosophie und Theologie* (Heidelberg, 1834/1837), pp. 267, 324; see Sengler, *Reden über die gegenwärtige Krisis der Weltgeschichte* (Freiburg, 1843).

3. Kurt Leese, *Philosophie und Theologie im Spätidealismus* (Berlin, 1929), p. 8; *DHS*, pp. 11ff.; on Schell and Sengler, *DHS*, pp. 7ff.; Franz Eichinger, "Jakob Sengler," in *CP* 1: 306ff.

4. *Über das Wesen* . . . , pp. xi, 96; see the review by H. Beckers in *Reportorium der in- und ausländischen Literatur der gesamten Philosophie* 1 (Nuremberg, 1839): 95ff.

5. Sengler, *Idee Gottes* (Heidelberg, 1847), 2: 376; Sengler, "Das Ich in seiner phänomenologischen und ontologischen Begründung," *Zeitschrift für Philosophie und philosophische Kritik* 45 (1864): 1ff.; 204ff.

6. *Idee Gottes* 2: 1; cf. J. Koch, "Die Entstehung des Gottesbegriffs der Selbstursache bei H. Schell," *ThQ* 98 (1916): 419ff.

7. *Idee Gottes* 1 (Heidelberg, 1845): 423ff.

8. *Erkenntnislehre* 1 (Heidelberg, 1858): 543.

9. *Erkenntnislehre* 1: 644. Vincent Berning, while noting links between Schell and Erich Przywara, Gustav Siewerth, Karl Rahner, and Heidegger observes the underlying influence of Schelling. *Gott, Geist und Welt* (Munich, 1978), pp. 10ff.

10. J. Hasenfuss, "H. Schells Synthese . . . ," in H. Fries, J. Ratzinger, eds., *Einsicht und Glaube* (Freiburg, 1962), pp. 385; on Schell, evolution, and Teilhard de Chardin, see H. Mynarek, *Der Mensch, Sinnziel der Weltentwicklung* (Munich, 1967); B. Janssens, *Metaphysisches Denken und heilsgeschichtliche Offenbarunq: Ihre Korrespondenz im Systemversuch Herman Schells* (Frankfurt, 1980); *DHS*, pp. 2f.

11. See G. Bleickert, "Herman Schell," *KThD* 3: 310ff.

12. See O. Kraus, "Biographical Sketch of Franz Brentano," and E. Husserl, "Reminiscences of Franz Brentano," in L. McAlister, *The Philosophy of Brentano* (London, 1976), pp. 3, 50; see E. Winter, *Franz Brentanos Ringen um eine neue Gottessicht: Nach dem unveröffentlichten Briefwechsel F. Brentano–H. Schell* (Vienna, 1941).

13. R. Schaeffler, *Die Wechselbeziehungen zwischen Philosophie und Katholischer Theologie* (Darmstadt, 1980), pp. 21, 30ff.; see J. Koch, "Herman Schell und Franz Brentano," *Philosophia Perennis* 1 (Regensburg, 1930): 340; the two scholars' correspondence is found in J. Hasenfuss, *Herman Schell als Wegbereiter zum II. Vatikanischen Konzil* (Munich, 1978).

14. "Everything must first be in the process of the soul and its inner experiences before presenting a point of view. Thus the principle: The origin of our ideas is the proof of their truth." *(Religion und Offenbarung* [Paderborn, 1901], p. 274). "The soul of spirit is the essential form of the human being, the determining law and penetrating power, the ideal and real principle which dominates all lower levels of being" (*KD* 2: 285).

15. Koch, "Herman Schell und Franz Brentano," p. 341.

16. Schell, *Die Einheit des Seelenlebens . . .* (Freiburg, 1873), p. 271.

17. *DHS*, p. 41.

18. T. Schäfer, *Die erkenntnistheoretische Kontroverse Kleutgen-Günther* (Paderborn, 1961), pp. 79ff. On Schell's time in Rome and its influences, see *DHS*, pp. 58ff.

19. For those by J. B. Heinrich and M. J. Scheeben, see *DHS*, p. 79; for Alois Schmid, see *Literarische Rundschau*, 1886, no. 8, p. 230.

20. Hettinger, *Die Reaction des sogenannten Fortschrittes gegen die Freiheit der Kirche und des religiösen Lebens* (Mainz, 1863); *Apologie des Christenthums* (Freiburg, 1879); *Lehrbuch der Fundamentaltheologie oder Apologetik* (Freiburg, 1913). See E. Biser, "F. S. Hettinger," *KThD* 2: 409ff.; J. Renninger, "Prälat Hettinger. Ein Lebensbild," *K* 70 (1890): 385ff.

21. For this intrigue, see G. Bleickert, "Herman Schell," pp. 305ff.

22. *DHS*, p. 155; on Kuhn and Schell, pp. 136–149.

23. *KD* 2, pp. 140f.; V. Berning, *Systematisches Philosophieren zwischen Idealismus und Neuscholastik um die Jahrhundertwende* (Munich, 1984), p. 169; "Hackels Monism und der christliche Glaube an Gott und Geist," *KL*, pp. 322ff.; *KD*, 3:2, p. x. "Idealism is a one-sided opposite to naturalism. It explains the world from ideas and ideals, employs images and necessary concepts, set adrift from Spirit which is active thought and will" ("Das Problem des Geistes," *KL*, p. 202). Clearly, this speculation on the life of God whose depth results in a Trinity finds precursors in Hegel and particularly Schelling where the life of consciousness, history, and religion are theogony. Berning sees an influence of Schelling's *Philosophy of Revelation* at work in the early theology of the Trinity so that it, aided perhaps by the Greek fathers, moves relationship and substance from the center of consideration; in fact the work on the Trinity contains little philosophical speculation. The two directions reach a different combination in *Gott und Geist* (Paderborn, 1895–1896) which presents its theology within an implicit meeting of Brentano, Günther, and Kuhn; *DHS*, p. 45.

24. Lectures of 1905/06 cited in "Einleitung," *KD* 2: xxi; cf. *DHS*, p. 199f.; Berning, *Systematisches . . .*, pp. 60ff.

25. On Schell and Molinist theologians, cf. *DHS*, pp. 82f. and Alois Schmid's review of *KD* in *Literarische Rundschau* 16 (1890): 204.

26. "Das Problem des Geistes," *KL*, pp. 217ff. "That freedom, which vitalized medieval scholasticism, even within a strict ecclesial world enabled the most diverse views of the teachings of faith. This makes it a priori impossible to advocate *one* theological way of thinking as *the scholastic* one and to make it the criterion of ecclesial membership. I have often noticed in controversies between important neoscholastics a rudeness even when the issue was treated objectively and peacefully. There is not one teacher, not one order, not one school whose name and doctrine can be equated with Catholic truth or church leadership" (*KD* 1, p. xiv).

27. F. X. Kiefl, "Herman Schell," *H* 3 (1906): 549.

28. *DHS*, p. 82.

29. H. Sinsheimer, *Gelebt im Paradies* (Munich, 1953), pp. 36ff.

30. "Der Katholizismus in Deutschland und die deutschen Universitäten," *KL*, pp. 151, 155, 162.

31. In 1869 in Prussian territories there were seven million Catholics and ten million Protestants, but out of 556 university professors only a tenth were Catholic; see Hans Rost, *Die Katholiken im Kultur- und Wirtschaftsleben der Gegenwart* (Cologne, 1908) and chapter eight of this book.

32. Schell, *Der Katholizismus als Princip des Fortschritts* (Würzburg, 1897).

33. *Münchener Neuesten Nachrichten* 167 (1986) cited in *Sp*, pp. 149f. *"Ideal* Catholicism is the goal for friend and foe and without concern over secular views. What is dangerous in identifying Catholicism as willed by God with that fashioned by humans is not so much that one idealizes reality and history but that the *ideal is forced to sink to the level of marked imperfection*..., the moves of religious actions and decisions which, though honorably meant, are the growth mainly of natural powers" (ibid., p. 14).

34. Ibid., p. 25.

35. Ibid., pp. 21, 41.

36. Ibid., p. 25.

37. Ibid., p. 54.

38. Ibid., pp. 88ff.

39. Schell, *Die neue Zeit und der alte Glaube* (Würzburg, 1898), pp. 98ff.

40. Ibid., p. 118.

41. Ibid., p. 120.

42. Ibid., p. viii.

43. Ibid., p. 158.

44. See K. Braun (the cathedral pastor in Würzburg), *Distinguo: Mängel und Übelstande im heutigen Katholizismus nach Prof. Dr. Schell in Würzburg und dessen Vorschläge zur Versöhnung der modernen Cultur und des Protestantismus mit der katholischen Kirche* (Linz, 1902); see G. Griener, "Herman Schell and the Reform of the Catholic Church in Germany," *Modernism: In Germany, In Spirituality* (Spring Hill, Ala., 1989), pp. 59ff.

45. A. Houtin, *Histoire du modernisme catholique* (Paris, 1913), p.59.

46. V. Berning, "Neue Zeit und alter Glaube," *Publik* 23 (1971): 19.

47. Against this theology, defended by Kiefl and other supporters of Schell, J. B. Stufler wrote *Die Heiligkeit Gottes und der ewige Tod* (Innsbruck, 1903); cf. *DHS*; "Pour où contre Schell," *Hoc* 3: 175ff. Others see these concrete theological topics as simply the examples of deeper Vatican concerns concerning progressive Catholicism and dialectics and subjectivity in God; Berning, *Systematische*..., p. 354.

48. *DHS*, p. 221; see J. Kübel, *Geschichte des katholischen Modernismus* (Tübingen, 1909).

49. O. Schroeder, *Aufbruch und Missverständnis: Zur Geschichte der reform-katholischen Bewegung* (Graz, 1969), p. 377. On Schell's various procedures and condemnations, see Carl Hennemann, *Die Widerrufe Herman Schells?* (Würzburg, 1908); *DHS*, pp. 215ff.; F. X. Kiefl, *Die Stellung der Kirche zur Theologie von Herman Schell* (Mainz, 1908); "Herman Schell," *H* 3 (1906): 548ff. On Schell and Hertling and the Center Party, see *DHS*, p. 217.

50. An anonymous polemic was published by the Jesuit Josef Müller in the *Salzburger Kirchenzeitung* drawing on sermons by the Jesuits in Würzburg.

51. E. Commer, *Herman Schell und der fortschrittliche Katholizismus* (Vienna, 1908) 2nd ed. with the papal letter on pp. x, xi and Michael Glossner's seventy-page introduction.

52. Ibid., pp. 7ff., 29ff.

53. Ibid., pp. 24f.

54. Ibid., pp. 212f.

55. Ibid., p. 212; cf. pp. 139ff., 332; cf. the second book, *Die jüngste Phase des Schellstreites* (Vienna, 1909). Hennemann then published Commer's earlier, positive letters on Schell: *Ernst Commers Briefe an Herman Schell* (Würzburg, 1907); cf. his *Herman Schell im Lichte zeitgenössischer Urteile bei seinem Tode* (Paderborn, 1909).

56. In Hennemann, *Herman Schell im Lichte . . .*, p. 33 and Hasenfuss, *Herman Schell*, p. 26.

57. *W*, pp. 405f.

58. *KD* 3, part 1, p. ix.

59. "Vorwort," *KD* 1: 10.

60. *DHS*, p. 95; *Systematisches . . .*, p. 352.

61. *Gott und Geist* 2 (Paderborn, 1896): 92f.

62. *Systematisches . . .*, pp. 216ff.

63. "Das Problem des Geistes . . .," *KL.* p. 207.

64. *KD* 3: 21.

65. Bleickert, "Herman Schell," p. 315. The roots of this central concept lie in Greek patristic and medieval scholastic thought, and B. Casper has traced its presence in Descartes and Spinoza. Schell's idea in its formal aspect recalls Kant, and in its content Schelling. On the influence of Schelling on Schell, see B. Casper, "Der Gottesbegriff 'ens causa sui,'" *PhJ* 76 (1968/69): 315ff.

66. *KD* 2: 6.

67. "Das Problem des Geistes . . .," *KL*, p. 192.

68. Cf. Hennemann, "Nachruf," *Herman Schell im Licht . . .*, pp. 152f.; *Gott und Geist* 1: 175.

69. Schell, "Vorwort," *Religion und Offenbarung*, pp. vff. See the articles "Das Problem des Geistes," "Das erkenntnistheoretische Problem," "René Descartes," in H. Schell, *KL*.

70. H. Fries, "Herman Schell," *H* 52 (1959/60): 510.

71. "Christus und die Kultur," *KL*, pp. 384, 392f.

72. R. Stölzle, "Das Prinzip des Katholizismus und die Wissenschaft," in *HPBl* 124 (1899): 492 cited in *Religion und Offenbarung* (Paderborn, 1901), p. x.

73. "Vorwort," *Religion und Offenbarung*, p. xii.

74. Ibid., p. xiii.

75. Bleickert, "Herman Schell," p. 300.

76. The volume ended with various responses to critics like C. Pesch, M. Glossner, von Hartmann.

77. Schell was knowledgeable in Protestant theology and sometimes touched on Protestantism in his addresses and essays. The dogmatic libertarianism of liberal Protestantism was alien to him, although he appreciated Protestant theologians' dialogue with the times. His contemporary apologetic orientation dealt not with Protestant theology but with modernity itself. He surveyed the views of figures such as Delitzsch, Luthard, Hase, Tschackert and concluded that the fundamental interconfessional issue was the image of God. One group of critics accused Catholicism of being paganism with excessive mediations in church and worship; the second group accused it of being

Judaism tied to laws and works. Schell's apologetics attempted to correct their misconceptions. He stressed that the merits and work of Christ have as their climax our own activity; God cannot be more sublime than when he acts through grace in human beings. (See "Der Gottesbegriff im Katholizismus und Protestantismus," *KL*, p. 126.)

Schell agreed with Harnack that Christianity was a product of life and spirit and had an intrinsic history and that the gospel could be interpreted by various metaphysics. In the forward to his *Apologie*, he looked at what his approach shared with *Das Wesen des Christentums*. He objected to the principle that Chalcedon marked a fundamental hellenistic obscuring of Christ or that inspiration, canon, and tradition emerged and existed spiritually outside of church forms. Cf. K. Neufeld, *Theologie als Suche nach der Kirche* (Paderborn, 1977).

78. F. Kiefl, *Hermann Schell*, pp. 33f.; see Paul Schanz, review in *ThQ* 84 (1902): 299f., and Schanz, "Neue Tendenzen der philosophischen Apologetik," *ThQ* 78 (1896): 408f.

79. *Apologie des Christentums* 1: 418f.

80. *KD* 2: 157ff.

81. *KD* 3, part 2, p. 742.; *KD* 2: 330, 349, 359; see H. Rotter, "Das Problem der Sünde bei Herman Schell," *Zeitschrift für katholische Theologie* 89 (1967); 249ff., 385ff.; on Schell combating Molinism in Würzburg, see *DHS*, pp. 82f.

82. "There is then no opposition between creation by a free act of God and natural development in the sense of the empirical teaching of the natural evolution of the cosmos; rather, this demands even more the law-giving thought and the powerful, lastingly active will of the divine spirit as its unavoidable source" ("Schöpfung oder Entwicklung," *KL*, p. 254; and see *KD* 2: 92). Schell also explored the meaning of the world religions, set as they were, in a developmental context. Behind the doctrinal expositions and comparisons one senses a probing toward a relationship based upon not simply a known God but an active and present Trinity. See "Das Entwicklungsgesetz der Religion und deren Zukunft," "Die kulturgeschichtliche Bedeutung der grossen Weltreligionen," in *KL*; on Schell, evolution, and Teilhard see H. Mynarek, *Der Mensch, Sinnziel der Weltentwicklung* (Munich, 1967).

83. *Apologie* 2: 338.

84. *KD* 1: 103ff.

85. *KD* 3, part 1, pp. 26, 130f.; *Apologie* 2: 532.

86. *Christus* (Mainz, 1903), p. 120.

87. *Jahwe und Christus* (Paderborn, 1905), p. 446.

88. *KD* 3, part 1, p. 333. Schell certainly shocked the Vatican by distinguishing between a "Roman" and a "German" understanding of how authority should be exercised. The "Roman" ecclesiology does not reflect the Catholic essence and is responsible for the inferior status of German Catholics; *Der Katholizismus . . .*, pp. 11ff.

89. "Lehrende und lernende Kirche: Wissenschaft und Autorität," *KL*, pp. 471ff.

90. *KD* 3, part 1, pp. 426ff.

91. *Jahwe und Christus*, p. 469; cf. "Catholicismus und Protestantismus . . . Reich Gottes," *KL*, pp. 305ff. On Schell's consideration of, but opposition to, the ordination of women see P. Wacker, *Glaube und Wissen bei Herman Schell* (Paderborn, 1961), pp. 371ff.

92. Karl Mühlek, *Dynamische Gemeinschaft: Zur Lehre Herman Schell's von der Kirche* (Munich, 1973), p. 181. "Schell unfolds an ecclesiology which is classical in the centrality of function. But this is then placed in a climate of thought and speculation, and within the context of the creativity and liberty of the human person" (*C*, p. 460).

93. An extensive list of disciples can be found in *DHS*, pp. 227–239 and in *Systematisches* . . . , pp. 30f. Schell had criticized the separation between theology and the church year; one of his early students, Theodor Abele, brought together phllosophers and political scientists and then this circle had contact with those interested in liturgical renewal at Maria Laach; *DHS*, pp. 240f. and H. Platz "Von Schell zu Festugière, wie wir zur Liturgie gekommen sind," *Das Wort in der Zeit* 2 (1934/35): 331.

94. See Hasenfuss, *Herman Schell* . . . , p. 9.

95. Hasenfuss, "Einleitung: Leben und Wirken H. Schells," *KD*, p. xxi.

96. H. Fries, "Herman Schell," p. 507; agreeing is Leo Scheffczyk, "Einleitung," *Theologie im Aufbruch und Widerstreit* (Bremen, 1965), p. 45. Carl Muth summed up Schell's career in this way: "What Augustine accomplished in his late work *De civitate Dei* for the uncovering and combating of the errors of his age is what Schell accomplished in his critique of Eduard von Hartmann" (Carl Muth's notes published in *H* 46 [1953/54], 240).

7. Carl Braig: On the Boundary in Freiburg

1. Braig is a notable omission from Fries-Schwaiger, *KThD*, but a recent brief article is devoted to him in *CP* 1: 409ff.; see also *Freiburger Diözesan-Archiv, NF* 27 (1926): 28ff; *Badischer Beobachter* 53 (March 31, 1925); F. Stegmüller, "Carl Braig," *Oberrheinisches Pastoralblatt* 54 (1953): 3ff.

2. Braig, *Apologie des Christentums* (Freiburg, 1889), p. xxxiii.

3. Braig, "Natürliche Gotteserkenntnis nach Thomas von Aquin," *ThQ* 63 (1881): 595; cf. Braig, *Gottesbeweis oder Gottesbeweise* (Stuttgart, (1887).

4. K. Leidlmaire, "Carl Braig (1853–1923)," *CP* 1, p. 410.

5. As we saw in the previous chapter, Wörter succeeded Staudenmaier in 1855 and taught until 1897. A student of Kuhn and Staudenmaier, he solidified the Tübingen influence at Freiburg. An expert on semi-Pelagianism, he resisted the arrival of the neoscholastic Schäzler and included in dogmatics the historical and the patristic. B. Welte writes: "We do note a certain shift from the characteristics of the Tübingen school and so we call Wörter a late idealist. This means there is still the search to understand everything through living ideas, but this attempt has reached a late and critical stage. In Wörter historical material plays a greater role than with the old Tübingen theologians; important ideal moments, while vital for him, have diminished attraction and power" ("150 Jahre Theologische Fakultät Freiburg als Exempelfall theologischer Entwicklung," *Zwischen Zeit und Ewigkeit* [Freiburg, 1982], pp. 144f.

6. see ibid, pp. 135ff.

7. Braig, *Die Grundzüge der Philosophie* (3 vols.): *Vom Denken; Vom Erkennen; Vom Sein* (Freiburg, 1896–1897).

8. Braig, *Jesus Christus ausserhalb der katholischen Kirche im neunzehnten Jahrhundert* (Freiburg, 1911); *Die Gotteslehre* (Freiburg, 1912).

9. Sections of Braig's *Jesus Christus*; the edition of his *Apologie des Christentums; Uber Geist und Wesen des Christentums* . . . (Freiburg, 1902); *Das Dogma des jüngsten Christentums* (Freiburg, 1907).

10. Braig, *Die Freiheit der philosophischen Forschung* (Freiburg, 1894); *Der Papst und die Freiheit* (Freiburg, 1903); *Zur Erinnerung an F. X. Kraus* (Freiburg, 1902); *Der Modernismus und die Freiheit der Wissenschaft* (Freiburg, 1911).

11. "Natürliche Gotteserkenntnis," p. 527.

12. Ibid., p. 588.

13. Ibid., p. 596.

14. John Caputo, "Heidegger and the Catholic Theology of Carl Braig," in his *Heidegger and Aquinas; An Essay on Metaphysics* (New York, 1982), pp. 45–57.

15. Braig, *Die Zukunftsreligion des Unbewussten und das Princip des Subjektivismus* (Freiburg, 1882); *Modernstes Christentum und moderne Religionspsychologie* (Freiburg, 1907); *Der Ursprung der religiösen Vorstellungen und der Phantasie* (Freiburg, 1907).

16. In 1869 Hartmann published a study on Schelling's later philosophy, the first major one in some years: *Schellings Positive Philosophie* (Berlin, 1869). He observed that between the two poles of Hegel and Schopenhauer, Schelling "holds the key" because he transcends panlogism and will (pp. 3ff.) and offers spirit and nature, mind and will in a dialectical unity. So Hartmann's goal (which was more than presenting the positive philosophy of Schelling and the earlier philosophy of identity) was "to accept the absolute, substantial subject of theism, without moving its consciousness, self-awareness, and personality into pantheism" (*Das Philosophische Dreigestirn des 19. Jh. Gesammelte Studien und Aufsätze* [Leipzig, 1888], p. 549ff.). In 1890 Hartmann began a "philosophy of the unconscious" by outlining his sources in earlier philosophers; *Philosophie des Unbewussten* 1 (Leipzig, 1888): 1–35. There was also a lengthy treatment of Schelling in *Geschichte der Metaphysik* (Leipzig, 1900) 2: 89–304. *Die Selbstzersetzung des Christenthums und die Religion der Zukunft* (Berlin, 1874) concluded with a version of Schelling's and Baader's doctrine of the dialectic of churches: Petrine, Pauline, and Johannine.

17. Braig, *Die Krisis des Christenthums in der modernen Theologie* (Berlin, 1880), p. 84.

18. In Braig's introduction to Duilhé the word "modernism" appeared again; some mistakenly see there its first appearance: F. Stegmüller, "Karl Braig," *Oberrheinisches Pastoralblatt* 54 (1953). Noting the earlier appearance in *Die Zukunftsvision* is E. Fastenrath, "Christologie im Zeitalter des Modernismus: Die Analyse der Problematik in den Schriften des Freiburger Dogmatikers Carl Braig," *MThZ* 34 (1983): 84.

19. Review in *Literarische Rundschau* 28 (1902): 20.

20. *Das Dogma* . . . , pp. 78ff.; *Jesus Christus* . . . , p. 120.

21. Ibid., p. 70.

22. Braig, "Eine Antwort," *PhJ* 12 (1899): 350. "St. Thomas Aquinas, if today he entered certain circles of those who are considered to be his disciples, would be

the first to say: 'Friends, what a mess you have made of my thought. Don't you see what a danger it is to lay claim to an exclusivity in the church for those who share your views'" (*Literarische Rundschau* 28 [1902]: 78).

23. Stegmüller, p. 6. It would be interesting to know what Braig thought of Brentano, whose influence was so extensive, reaching from Freiburg to Vienna and Prague, and ultimately influencing neo-Aristotelianism, phenomenology, and existentialism.

24. For a neoscholastic reaction to Braig, see Michael Glossner's review of *Vom Sein* in *JPsT* 13 (1898): 59ff; 14 (1900): 204ff. See his reply to Braig's "Eine Frage," in *JPsT* 13 (1899): 86ff., and further "Ein Zweites Wort an Prof. Dr. Braig," *JPsT* 14 (1900): 248ff. For how a strict neo-Thomist viewed the entire Tübingen history, see Glossner's "Die Tübinger katholische Schule, vom spekulativen Standpunkt kritisch beleuchtet," *JPsT* 15 (1901): 166ff.; 16 (1902): 1ff; and particularly, "Die Epigonen: Schanz, Braig, Schell," *JPsT* 17 (1903): 2ff.

25. "Wie sorgt die Enzyklika gegen den Modernismus für die Reinerhaltung der christlich-kirchlichen Lehre?" *Jesus Christus*, p. 420.

26. Ibid., p. 418.

27. Braig, "Über Geist und Wesen des Christenthums, eine Studie zu Chateaubriand's *Genie du Christianisme* und verwandte Erscheinungen," in *Festschrift . . . des Grossherzogs Friedrich* (Freiburg, 1902), p. 42.

28. *Jesus Christus*, p. 185; cf. Braig, "Die jüngste Leugnung der geschichtlichen Existenz Jesu und ihr letzter Grund," *K* 91 (1911): 81ff., 168ff. Braig's *Abriss der Christologie* is a record of his lectures on christology assembled by students and published in a manuscript form in 1907. There is also an *Abriss der Gotteslehre* from 1912; see Fastenrath (note 18 above), p. 117.

29. Review of Schell's *Christus* in *Literarische Rundschau* 29 (1903): 147.

30. "Über Geist und Wesen des Christenthums . . . ," pp. 15–62.

31. Harnack was also treated in the rectorate address (*Das Dogma des jüngsten Christentums*) and in *Das Wesen des Christentums an einem Beispiel erläutert oder Adolf Harnack und die Messiasidee* (Freiburg, 1903). Curiously Harnack mentioned Catholic romanticism and Chateaubriand in his *Wesen*. "At the beginning of this century Catholicism was reintroduced in Germany and in France through the romantics and, above all, Chateaubriand, who could not do enough for its glorification and for his self-perception as a Catholic. But a perceptive critique explains that Chateaubriand erred in his sensitivity: he thought he was a real Catholic but in fact he stood before the old ruin of the church and exclaimed, 'How beautiful!' That is one of the ways by which one can value a religion without being inwardly touched by it" (*Das Wesen des Christentums* [Leipzig, 1901], p. 124); Cf. Braig's review of a study on Chateaubriand in *Literarische Rundschau* 29 (1903): 216f.

32. "Über Geist . . . ," p. 18.

33. Ibid., p. 32.

34. Staudenmaier, *Darstellung und Kritik des Hegelschen Systems* (Mainz, 1844), p. 5. See also B. Casper, ed., F. A. Staudenmaier, *Frühe Aufsätze* (Freiburg, 1974); A. Franz, *Glauben und Denken* (Regensburg, 1983) (on Hegel); W. McConville, *Theology and Encyclopedia* (Vanderbilt, 1983); H. Ploch, *Feier der Versöhnung*

und des göttlichen Lebens (Münster, 1978); B. Schrott, *Die Idee in der Geschichte* (Essen, 1976); Thomas O'Meara, "Between Schelling and Hegel: The Catholic Tübingen School," in *Romantic Idealism*, pp. 139–147.

35. Über den Geist. . . , p. 25.

36. Ibid., pp. 27, 29.

37. Ibid., pp. 51, 46.

38. See Braig's review of J. M. Pernter, *Voraussetzunglose Forschung, freie Wissenschaft und Katholizismus* (Vienna, 1902) in *Literarische Rundschau* 28 (1902): 78.

39. Braig, *Die Freiheit der philosophischen Forschung in kritischer und christlicher Fassung* (Freiburg, 1894), pp. 53, 58. See Alois Schmid's review in *Literarische Rundschau* 20 (1894): 284.

40. Braig, *Der Papst und die Freiheit* (Freiburg, 1903).

41. Braig, *Was soll der Gebildete von dem Modernismus wissen?* (Kamm, 1908), p. 3.

42. Ibid., pp. 12ff.

43. *Apologie*, p. lxxiii.

44. Braig, *Der Modernismus und die Freiheit der Wissenschaft* (Freiburg, 1911), p. vi.

45. *Literarische Rundschau* 28 (1902): 86.

46. Ibid.; see also further reviews of *Christus* and *Jahwe und Christus* in *Literarische Rundschau* 29 (1903): 145f.; 35 (1909): 5540f.; and see Braig's views on the reactionary essays in C. Pesch's multivolume *Theologische Zeitfragen* (Freiburg, 1900–1916), some of which criticized Schell; *Literarische Rundschau* 28 (1902): 86f., 331f. He generally praised Paul Schanz but with the reservations that he was an eclectic, too concerned with the natural sciences, and shallow in terms of philosophical depth. See *Gottesbeweis oder Gottesbeweise?* p. 2.; and reviews in *Literarische Rundschau* for 1898, 1900, 1903.

47. Review of *Christus* in *Literarische Rundschau* 29 (1903): 145ff.

48. Braig, *Zur Erinnerung an F. X. Kraus* (Freiburg, 1902). But he is critical of J. Schnitzer who leaves the church in the aftermath of *Reformkatholizismus*; (*Jesus Christus . . .* , p. 127).

49. *Zur Sache des Denkens* (Pfullingen, 1969), p. 82.

50. M. Heidegger, "Mein Weg in die Phänomenologie," *Zur Sache des Denkens* (Tübingen, 1969), p. 82. "The decisive, and therefore ineffable, influence on my later academic career came from two men who should be expressly mentioned here in memory and gratitude; the one was Carl Braig, professor of systematic theology, who was the last in the tradition of the speculative school of Tübingen, which gave significance and scope to Catholic theology through its dialogue with Hegel and Schelling" ("A Recollection [1957]," in *Heidegger, the Man and the Thinker* [Chicago, 1981], p. 22). Cf. F. Volpi, "Alle origini delle concenzione Heideggeriane dell' essere: Il trattato *Vom Sein* di C. Braig," *Rivista critica di storia della filosofia* 34 (1980): 183ff. Heidegger was supported for several years by a stipend from the von Schäzler foundation in Freiburg.

Heidegger was also influenced by Schell: "I entered the University of Freiburg in Breisgau in the winter semester of 1909. . . . At first I studied theology. . . [and] resorted to studying scholastic textbooks on my own. They provided me with a certain formal-logical schooling, but as regards philosophy they did not give me what I was looking for, and what, in the area of apologetics, I had already found in the works of Herman Schell" (*"Heidegger's Lehrjahre,"* in J. C. Sallis, ed., *The Collegium Phaenomenologicum* [Boston, 1988], p. 79). See also J. Caputo, *Heidegger and Aquinas* (New York, 1982), pp. 46ff.; H. Ott, *Martin Heidegger: Unterwegs zu seiner Biographie* (New York, 1988); T. O'Meara, "Heidegger and His Origins: Theological Perspectives," *Theological Studies* 47 (1986): 205ff. Braig's first essays showed some possible influence upon Heidegger: an insistence upon Plato along with Aristotle, the critique of mathematical and Aristotelian conceptions of truth, the links of attitudes to knowing. "Die natürliche Gotteserkenntnis. . . ," pp. 528, 569, 593.

51. Stegmüller listed Guardini as having promoted under Braig—as does W. Ferber in "Romano Guardini," *Zeitgeschichte in Lebensbilder* (Mainz, 1973), p. 388—but H. B. Gerl described that as a widespread inaccuracy in *Romano Guardini* (Mainz, 1985), pp. 83ff.

52. "Die natürliche Gotteserkenntnis. . . ," p. 595.

53. On some links between the Tübingen school's view of truth and subjectivity and Heidegger, see W. Kasper, *Das Absolute in der Geschichte* (Mainz, 1965), pp. 423ff. Stegmüller, Fastenrath, and Caputo conclude, after studying Braig's writings, that the impact of his teaching in style and personal contact exceeded that of the printed page.

54. Welte (note 5 above), p. 150.

8. Reform for the Next Century (1898–1906)

1. Schanz, "Die alte und neue Weltanschauung," *ThQ* 72 (1890): 437.

2. Addressing the minority status of Catholics in the Protestant Reich were: C. Moufang, *Einige Irrthümer bezüglich der socialen und religiösen Frage* (Würzburg, 1877); O. Hanson, " 'Verjüngert' Katholicismus?" *Die Kultur* (Vienna, 1900) 1: 48ff.; H. Rost, *Die Katholiken im Kultur- und Wirtschaftsleben der Gegenwart* (Cologne, 1908); W. Lossen, *Der Anteil der Katholiken am akademischen Lehramt in Preussen* (Cologne, 1901); R. Hillebrand, "Katholische und Protestantische Wahrheitsliebe," *Der Katholik* 79 (1899), 1ff., 117ff., 227ff.; H. Kuhn, "Der internationale wissenschaftliche Katholikencongress zu München," *Der Katholik* 81 (1901), 34ff., 121ff., 212ff.; C. Braig, "Der Katholicismus im Spiegel der neuesten Protestantischen Kritik," *Literarische Rundschau* 29 (1903): 1ff. Articles on these deficiencies appear in *Historisch-politische Blätter* in vols. 117 (1887) through 120 (1894).

3. T. Nipperdey, *Religion im Umbruch. Deutschland 1870–1918* (Munich, 1988), pp. 38f.; A. Kraus, *Geschichte Bayerns* (Munich, 1983), p. 587. "At the Universities of Greifswald and Königsberg the Catholics were granted one professorship (usually in medicine or natural science). Elsewhere, for instance in Leipzig, all the humanities were reserved to Protestants" (*Sch*, p. 181). Among 90 Prussian ministers between 1888 and 1914 only four were Catholics" (H. Lutz, *Demokratie in*

Zwielicht [Munich, 1963], p. 16). K. E. Lönne sees an early cause for this to be in the secularization in Catholic lands of the educational institutions run by the religious orders and a proximate cause to be in the lack of individuality and openness to modernity; *Politischer Katholizismus im 19. und 20. Jahrhundert* (Frankfurt, 1986), p. 25f. See also G. E. Windell, *The Catholics and German Unity, 1866-1871* (Minneapolis, 1954); U. von Hehl, K. Repgen, eds., *Der deutsche Katholizismus in der zeitgeschichtlichen Forschung* (Mainz, 1988); K. Schatz, *Zwischen Säkularisation und Zweitem Vatikanum: Der Weg des deutschen Katholizismus im 19. und 20. Jahrhundert* (Frankfurt, 1986); R. Morsey, "Die deutschen Katholiken und der Nationalstaat zwischen Kulturkampf und erstem Weltkrieg," *Historisches Jahrbuch* 90 (1970): 35ff.; M. Baumeister, *Parität und katholische Inferiorität: Untersuchungen zur Stellung des Katholizismus im Deutschen Kaiserreich* (Munich, 1987).

4. Schwaiger, *Geschichte der Päpste im 20. Jahrhundert* (Munich, 1968), p. 64.

5. *J* 6 no. 2: 439; "Der Kampf gegen den Zölibat," *Hgn*, pp. 183ff.

6. Müller, *Der Reformkatholizismus: Die Religion der Zukunft* (Würzburg, 1899). V. Berning believes that the term's origin lies with E. Spranger and that Müller's usage was associated from the beginning with radical groups; "Modernismus und Reformkatholizismus in ihrer prospektiven Tendenz," *Die Zukunft der Glaubenunterweisung* (Freiburg, 1971), p. 19. See also O. Schroeder, *Aufbruch und Missverständnis: Zur Geschichte der reformkatholischen Bewegung* (Graz, 1969); A. Kolping, *Katholische Theologie Gestern und Heute* (Bremen, 1964), p. 47; G. Maron, "Reformkatholizismus," *Religion in Geschichte und Gegenwart*, 3rd ed., 5: 896ff.

7. Müller "Deutschtum und Luthertum," *HPBl* 123 (1899): 55ff.; and *Die Jesuiten* (Würzburg, 1891).

8. *Reformkatholizismus* (Würzburg, 1899), p. 5.

9. See K. Bachem, *Vorgeschichte, Geschichte und Politik der deutschen Zentrumspartei* 7 (Cologne, 1930); A. ten Hompel, *Indexbewegung und Kulturgesellschaft* (Bonn, 1908).

10. *Akten des fünften internationalen Kongresses katholischer Gelehrter in München* (Munich, 1901); on the Isarlust meeting, *Hgn*, pp. 19ff. On Schell as a modernist see Da Veiga Coutinho, *Tradition et Histoire dans la controverse moderniste 1898–1910* (Rome, 1954), pp. 71ff.; X. M. Le Bachelet, "Catholicisme et progrès: Le mouvement Schell," *Études* 78 (1899): 622ff.; W. Sapel, "H. Schell und der Reformkatholizismus," *Fränkische Heimat* no. 17 (1966), 23f.; P. Schanz, "Die katholische Tübigen Schule," *ThQ* 78 (1896): 27f.

11. Glossner, "Scholastik, Reformkatholicismus und Reformkatholische Philosophie," *JPsT* 13 (1899): 393.

12. On the lecture, see A. Gisler, *Im Kampf gegen Modernismus* (Stans, 1913), pp. 150ff.; H. Schiel, "Tübinger Theologen in Verbindungen mit F. X. Kraus," *ThQ* 137 (1957): 18ff., 168ff., 289ff.

13. A. Walz, *Andreas Kardinal Frühwirth* (Vienna, 1950).

14. See *Tr*, p. 43.

15. Franz Xaver Kraus (1840–1901) was a brilliant and engaging professor of church history and a pioneer in the fields of archaeology and Christian art. He joined the Freiburg theological faculty in 1878, becoming its guiding spirit. He was an adviser

to the Berlin government, although his loyalty to the Catholic church was irrevocable. An emotional essayist, author of a kind of column, "Spectator Letters" from 1896 to 1900, he easily slipped into a polemical misunderstanding of his opponents. He generally refrained from speculative theological and philosophical issues.

Deeply convinced that the policies of the Curia would severely injure the life of the church in Germany, he advocated pastoral reforms, and a distinction between "religious" and "political" Catholicism (which he drew from his long-term and respected research into Dante; like Schnitzer and others he saw Savonarola as a model). He worked in the spirit of Rosmini and Montalambert: in 1904 Bavarian Catholics founded a Krausgesellschaft, "a society for the advancement of religion and culture," advocating freedom of scholarly research and anti-Roman reforms.

Viewed by some as the creator of a mystical, culture-Catholicism, he advocated a liberal church but a conservative state. Bishop P. W. Keppler defended Kraus in 1899 but advised him to make a "heroic decision" to leave the arena of journalism concerning church politics and church reform. Kraus wrote in his diary in 1900: "I became convinced that these treatments of church politics were so uncomfortable to Vatican Pharisaism that they would not stop at forbidding attendance at my lectures but would censure or excommunicate me." Carl Braig delivered at Freiburg a lengthy address defending Kraus' gifted union of scholarship, creativity, and fidelity. See *Hgn*, pp. 11ff.; E. Hauvillier, *F. X. Kraus. Ein Lebensbild aus der Zeit des Reformkatholizismus* (Colmar, 1904); H. Schiel, *Im Spannungsfeld von Kirche und Politik. F. X. Kraus* (Trier, 1951); H. Schiel, *F. X. Kraus und die Tübinger Schule* (Ellwangen, 1958); O. Köhler, "F. X. Kraus (1840–1901)," *KThD* 3: 241ff.

16. Sebastian Merkle (1862–1945) was born at Ellwangen in 1862. Professor of church history at Würzburg from 1898 to 1933, he pioneered a new Catholic view of Luther and wrote on Catholicism in the ages of *Aufklärung* and of *Romantik*. He was able to combine the scholarly editorship of the diaries of the Council of Trent with an active engagement in issues about Catholic identity. In 1905 he wrote a defense of theological faculties at state universities and of religious freedom for Catholics. When the plan for a Catholic university was brought up again in 1912, he opposed it. His lectures led at times to conflicts between the directors of the university's seminary and the seminarians' bishops. Church leaders began to notice how many of his students were active in the reform movements. He delivered the funeral address for Schell and led the controversial movement to establish a modest monument to him; *Hgn, passim*.

Philipp Funk (1884–1937), editor of newpapers in Munich and Augsburg, followed the approach of Carl Muth, steering Catholicism through the shoals of liberalism and historical relativism. A Tübingen education and Schell's stimulating addresses influenced Funk in a career which began with an article in Müller's *Renaissance* in 1906 on the state of exegesis and on *Pascendi*'s view of the Bible. Trained as a historian, he wrote on baroque and medieval piety as well as on the passage of Catholicism from the Enlightenment into the Bavarian romantic restoration in the years around 1800. He became professor of history in Freiburg in 1929. See *KThD* 3: 272ff.; *Hgn*, 97ff.

17. Otto Sickenberger (1867–1918), teacher in a Passau gymnasium, was a vocal leader of reform and published a large irenical theology aimed at joining positively Catholics and Protestants. He criticized Keppler's turn to conservatism in

Falsche Reform? (Augsburg, 1903) and *Veritas et Justitia* (Augsburg, 1903). Advocating an ecumenical council of reform, he traveled to Rome twice seeking a change in the discipline of priestly celibacy. He eventually left the priesthood and married; *Der Zölibatszwang und Bischof Keppler* (Würzburg, 1911); see *Hgn*, pp. 38ff., 193f; J. Kübel, *Geschichte des katholischen Modernismus* (Tübingen, 1909), p. 69.

Thaddaeus Engert (1875–1945) published in the area of exegesis and science and was excommunicated for his views in 1907. He edited *Das Zwanzigste Jahrhundert* up to his entry into the Protestant church where he served as a pastor; see *Tr*, p. 38. On other figures of Reform-Catholicism, see *Hgn*, pp. 97ff.

18. Other examples of this genre addressing the new century are: P. Schanz, "Die geistigen Strömungen der Gegenwart," *Die Kultur* 1 (1900): 1ff.; Schanz, "Die Weltausstellung der Gegenwart und die Zukunft des Katholicismus," *HPBl* 126 (1900): 10ff.; the addresses at the *Katholikentag* in the years from 1892 to 1894; K. Gebert, *Katholischer Glaube und die Entwicklung des Geisteslebens* (Munich, 1905); E. Jung, *Radikaler Reform-Katholizismus* (Munich, 1906). Conservatively critical of these essays are the Dominican A. Weiss, "Eine theologische Aufgabe für das kommende Jahrhundert," *HPBl* 125 (1900): 131ff., and the Jesuit R. Nostiss, "Von der Wiedergeburt katholischen Lebens im XIX Jh.," *HPBl* 121 (1898): l2ff.; Emil Jung, *Radikaler Reform-Katholizismus: Grundlage einer deutschkatholischen Kirche* (Munich, 1906).

19. Alois Dempf, *Albert Ehrhard* (Colmar, 1944), pp. 34f.; see F. Loidl, "Ehrhard, Albert Joseph Maria," *LThK* 3: 719; *Hgn*, pp. 21ff.

20. Ehrhard, *Der Katholizismus und das 20 Jh. im Licht der kirchlichen Entwicklung der Neuzeit* (Vienna, 1901); see *Tr*, pp. 113f. Typical of literature on the renewal of Catholicism would be: J. Hillebrand, "Katholische und Protestantische Wahrheitsliebe," *K* 79 (1899); 1ff., 117ff., 227ff,; H. Kuhn, "Der internationale wissenschaftliche Katholikencongress zu München," *K* 81 (1901): 34ff., 121ff., 212ff,; C. Moufang, *Einige Irrthümer . . .* (note 2 above); O. Hanson, " 'Verjüngert' Katholicismus?" (note 2 above) 1:48ff.; C. Braig, "Der Katholicismus . . ." (note 2 above).

21. *Der Katholizismus . . .* , pp. vii, 1. "Nothing is more difficult for the historian than to determine the hour in which an era is born . . . coming as its does from the working together of *a dual moment*, the ideal and the real. The ideas and movements of significant facets condition the historical process whose fall-out forms the facts" (ibid., p. 55).

22. Ibid., pp. 3ff.

23. Ibid., pp. 70f.

24. Ibid., p. 226. Ehrhard only briefly acknowledged the role of romanticism and moved quickly to those condemned distractions: Hermes and Günther. The Tübingen and Munich schools are briefly sketched without an analysis of either history or philosophy. One phenomenon of the controversies at the beginning of the century is the German hostility toward the Jesuits. Ehrhard analyzed the origin and history of Ignatius and his order to combat "this lamentable phenomenon" (ibid., p. 138).

25. Ibid., p. 242.

26. Ibid., pp. 243ff. Neoscholasticism achieved success as a reaction to philosophy after Kant. An early victory by neoscholasticism was held off by Kuhn of

Tübingen. Louvain's ontologism was an attempt to draw post-Kantian conclusions from neoscholastic epistemologies. Ehrhard criticized the attempt to "dogmatize" the theological system of Aquinas. "The Catholic church never identified itself fully with a particular philosophical and theological school and such an identification cannot occur. It is a mistake to imply that philosophy and theology in Catholicism can only be done through a scholastic mentality; in fact, scholasticism within a century had ended up in the disastrous shipwreck of nominalism. . . . Thomas Aquinas is a lighthouse, not a fence" (pp. 248–253).

27. Ibid., p. 218.

28. Ibid., pp. 291f.

29. Ibid., p. 307.

30. Ibid., pp. 336f.

31. Ibid., pp. 345, 379ff. "The attempt to construct the theoretical worldview from the thinking subject while setting aside every tradition and the historically formed philosophical systems was occasioned by the events I described earlier and could not have been avoided from a psychological point of view" (p. 345).

32. Ehrhard offered interesting remarks on the relationship of Catholicism to art, past and modern. The arts contained the total cultural world. Art was not simply a question of an aesthetics made concrete but of the disclosure of values, insights, and perspectives. Modern art was already presenting challenges in terms of its forms and content; ibid., pp. 393ff.

33. *Tr*, pp. 115ff.

34. See T. M. Loome, "Die Trümmer des liberalen Katholizismus," in M. Schmidt and G. Schwaiger, *Kirchen und Liberalismus im 19. Jahrhundert* (Göttingen, 1976), pp. 207ff.

35. Dempf, pp. 115ff.; *Tr*, pp. 117f.; A Rosler, *Für und Wider in Sachen der katholischen Reformbewegung der Neuzeit* (Freiburg, 1903).

36. Dempf, pp. 125ff.

37. Keppler, *Wahre und falsche Reform* (Freiburg, 1903), pp. 34ff.; Keppler-*Nachlass* cited in Loome, p. 213, n. 37; see *Hgn*, pp. 21ff., 162ff. And see A. Donders, *Bischof Keppler* (Freiburg, 1935). Rompola's letter of February 1, 1899, is cited in H. Schiel, *Franz Xaver Kraus und die Tübinger Schule* (Ellwangen, 1958), p. 89. Sickenberger wrote: "Your grace accuses your own friend Kraus of furthering inner untruthfulness and pharasaism with the slogan of religious Catholicism. You did not at all do justice to the true tendencies of that significant man. You could know what he meant: a church activity and life which make the purely religious its main interest and which renounce external power and glitter." Open letter in O. Sickenberger, *Falsche Reform?*, p. 1.

38. Ehrhard (Stuttgart, 1902). Surveying the controversy (strongest in Austria) is H. Dachs, "Albert Ehrhard—Vermittler oder Verräter?" in E. Weinzierl, *Der Modernismus: Beiträge zu seiner Erforschung* (Graz, 1970), pp. 221ff.; "Bischof Keppler und Albert Ehrhard," *Hgn*, pp. 21ff. In the controversy from 1902 to 1905 supporting Ehrhard are Sickenberger, Kiefl, and M. Spahn; typical of a conservative critique would be Matthias Hoehler, *Fortschrittlicher "Katholizismus" oder Katholischer Fortschritt?* (Trier, 1897).

39. "Die internationale Lage der katholischen Theologie," *Internationale Wochenschrift für Wissenschaft, Kunst und Technik* 1 (1907): 231ff. Ehrhard published in 1907 *Katholizismus und Kultur* (Mainz, 1907), a small handsomely bound book whose theme was the "ideal power and inspiring beauty of Catholicism" and whose frontispiece had a reproduction of Friedrich Overbeck's painting "The Covenant of Religion with Culture."

40. "Die neue Lage der katholischen Theologie," *Internationale Wochenschrift für Wissenschaft, Kunst und Technik* 2 (1908): 65ff.

41. Letter of September 1919 cited in *Tr*, p. 151.

42. Dempf, p. 11.

43. See J. M. Hausladen, "Hertling, Georg Freiherr von," *LThK* 5: 282; L. Wahl, *Das kulturpolitische Program des Freih. von Hertling* (Würzburg, 1913); W. Polle, "Hertling als Sozialphilosoph," (Diss., Würzburg, 1933); J. Schink, "Graf von Hertling als Sozialpolitiker (Diss., Cologne, 1924); M. Spindler, "Die kirchlichen Erneuerungsbestrebungen in Bayern im 19 Jahrhundert," *Historisches Jahrbuch* 70 (1951): 260ff; E. Deuerlein, "Verlauf und Ergebnis des Zentrumstreites (1906–09)," *Stimmen der Zeit* 156 (1954/55): 103ff.; articles by H. Eisele and M. Ettlinger in *Hochland* from 1912 to 1914; M. Schneidewin, *Der katholische Reichskanzler und die geistige Freiheit* (Hameln, 1918); J. Hessen, *Graf von Hertling als Augustinusforscher* (Düsseldorf, 1919).

44. Hertling, *Reden, Ansprache und Vorträge mit einigen Erinnerungen*, ed. A. Dryoff (Cologne, 1929).

45. A. Kraus, *Geschichte Bayerns*, p. 602.

46. Hertling, *Erinnerungen aus meinem Leben* (Kempten, 1919) 2: 242f.

47. Hertling, *Das Prinzip des Katholicismus und die Wissenschaft* (Freiburg, 1899), p. 2.

48. Ibid., p. 22.

49. Ibid., pp. 11f.

50. Ibid., p. 39.

51. Ibid., p. 43.

52. Ibid., pp. 82f. "For a long time I was considering Tübingen...with its shining trinity in the Catholic theological faculty of Kuhn, Hefele, and Aberle..." (*Erinnerungen*, 1: 37f.).

53. *Das Prinzip*..., p. 101.

54. Ibid., pp. 75f.

55. *Sp*, p. 266.

56. *HPBl* 122 (1898): 548ff., 634ff.; on Schnitzer, see *Tr*, pp. 267–404.

57. Cited in *Tr*, p. 283.

58. "Die Enzyklika Pascendi und die katholische Theologie," *Internationale Wochenschrift für Wissenschaft, Kunst und Technik* 2 (1908): 129ff.

59. A. Houtin, *Histoire du modernisme catholique* (Paris, 1919), p. 228.

60. Schnitzer, *Der katholische Modernismus* (Berlin, 1912).

61. (Augsburg, 1910).

62. (Munich, 1924).

63. Cited in *Tr*, p. 397.

64. *Tr*, p. 402.
65. See *J*, 6: 2, p. 446.
66. Dachs, "Albert Ehrhard—Vermittler oder Verräter?" p. 213.

9. Through and beyond Modernism (1907–1914)

1. R. Aubert, "Modernism," in Karl Rahner, *Sacramentum Mundi* (New York, 1968) 4: 99. Cf. R. Scherer, "Modernismus," *LThK* 7: 513. For a history of the word beginning with Luther see A. Houtin, *Histoire du modernisme catholique* (Paris, 1913), pp. 81ff. "Recourse was constantly being had to 'isms' of every kind. Blondel's *L'Action*, for example, was condemned as Kantianism, psychologism and subjectivism. References to life and experience were rejected as fideism, false mysticism and pragmatism. Laberthonniere repudiated scholasticism under whatever form as intellectualism, and Tyrrell called the system that challenged him Vaticanism, Jesuitism and Medievalism" (D. Donovan, "Church and Theology in the Modernist Crisis," *Proceedings of the Catholic Theological Society of America* 40 [1985]: 155).

2. *Syllabus Errorum* (Denziger-Schönmetzer, 2901). "As a result of the dominance of those erring and of the careless argument of those unreflective, an atmosphere of ruin has been created penetrating all and spreading like the plague" (*Acta Apostolicae Sedis* [hereafter *AAS*] 40 [1907]: 626).

3. E. Poulat, *Histoire, dogme et critique dans la crise moderniste* (Casterman, 1962), p. 9.

4. A collection of the main documents issued by the Vatican against modernism can be found in A. Vermeersch, *De modernismo* (Bruges, 1910).

5. Houtin, *Histoire du modernisme*, p. 123.

6. *E Supremi Apostolatu, Acta Sanctae Sedis* [hereafter *ASS*] 16 (1883): 113.

7. E. Commer, *Hermann Schell und der fortschrittliche Katholizismus* (Vienna, 1907); for the letter to Commer, see *ASS* 40 (1907): 392.

8. To the committee protesting this insult, the cardinal secretary of state had to write: "The Holy Father is convinced that you have wished to make only an act of human piety toward someone dead. . . . His Holiness has clearly expressed his opinion in saying that one should make a difference between the private life of Herman Schell and the works he published" (Houtin, p. 160). The monument was constructed.

9. *Accogliano Colla Piu . . .*" *ASS* 40 (1907): 266f.

10. R. Aubert, "Eingriff der kirchlichen Obrigkeit und die integralistische Reaktion," *J* 6 part 2: 483.

11. R. Aubert, "Aux origines du modernisme," *EThL* 37 (1961): 557ff.; cf. F. Heiner, *Der neue Syllabus Pius X* (Mainz, 1907); J. Riviere, *Le modernisme dans l'église* (Paris, 1929).

12. *Pascendi . . . , ASS* 40 (1907): 593. In November Pius issued a *motu proprio* (*Praestantia Scripturae*) stating that Catholics were bound to submit to decrees of the Pontifical Biblical Commission.

13. P. Sabatier cited in Aubert, "Eingriff der kirchlichen Obrigkeit," p. 479.; A. Loisy, *Simples reflexions sur le Decret du Saint-Office Lamentabile sane exitu et sur l'Encyclique Pascendi dominici gregis* (Ceffods, 1908), pp. 149f. See J. Kübel,

Geschichte des katholischen Modernismus (Tübingen, 1909); C. Braig, *Der Modernismus* (Freiburg, 1911); A. Gisler, *Im Kampfe gegen Modernismus* (Stans, 1913); A. Gisler, *Der Modernismus* (Einsiedeln, 1912); F. Heiner, *Die Massregeln Pius X* (Paderborn, 1910); J. Bessmer, *Philosophie und Theologie des Modernismus* (Freiburg, 1912); M. Grabmann, *Der Modernismus* (Eichstatt, 1911); J. Müller, *Die Verurteilung des Modernismus durch Pius X* (Munich, 1908); A. d'Alès, "Modernisme," *Dictionnaire apologétique de la foi catholique* 3 (1912): cols. 591–612; J. Schnitzer, *Der katholische Modernismus* (Berlin, 1912); John A. Bain, *The New Reformation: Recent Evangelical Movements in the Roman Catholic Church* (1906); *Hgn*, pp. 62ff.; E. Weinzierl, ed., *Der Modernismus: Beiträge zu seiner Erforschung* (Graz, 1974); E. Poulat, *Histoire, dogme et critique dans la crise moderniste* (Tournai, 1979); L. Kurtz, *The Politics of Heresy* (Berkeley, 1986).

14. Houtin, *Historie du modernisme*, p. 217; on Troeltsch's views, see E. Herms, "Theologischer 'Modernismus' und lehramtlicher 'Antimodernismus' in der römischen Kirche am Anfang des zwanzigsten Jahrhunderts," in H. Renz, ed., *Umstrittene Moderne: Die Zukunft der Neuzeit im Urteil der Epoche Ernst Troeltschs* (Gütersloh, 1987), pp. 41ff.

15. Holl, *Der Modernismus* (Tübingen, 1908), pp. 39, 66.

16. J. Mausbach writing in 1905 cited in Houtin, *Historie du modernisme*, p. 224.

17. For a detailed study of Kantianism in the French scene in terms of epistemology, revelation and dogma see P. Colin, "Le Kantisme dans la crise moderniste," in D. Dubarle, ed., *Le Modernisme* (Paris, 1980).

18. Peter Neuner, "Was ist Modernismus?" H. Renz, ed., *Umstrittene Moderne*, p. 61.

19. R. Aubert, "Eingriff . . . ," p. 484.

20. M. Pernot, *La Politique de Pie X (1906–1910): Modernistes* (Paris, 1910), p. 84.

21. *AAS* 2 (1910): 655f. In 1931 Pius XI prescribed it for those attaining advanced ecclesiastical degrees and assuming positions in seminaries. Neither the code of 1917 or the recent code mentions the anti-modernist oath. The oath remained in force until Vatican II.

22. "Der Antimodernisteneid und die theologischen Fakultäten," *Katholische Kirchenzeitung für Deutschland* 1 (1910): 83f. After this Adam was frequently in trouble with church authorities. Although his writings by the 1950s had assumed an almost devotional tone, books like *Christ Our Brother* were corrected by Vatican censors up to 1934. H. Kreidler, "Excurs über Karl Adam und die kirchliche Autorität: Der Modernismusverdacht," *Eine Theologie des Lebens* (Mainz, 1988), pp. 296ff.; Robert Krieg, *Karl Adam* (Notre Dame, Ind., 1992).

23. Typical of a strict ecclesiastical defense of the oath are Reginald Schultes, *Was beschwören wir im Antimodernisteneid?* (Mainz, 1911) and J. M. Verweyen, *Philosophie und Theologie im Mittelalter* (Bonn, 1911). Opposing the oath were Adam's "Der Antimodernisteneid." See also, *Eine deutsche Abrechnung mit Rom* (Munich, 1911); M. Leitner, *Legt der Antimodernisteneid neue Glaubenspflichten auf?*

(1911); H. Mülert, *Anti-Modernisteneid, freie Forschung und theologische Fakultäten* (Breslau, 1911); T. Engert, *Eid oder Meineid* (Würzburg, 1911); F. X. Kiefl, *Gutachten den durch den päpstlichen Motu Proprio* . . . (Kempten, 1911); C. Meurer, *Der Modernisteneid und das Bayerische Plazet* (Würzburg, 1911); J. Marx, *Der Eid wider den Modernismus* (Trier, 1911); J. Mausbach, *Der Eid wider den Modernismus und die theologische Wissenschaft* (Cologne, 1911).

24. *Hgn*, p. 73.

25. The encyclical is printed in *AAS* 2 (1910): 357ff. See G. Knopp, "Die 'Borromäusenzyklika' Pius X. als Ursache einer kirchenpolitischen Auseinandersetzung in Preussen," in G. Schwaiger, ed., *Aufbruch ins 20. Jahrhundert: Zum Streit um Reformkathoizismus und Modernismus* (Göttingen, 1976), pp. 56ff.; M. Hage, *Die Borromäus-Enzyklika und ihre Gegner* (Wiesbaden, 1910); Clericus Rhenanus, *Der h. Karl Borromäus und das Rundschreiben Pius X. vom 26. Mai, 1910* (Mainz, 1910); B. Mock, *Die Hetze gegen die Borromäus-Enzyklika* (Paderborn, 1910); J. Diefenbach, *Rechtfertigung der Borromäus-Enzyklika durch evangelische Prediger und Gelehrte* (Mainz, 1910); J. Schnitzer *Borromäus-Enzyklika und Modernismus* (Frankfurt, 1911); J. Winter, *Das Zentrum und die Borromäus-Enzyklika* (Halle, 1911). This encyclical had nothing to do with the liberal and influential *Borromäus-Verein* (*Sp*, pp. 121ff.).

26. *Osservatore Romano*, June 16, 1910.

27. L. Altzberger, *Was ist der Modernismus* (Cologne, 1908), pp. 18f. Anton Eisler in *Der Modernismus* (Einsiedeln, 1912) traced modernism to a syncretistic origin in Protestantism and to a complicating of reason by "Kantian" idealism and to the introduction of the new immanentist apologetics. All these alter the ideas of God and dogma; cf. C. Pesch, *Glaube, Dogmen und geschichtliche Tatsachen: Eine Untersuchung über den Modernismus, Theologische Zeitfragen* 4 (1908); A. M. Weiss, *Die religiöse Gefahr* (1904); E. Commer, *Hermann Schell* . . . .

28. *Tr*, p. 406

29. *Sp*, p. 170; *Hgn*, p. 40.

30. Przywara, "Modernismus," *Staatslexikon* 3 (Freiburg, 1929), 1373ff.

31. "La nouvelle théologie ou va-t-elle?" *Angelicum* 23 (1946), 126ff.

32. Poulat, *Histoire* . . . , (n. 13 above), pp. 613ff., 620.

33. "Ultimately there can be no theology which does not come to grips and somewhat resolve the problems which appeared at the beginning of this century in the so-called modernism in Catholic theology. These problems are in my view still not worked out sufficiently for the greater public of educated Christians . . . . [They are] all summed up in the uniqueness of Christianity without obscuring or overlooking its historical connections with the totality of the history of religion" (Rahner, "Eine Theologie mit der Wir Leben Können," *Schriften zur Theologie* 15 [Zurich, 1983]: 113f.).

34. See *Sch*, pp. 166f.; F. Vigener, *Ketteler* (Munich, 1924); J. Hoeffner, *W. E. von Ketteler und die Katholische Sozialbewegung im 19. Jahrhundert* (Wiesbaden, 1962); Ketteler opposed the declaration of infallibility and then interpreted it in a sense including other aspects of the church; K. J. Rivinius, *Bischof W. E. von Ketteler und die Infallibilität des Papstes* (Bern, 1976).

35. See Knopp, "Die 'Borromäusenzyklika' Pius X. . . . ," p. 57; T. Loome,

"Die Trümmer des liberalen Katholizismus," in M. Schmidt and G. Schwaiger, *Kirche und Liberalismus im 19 Jahrhundert* (Göttingen, 1976), pp. 210f.

36. R. Lill, "Der deutsche Katholizismus...," *J* 6 no. 2: 516.

37. R. Morsey, "Die deutschen Katholiken und der Nationalstaat zwischen Kulturkampf und erstem Weltkrieg," *Historisches Jahrbuch* 90 (1970): 53. "Of the 65 million Germans in 1910 about 34 million, i.e., 36 percent were Catholics, and in Prussia the percentage was the same.... Among 90 Prussian ministers between 1888 and 1914 only four were Catholics" (H. Lutz, *Demokratie in Zwielicht* [Munich, 1963], p. 16).

38. E. Gatz, "Caritas und soziale Dienst," *R* 2, pp. 312ff.; *Sp* pp. 19f. See various essays (especially upon Ketteler) in E. Iserloh, *Kirche—Ereignis und Institution* 1 (Münster, 1985), pp. 259ff. On the *Vereine*, see H. Hürten, "Katholische Verbände," *R* 2: 215ff.; Lönne, (see above, chap. 8, n. 5), pp. 182ff.

39. H. Brauweiler, "Der Kern und die Bedeutung des Zentrumstreites," *H* 2 (1914): 75–90.

40. A. Kolping, *Katholische Theologie Gestern und Heute* (Bremen, 1964), pp. 40, 45.

41. Lönne, p. 184; on the first unions and their "red chaplains" see *Sp*, pp. 35ff.; *Hn*, pp. 165ff.

42. Lill, "Der deutsche Katholizismus...," *J* 6 part 2: 524; see R. Brach, *Deutscher Episkopat und Gewerkschaftstreit 1909–1914* (Cologne, 1976).

43. "Zentrum und kirchliche Autorität," *Gegen die Quertreiber* (Freiburg, 1914); Wacker, *Friede Zwischen Berlin und Rom* (Freiburg, 1879); J. Schofer, *Theodor Wacker* (Karlsruhe, 1921); H. Sacher, "T. Wacker," *LThK* 10: 906.

44. H. Pesch cited in *Hn*, p. 177.

45. *AAS* 4 (1912): 657ff.

46. See O. Roegele "Presse und Publizistik des deutschen Katholizismus, 1803–1963," *R* 2: 395ff.; *Sp*, p. 129. On Görres, see O'Meara, *Romantic Idealism and Roman Catholicism*, pp. 51ff., 126ff. J. E. Jörg, a product of the Görres circle and at first a collaborator of Döllinger, continued this direction as the editor of and frequent contributor to the *Historisch-politische Blätter* from 1852 until his death in 1901. Here for half a century he presented the political, ecclesiastical, and social movements of the day. His pictorial and enthusiastic language analyzed the great movements of the century in a perspective which was Catholic, increasingly conservative, and German. See M. Doberl, "J. E. Jörg," *Biographisches Jahrbuch* 4 (1904): 429ff.,; M. Spahn, "E. Jörg," *Hochland* 17 (1919/20): 273; 434ff.; F. Wöhler, *J. E. Jörg und die sozial-politische Richtung im deutschen Katholizismus* (Leipzig, 1929).

47. Veremundus, *Steht die katholische Belletristik auf der Hohe der Zeit?*" (Mainz, 1898); see "C. Muth und seine Zeitschrift 'Hochland' als Vorkämpfer für die innere Erneurung Deutschlands" (Diss., Munich, 1952); E. Hanisch, "Der Katholische Literaturstreit," in E. Weinzierl, ed., *Der Modernismus*..., pp. 125ff.; E. Streng, *Wiederbegegnung von Kirche und Kultur in Deutschland* (Carl Muth *Festschrift*) (Munich, 1927); A. W. Hüffer, *Carl Muth als Literaturkritiker* (Münster, 1959); O. Köhler, "Bücher als Wegmarken des deutschen Katholizismus," in *Der katholische Buchhandel Deutschlands: Seine Geschichte bis zum Jahre 1967* (Frankfurt, 1967), pp. 11ff.

A significant union of publishing enterprise with religious order was to be found in the Steyler missionaries; see *Arnold Janssen 1837–1909* (Nettetal, 1987).

48. C. Bauer, "Carl Muth und des Hochlands Weg aus dem Kaiserreich in die Weimarer Republik," *Hochland* 59 (1966): 234.

49. Richard von Kralik, *Die katholische Literaturbewegung der Gegenwart* (Regensburg, 1909); M. Enzinger, ed., *Gral und Romantik* (Graz, 1963); D. Pfister, *Die Diskussion über das katholische Schrifttum und die Jahrhundertwende* (Freiburg, 1952).

50. Entry for January 1910 in L. Pastor, *Tagebücher—Briefe—Erinnerungen*, W. Wuhr, ed. (Heidelberg, 1950), p. 513.

51. A. Walz, *Andreas Kardinal Frühwirth* (Vienna, 1950), pp. 307ff. Frühwirth protected Muth and *Hochland*; cf. E. Ritter, *Die katholisch-soziale Bewegung und der Volksverein* (Cologne, 1954), pp. 219ff.

52. Walz, pp. 332ff.

53. Ibid., pp. 345f.

54. T. Nipperdey, *Religion im Umbruch: Deutschland 1870–1918* (Munich, 1988), pp. 18ff.

55. Ibid., pp. 64ff., 157.

56. Lill, "Der deutsche Katholizismus . . . ," *J* 6 part 2: 523ff.

57. Cf. K. Epstein, *Matthias Erzberger und das Dilemma der deutschen Demokratie* (Berlin, 1962); J. Schauff, *Die deutschen Katholiken und die Zentrumspartei* (Cologne, 1928). G. Clemens, *Martin Spahn und der Rechtskatholizismus in der Weimarer Republik* (Mainz, 1983), pp. 9–48. There were also the "Unitarier" whose Unitas student movement, begun in 1834, found renewed prominence in 1860 and became particularly active from 1887 to the end of the war. Through the leadership of Carl Sonnenschein and Ludwig Windthorst it produced future cardinals (Bertram, Fischer) and theologians (Heinrich Pesch, Ehrhard, Mausbach) imbued with an openness for change and a deep fidelity to church.

58. Cited in R. Morsey, "Der Kulturkampf," *R* 1: 106.

59. Cited in H. Hürten, "Katholische Verbände," *R* 2: 261.

Conclusion

1. R. Schaeffler, *Die Wechselbeziehungen zwischen Philosophie und katholischer Theologie* (Darmstadt, 1980), pp. 140ff.; see also pp. 60ff.

2. *C*, pp. 450, 368, "If, in the first half of the century, episcopalist and anti-infallibilist ideas were still quite powerful (not only in Germany but in France and sporadically in Italy and the United States), ultramontane ideas achieved a substantial advance in the course of the second third of the century. We see this advance in the inevitably Roman direction of theological textbooks, in a similar theology introduced into catechisms, in provincial councils usually corrected by Rome after 1850, in the elimination of local liturgies to the benefit of the one Roman rite, in the diffusion of Italian forms of piety . . . , and finally, in the multiplication of publications favorable to papal points of view" (*C*, p. 427). See A. Kolping, *Katholische Theologie Gestern und Heute* (Bremen, 1964), pp. 31ff.

3. H. Jedin, "Die Vertretung der Kirchengeschichte in der katholisch-theologischen Fakultät Bonns, 1823–1929," *Annales des Historischen Vereins für den Niederrhein* 155/56 (1954): 411f.; *HOC* 3: 37ff., 84f.

4. G. McCool, *Catholic Theology in the Nineteenth Century* (New York, 1977), p. 238.

5. *C*, p. 456. Interestingly, around 1900 the topic of the salvation of those living and dying outside of baptism was widely discussed. This is not surprising, for an emphasis upon apologetic conversion through explicit faith easily isolates the number of those open to salvation, and colonial exploration brought to awareness the issue of grace in a wider world. Schell discussed the topic, offering the original idea of the death of every person of good will participating in the salvific mystery of Christ's death. J. B. Heinrich, C. Gutberlet, C. Pesch and others wrote compendious studies struggling with the issue. While the ecclesiastical and apologetic atmosphere urged a conservative position, the easy condemnation of non-Christians was not part of the Catholic tradition and had been rejected by Pius IX in 1863 [*Denzinger-Schönmetzer*, 1677]. See *Hoc* 3: 245ff.; S. Harent, "Infidèles (Salut des)," *Dictionnaire de théologie catholique* 7 part 2: 1900ff.

6. E. Hanisch, "Zur Kritik des katholischen und sozialistischen Staatsdenkens im 19. Jahrhundert," *Heuresis* (Salzburg, 1969), p. 261.

7. Typical of this hardening of Protestant evaluations of Catholicism is D. F. Loofs, *Symbolik oder christliche Konfessionskunde* (Tübingen, 1902); and see the review by Carl Braig in *Literarische Rundschau* 29 (1903): 1ff.

8. H. Lutz, *Demokratie im Zwielicht: Der Weg der deutschen Katholiken* (Munich, 1963), pp. 18f., 20f. "Without this need to escape the isolation of the Kulturkampf and to be recognized as a full member of national life, the national 'fulfillment of duty' without any reservation of German Catholics in World War I makes no sense. . . .
Critical powers against nationalism and militarism of the Kaiser, which were certainly still present in Catholic tradition in 1890 were neutralized" (*Sch*, p. 188). "There seemed to be no counter-influence coming from the fact that German Catholics were members of an international religious community and had been attacked precisely because of their links with the papacy. . . . Consciously or unconsciously Catholics hoped for a final equality to be achieved in the war" (K.-E. Lönne, *Politischer Katholizismus im 19. und 20. Jahrhundert* [Frankfurt, 1986], p. 189). See also A. C. Baudrillart, *La Guerre allemande et le catholicisme* (Paris, 1915); G. Pfeil-Schifter, *Deutsche Kultur, Katholizismus und Weltkrieg* (Freiburg, 1915).

9. Hanisch, "Zur Kritik . . . ," p. 261.

10. Thomas Sheehan, "Heidegger's *Lehrjahre*," *The Collegium Phaenomenologicum* (Boston, 1988), pp. 77ff.

11. See J.-C. Pinto de Oliveira, "L'Esprit agit dans l'Histoire. La totalisation hégélienne de l'histoire confrontée avec les perspectives du Concile de Vatican II," in *Hegel et la théologie contemporaine* (Neuchâtel, 1977), pp. 54ff.

12. *W*, pp. 407f.; cf. "Die Problematik der Neuscholastik," *Kant-Studien* 33 (1928); 97.

13. Vincent Berning notes the similarity of Schell's view to that of Rahner regarding nature and grace, and Schell's anticipation of the dialogue between Aristotle and Aquinas, and transcendental philosophy in various forms ranging from Schelling to Heidegger. Berning, *Gott, Geist und Welt* (Munich, 1978), pp. 88ff.

Nor can the similarities between J. E. Kuhn and Rahner be overlooked: the omission of Molina and Suarez, the intention to think through theology in terms of process and subjectivity; theology as anthropology; a shift of grace from an extrinsic, efficient, physical causality, to a formal presence within the various activities of consciousness. "We emphasize that the divine predestination should be kept in view here as an immediate relationship of God to God's rational creature; we should be less concerned with the divine grace mediated through temporally and geographically limited proclamations of the Gospel. . . . As the basic truth [of predestination]: God wills that all human beings are saved: Christ, through whom alone we can be saved, has died for all. From this point we move to the further and consequently secondary truth that God effects—immediately and efficaciously—the salvation of individuals, of all who really attain salvation." *KD* 1: 368, 436f. On the relationship of the Tübingen school to Henri de Lubac and Rahner, see E. Klinger, "Gnade—Natur—Geschichte: Über ein Grundproblem der alten katholischen Schule in Tübingen und seine aktuelle Bedeutung," *Theologie und Philosophie* 45 (1970): 551ff.

14. Mann, *Der Zauberberg* (Munich, 1967) 2: 419.

15. Hugo von Hofmannsthal, "Der Dichter und diese Zeit," in *Gesammelte Werke* 2 (Frankfurt, 1951): 268, 287, 293.

16. *W*, pp. 400f.

17. Ibid., p. 408.

BIBLIOGRAPHY

R. Aubert, "Die Modernistische Krise: Der Reformkatholizismus in Deutschland";
R. Lill, "Der deutsche Katholizismus zwischen Kulturkampf und 1. Weltkrieg";
O. Köhler, "Das Lehramt und die Theologie"; and Köhler, "Neuthomismus,
Scholastik und die neuen Philosophen,'" all in H. Jedin, ed., *Handbuch der
Kirchengeschichte* 6 part 2 (Freiburg, 1973): 437ff., 515ff., 316ff.

J. Bellamy, *La Théologie catholique au XIXème siècle* (Paris, 1904).

R. Bubner, *Modern German Philosophy* (New York, 1981).

E. Coreth, ed., *Christliche Philosophie im katholischen Denken des 19. und 20.
Jahrhunderts*, 3 vols. (Graz, 1987, 1988, 1990).

K. Eschweiler, *Die zwei Wege der neueren Theologie* (Augsburg, 1926).

H. Fries and G. Schwaiger, eds. *Katholische Theologen Deutschlands im 19. Jahrhundert*, 3 vols. (Munich, 1977).

F. Fuchs, *Die deutschen Katholiken und die deutsche Kultur im 19. Jh.* (Würzburg, 1927).

P. Funk, *Der Gang des geistigen Lebens in Deutschland* (Würzburg, 1922).

J. A. Gallagher, *Time Past, Time Future* (New York, 1990).

M. Grabmann, *Die Geschichte der katholischen Theologie seit dem Ausgang der
Väterzeit* (Freiburg, 1933).

L. Grane, *Die Kirche im 19. Jahrhundert* (Göttingen, 1986).

G. Grupp, *Die Kulturperioden des 19. Jahrhunderts* (Frankfurt, 1896).

Histoire de la Philosophie, vol. 3 (Paris, 1974).

U. von Hehl, ed., *Der deutsche Katholizismus in der zeitgeschichtlichen Forschung*
(Mainz, 1988).

E. Hocedez, *Histoire de la théologie au XIXème siècle*, 3 vols. (Paris, 1947–1952).

K. Hoeber, *Die Rückkehr aus dem Exil* (Dortmund, 1926).

B. Hubensteiner, *Bayerische Geschichte: Staat und Volk, Kunst und Kultur* (Munich,
1985).

H. Hürten, *Geschichte des deutschen Katholizismus* (Mainz, 1986).

A. Kerkvoorde, O. Rousseau, eds. *Le Mouvement théologique dans le monde contemporain* (Paris, 1969).

A. Kolping, *Katholische Theologie Gestern und Heute* (Bremen, 1964).

A. Kraus, *Geschichte Bayerns* (Munich, 1983).

G. La Piana, "Recent Tendencies in Roman Catholic Theology," *Harvard Theological
Review* 15 (1922): 122ff.

K.-E. Lönne, *Politischer Katholizismus im 19. und 20. Jh.* (Frankfurt, 1980).

F. Loofs, *Grundlinien der Kirchengeschichte* (Halle, 1901).

H. Lutz, *Demokratie im Zwielicht. Der Weg der deutschen Katholiken* (Munich, 1963).

G. McCool, *Nineteenth-Century Scholasticism* (revision of *Catholic Theology in the Nineteenth Century*) (New York, 1989).

—— *From Unity to Pluralism: The Internal Evolution of Thomism* (New York, 1989).

G. Maron, *Die römisch-katholische Kirche von 1870 bis 1970* (Göttingen, 1972).

R. Morsey, *Zeitgeschichte in Lebensbildern: Aus dem deutschen Katholizismus des 20. Jahrhunderts*, 6 vols. (Mainz, 1975).

—— "Die deutschen Katholiken und der Nationalstaat zwischen dem Kulturkampf und dem ersten Weltkrieg," *Historisches Jahrbuch* 90 (1970): 267ff.

T. Nipperdey, *Religion im Umbruch: Deutschland 1870–1918* (Munich, 1988).

A. Rauscher, *Der soziale und politische Katholizismus: Entwicklungslinien in Deutschland, 1803 bis 1963*, 2 vols. (Munich, 1981).

K. Repgen, U. von Hehl, *Der deutsche Katholizismus in der zeitgeschichtlichen Forschung* (Mainz, 1988).

J. Roberts, *German Philosophy* (Atlantic Highlands, N.J., 1988).

R. Schaeffler, *Die Wechselbeziehungen zwischen Philosophie und katholischer Theologie* (Darmstadt, 1980).

K. Schatz, *Zwischen Säkularisation und II Vatikanum: Der Weg des deutschen Katholizismus in 19. und 20. Jahrhundert* (Frankfurt, 1986).

L. Scheffczyk, "Der Weg der deutschen katholischen Theologie im 19. Jh.," *Theologie im Aufbruch und Widerstreit: die deutsche Theologie im 19. Jahrhundert* (Bremen, 1965).

H. Schnädelbach, *Philosophy in Germany, 1831–1933* (Cambridge, 1984).

I. Silbernagl, *Die kirchenpolitischen und religiösen Zustande im 19. Jh.* (Landshut, 1902).

W. Spael, *Das Katholische Deutschland im 20 Jh.* (Würzburg, 1964).

J. Sperber, *Popular Catholicism in Nineteenth-Century Germany* (Princeton, 1984).

M. Spindler, *Handbuch der bayerischen Geschichte* (Munich, 1974).

N. Trippen, *Theologie und Lehramt im Konflikt: Die kirchlichen Massnahmen gegen den Modernismus im Jahre 1907 und ihre Auswirkungen* (Freiburg, 1977).

B. Welte, "Zum Strukturwandel der katholischen Theologie im 19. Jahrhundert," *Auf der Spur des Ewigen* (Freiburg, 1965).

G. G. Windell, *The Catholics and German Unity, 1866–1871* (Minneapolis, 1954).

W. Zorn, *Bayerns Geschichte im 20. Jahrhundert* (Munich, 1986).

Index